Civil–Military Relations in Russia and Eastern Europe

This book examines how civil–military relations have been transformed in Russia, Poland, Hungary and Ukraine since the collapse of the Soviet Union and the Warsaw Pact in 1991. It shows how these countries have worked to reform their obsolete armed forces, and bring them into line with the new economic and strategic realities of the post-Cold War world, with new bureaucratic structures in which civilians play the key policy-making roles, and with strengthened democratic political institutions which have the right to oversee the armed forces.

David J. Betz is a lecturer in the Department of War Studies, King's College London.

RoutledgeCurzon Contemporary Russia and Eastern Europe Series

1 **Liberal Nationalism in Central Europe**
Stefan Auer

2 **Civil–Military Relations in Russia and Eastern Europe**
David J. Betz

Civil–Military Relations in Russia and Eastern Europe

David J. Betz

RoutledgeCurzon
Taylor & Francis Group
LONDON AND NEW YORK

First published 2004
by RoutledgeCurzon
11 New Fetter Lane, London EC4P 4EE

Simultaneously published in the USA and Canada
by RoutledgeCurzon
29 West 35th Street, New York, NY 10001

RoutledgeCurzon is an imprint of the Taylor & Francis Group

Typeset in Times by
Keystroke, Jacaranda Lodge, Wolverhampton
Printed and bound in Great Britain by
Antony Rowe Ltd, Chippenham, Wiltshire

British Library Cataloguing in Publication Data
A catalogue record for this book is available from the British Library

Library of Congress Cataloging in Publication Data
A catalog record for this book has been requested

ISBN 0–415–32477–7

Contents

Preface

This book had its beginning in 1996 when I was the programme officer on the Canadian Department of National Defence's Democratic Civil–Military Relations Programme. This programme which brought twenty or so East European defence officials to Canada annually for approximately one month of seminars, government briefings and visits to various Canadian academic departments, governmental and non-governmental agencies having to do with civil–military relations was aimed at assisting in a small way the transformation of civil–military relations in the former Soviet bloc. A curious fact struck me at that time – and not only me, I must admit. While both civilian and military defence officials in the transition states faced a great challenge in learning to manage civil–military relations under the rules of a democratic game, civilians faced a double challenge. For them, military matters had long been a kind of terra incognita because under the old system such things were traditionally the preserve of men in uniform.

The gap in confidence, and competence, between the average military participant and the average civilian participant in the programme was usually quite apparent. Generally, the military participants had better language skills, better knowledge of international affairs, more familiarity with the theory and practice of civil–military relations in the West, a much better sense of strategy (naturally enough), and certainly no less – and often more – of an understanding of democratic governance than their civilian counterparts. Practical reasons why this should be the case were not hard to find. Many military officers had received language training in military academies. Most, having joined the military during times when a military career was a relatively socially and financially rewarding occupation represented the privileged and educated stratum of their societies. By the mid-1990s many had already had opportunities to interact with their counterparts in the West through any one – and quite often several – of a multitude of military to military exchanges, bilateral or through the auspices of the Partnership for Peace. Civilian officials, on the other hand, generally shared few of these advantages. Many obtained their positions precisely because they had opposed the former regime and did not profit from the study of foreign languages, let alone international relations, strategy or defence studies, in its elite institutes. For most, the only experience they had of military life was a decidedly negative experience of conscript service in the lower ranks. And there were relatively fewer opportunities for civilian officials to interact with their counterparts in the West.

It is a truism that there is no such thing as a democratic army. Armies by nature are authoritarian and hierarchical; this must be the case if they are to perform their essential function of fighting wars, whether they do so on behalf of a democratic regime or a regime constituted in some other way. Leaving aside its many demerits, one great virtue of the Soviet system of civil–military relations was its incorporation at a deep level of a professional military ethic of civilian supremacy. Post-communist armies had to readjust their notions of to whom, or rather to what, they owed loyalty as the legal command authority. Civilians, working from a lesser base of knowledge in most cases, had to actually *constitute* that authority, make it real not only in law but also in practice – and at a time when there were many other pressing issues on the public agenda. Not to make light of the many challenges to the traditions and prejudices of military men that came in the wake of the democratic revolutions in Eastern Europe the challenges to civilians were greater.

In other words, it struck me in 1996 that the main problems of reforming civil–military relations in Eastern Europe centred on the civilian side of the civil–military equation. Exploring that idea, explaining why that might be the case, and reflecting on what that might suggest about post-communist transition and the corpus of thinking on civil–military relations more generally is the focus of this book.

This is not a book about the minutiae of defence reform or the specifics of defence policy in the four countries under review, Poland and Hungary, Russia and Ukraine – though that is the subject of Chapter 2, 'Security policy-making and defence reform'; rather, it is an investigation of the *process* of defence policy formulation and a discussion of what that says about the functioning of civilian control of the military. A major focus of the book is on the organisation of the defence establishment in the countries under review – specifically the ministries of defence and the role of civilians within them. But the object of Chapter 3, 'Civilian integration in the Ministry of Defence', is not merely to discuss organisation; rather it is to probe beneath the organisational chart and clarify the real patterns of authority and work in these ministries. Finally, while in Chapter 4, 'Agencies of civilian oversight', I examine the legal architecture of civilian control my aim is not just to describe the legal competencies of various actors but to probe their actual competency to perform their legislated duties.

In short, I aim in this book to penetrate beneath the rhetoric to explore the reality of civil–military relations in Eastern Europe at a time of great change. I could not have done that without the insight I gained through approximately 120 interviews conducted by me with elite politicians, military officers, defence analysts, and journalists in each of the countries in the study between 1998 and 2001. Most of these interviewees are quoted by name and position, others are identified only in general terms in accordance with their wishes. I am grateful to all my interlocutors who were in general very forthcoming and helpful. Any errors of fact or interpretation are entirely mine.

Acknowledgements

I am greatly indebted to Professor Harald Von Riekhoff of Carleton University (Ottawa, Canada) for being a mentor and friend since 1992. His dedication to his craft and his students is a great inspiration to me. I also deeply appreciate the many hours of patient advice and criticism given to me by Professor John Löwenhardt, formerly Alec Nove Professor of Russian and East European Studies of Glasgow University.

In the conduct of the research a few people offered substantial assistance in providing contacts, making introductions and giving advice. I would not have been able to do the work without the very great help given to me by Leonid Polyakov in Kiev, Wladyslaw Staron in Warsaw, Zoltan Szenes in Budapest and Valeriy Volkov in Moscow.

Much of my research dovetailed with the research programme of the Canadian Department of National Defence's Democratic Civil–Military Relations Programme (DCMRP). In 1997–1998 I was the programme officer for DCMRP, and in 1999 I was a researcher on its Russian and Czech portions. DCMRP proved invaluable to me in the building of the network of contacts throughout Eastern Europe on which this book is based. I am grateful to the Department of National Defence.

Above all I am grateful to my wife, Taisha, for her patience, support and love.

Introduction

The transition of the post-communist regimes of Eastern Europe[1] to democracy in the 1990s was one of the most consequential events of the twentieth century. In this book I look at an aspect of that change – the transformation of civil–military relations in Poland, Hungary, Ukraine and Russia between the dissolution of the Warsaw Pact in July 1991 and the first enlargement of NATO in March 1999[2] – through the prism of in-depth interviews with the military, political and academic elite in each of the countries in the study. My main concern is with how these states built qualitatively new regimes of civil–military relations during a time of great upheaval; my main object is to better understand why actors in this process chose various paths of reform and to explain how and why they accomplished, or failed to accomplish, the building of democratic civil–military relations. This issue has received comparatively less scholarly attention than have other aspects of post-communist transition such as the change from a planned to a market economy, the building of representative democratic institutions, the fostering of civil societies, and so on. Yet it is a matter of great importance. As Christopher Donnelly wrote 'defence transformation, good civil–military relations and democratic control are problems which must be solved . . . or they will destabilise society'.[3]

Somewhat in contrast with conventional wisdom, the work proceeds from the understanding that the problems of transforming civil–military relations in the countries under review were rather the same at a basic level. In order to build democratic civilian control all the states under review had to:

1 reform their obsolete armed forces, bringing them into line with the new economic and strategic realities of the post-Cold War world;
2 create new bureaucratic structures for their defence establishments in which civilians played the key policy-making roles; and,
3 strengthen political institutions tasked with oversight of the armed forces.

Accordingly, the book addresses each of these tasks in its three main chapters: 'Security policy-making and defence reform', 'Civilian integration in the ministry of defence' and 'Agencies of civilian oversight'. The reader may note from the chapter headings that the analytical focus of the work is on the civilian side of the civil–military equation. This is deliberate. While it is true that the military cultures in the region were, and are, to some extent misaligned with democratic norms, the most significant and enduring challenges for the reform of civil–military relations were faced by the new civilian elites whose ‘learning curves’ were much steeper than those of the military. The main reason for comparing these particular countries is that they are emblematic of an emerging dichotomy in Europe between ‘outsiders’ and ‘insiders’.[4] On the one hand are two countries – Poland and Hungary – which have returned to the ‘European fold’ and whose *comparatively* successful transformations were supported by the expansion of NATO and the prospect of inclusion in the European Union. On the other hand are two countries – Russia and Ukraine – whose problematic transformations have been complicated by NATO expansion and which seemed to be growing more and more distant from the ‘New Europe’ by the end of the 1990s.

The central argument of the work is that variation in the state of civil–military relations among the states under review is explained by the interaction of three factors. First, in Poland and Hungary the external incentives to reform were mainly positive. Establishing democratic control was intimately linked with their obtaining membership of NATO which, in turn, was connected to their aspirations to join the European Union. In Russia, on the other hand, the external incentives to reform were mostly negative. NATO membership was not a Russian goal in the period under review and thus meeting its admission criterion was not a stimulus for change; on the contrary, the legacy of rivalry and confrontation with the West continued to inform the thinking of Russia’s military policy-makers.[5] Ukraine’s external incentives to reform were more neutral: building good relations with NATO was a main goal, but the nature of Ukrainian domestic politics constrained the capacity of policy-makers to openly seek membership.

Second, the attitude of the political and military elite in Poland and Hungary was more open to the adoption of new norms of civil–military relations than was that of the elites in Russia and Ukraine. The Polish and Hungarian elites were more unified, had a stronger sense of a ‘return to Europe’, were prone to emotional backlash against anything cognitively socialist, and desired to protect themselves from a resurgence of Russian influence. By contrast, the Russian and Ukrainian elites were more fractured, suffered less emotional backlash against past practices, were not part of a ‘return to Europe’, and, in Russia, had pretensions to great power status.

Third, in Poland and Hungary the state of the polity and economy presented a less significant internal constraint on reform because the economic downturn at the beginning of transition was not as long or as pronounced as it was in Russia and Ukraine. Moreover, due to the greater degree of militarisation in the Soviet Union the problems of military transformation were of a greater magnitude.

Context of civil–military reform in Eastern Europe

The context of the reform of civil–military relations in Eastern Europe differs from that of previous transformative waves such as in Latin America and Southern Europe. There are specificities of post-communist transition which make the transformation of civil–military relations in Eastern Europe different, including: its non-military and non-violent nature; the (despite appearances) non-revolutionary way in which the old regimes collapsed; the simultaneity and inter-connectedness of reform tasks which overcrowded the transitional agenda; and, the salient fact that, while not of a democratic type, civilian control of the armed forces was a characteristic feature of the old political order.

The collapse of socialism in the states under review was relatively peaceful. The Polish and Hungarian armed forces neither tried to bring about the downfall of the old regime nor attempted to reverse its decline by putting down the reformist movements; they were either passive observers of events or played an instrumental role in negotiating communist retreat from power rather than being players in their own right.[6] The Soviet military was more involved in the collapse of the old regime. Yet despite its participation in the August Putsch of 1991, it too tended toward a position of neutrality between opposing civilian actors who sought to use the military for their own ends. Although some of the coup leaders were prominent military men, including the minister of defence, Marshal Dmitri Yazov, ultimately the coup failed because the bulk of the army was unwilling to use force to prop up the failing Soviet state while a few military units appeared ready to oppose the putsch.[7]

Whatever the reason for restraint, the passivity of the armed forces was a characteristic feature of civil–military relations in post-communist transition. Transition theory suggests, however, that until 1989, regime change tended to coincide with defeat in war or bloody popular revolution.[8] The trauma of regime change, in turn, is thought to have been a force which generated powerful political and institutional transformative efforts. In the peaceful Eastern European transition, however, regime change was less traumatic and consequently evinced less energetic transformative drives. In short, the passivity of the military provoked a lesser sense of urgency on the part of new leaders for institutional innovation, particularly in the sphere of civil–military relations. Indeed, as Donnelly wrote 'In many countries the problem is not appreciated, or its extent and complexity are not acknowledged. Sometimes it is denied that a problem even exists.'[9]

A second characteristic feature of post-communist transition was its non-revolutionary nature.[10] Strictly speaking, a revolution should have a target regime which defends itself and an organised counter-elite which opposes it. In the aftermath of revolt, the old regime is thoroughly discredited – and the legitimacy of the revolutionary agenda is to a large extent signalled by its victory. Such was not the case in Eastern Europe. It is difficult to say that the almost completely unexpected collapse of communism – particularly in the USSR – was a result of the organised efforts of an internal actor; rather 'The spectacular if short-lived popular mobilisation of the last months of 1989 and the first months of 1990 followed and confirmed the self-abandonment of the ruling powers, rather than being the cause of their resignation.'[11]

In the absence of an organised, victorious counter-elite with a dominant political agenda, the result in Eastern Europe was political confusion. The old regime was dead, but who killed it and where to go from there was a matter of debate. Hence, transition was characterised by sharp political conflict amongst diffuse actors. In such a context, where the shape of the new system and the institutional patterns it would adopt were not agreed, the reform of civil–military relations was further delayed and complicated.

The sheer scope of the transformative agenda also distinguished post-communist transition. The new democratic states of Eastern Europe inherited a plethora of problems – dysfunctional economies and polities, weak civil societies, etc. Amongst the various reform tasks, incompatibilities and unwanted interactions inevitably occurred such as, for example, between liberalisation in the political sphere and economic reform. Conflicts over the speed and sequencing of reforms could not easily be resolved in a situation of sharp political struggle. A big problem was that no single actor was sufficiently powerful to impose its own agenda. Consequently, though it may have made sense to pursue economic reform before political reform or vice versa, in practice Eastern European elites did not have this luxury; all reforms were simultaneous, interacted with each other, and in some cases cancelled progress altogether. Military reform, for example, was an early casualty in the confrontation between presidents and parliaments for control of the defence establishment in all the states under review except Hungary.

The extreme tightening of military budgets in Eastern Europe was also different from transitions elsewhere and greatly complicated reform. Managing comprehensive, well-thought-out military reform in conjunction with severe budgetary restraint proved fiendishly difficult. Indeed, in Russia and Ukraine the tight fiscal straitjacket on spending caused by economic collapse all but completely derailed military reforms and radicalised increasingly shambolic, resentful and alienated armed forces. In Central Europe, balancing military reform with economic reform was somewhat more manageable due to better economic conditions than was the case in Russia and Ukraine.

Though it was not a liberal-democratic type of civil–military relations, communist armies were under firm civilian control. Zoltan Barany claims that the practice of civil–military relations during four decades of communism in Central Europe points to 'periodic meddling by the armed forces in politics',[12] but most authors conclude that civilian control was secure throughout Eastern Europe and that communist armed forces were loyal to the established social order. Thus, in Eastern Europe, transition did not entail a military 'return to barracks' because the military had never left the barracks. The problem was that communist armies were subordinated not to the state per se but to the national communist parties and by extension to the Communist Party of the Soviet Union (CPSU). Nearly all of the officer corps in Eastern European armies were communist party or communist youth league members; Party membership was a prerequisite for promotion and various inducements were employed to compel officers to identify their well-being with that of the regime.

The effect of past politicisation on reform of the military was extensive. Civil–military relations in transition were permeated by mutual mistrust: an emotional backlash by the military against politicisation engendered suspicion of the motives of civilian authorities to introduce civilians in defence;[13] while especially in Central Europe where the new elite were often former dissidents, there was a tendency to mistrust the military because of its perceived close connection with the old regime.

Another way in which the past system impacted on the transitional period was in the distinct lack of civilians qualified in security and defence. In the Soviet system the compartmentalisation of civilian and military tasks had the effect of concentrating nearly all military/strategic experts in the general staff[14] and military colleges of the armed forces. As a result, the Soviet Union and its client states produced very few civilian experts on defence matters since civilian educational institutions were not designed for such work.

Central issues of civil–military reform in Eastern Europe

The imperative of civil–military reform in Eastern Europe stemmed from a number of main issues. One of the main areas of concern was the problem of defence reform. James Sherr made the trenchant point that:

> if armed forces are to be 'tools of policy', then they must be subservient to the country's political authorities. But in itself such subservience does not guarantee that armed forces will be able to fulfil the roles assigned and entrusted to them. For this they must be effective, and a military establishment controlled without understanding, knowledge and judgement will prove to be as much of a threat to national security as a military establishment which answers only to itself.[15]

In other words, armed forces must be *effective* and *effectively managed*. It is no good saying 'we have good civil–military relations' if infantry soldiers are not trained to fight, if pilots do not fly, if sailors do not sail, if the equipment is obsolete and badly maintained, if the living conditions for soldiers and their families are squalid, and so on.

The second area of concern was the manner in which the ministry of defence was organised and manned. Military policy, as any policy, has three stages: policy design, followed by preparation, and then action. Ultimately, civilian politicians are accountable for policy outcomes and so the onus for decision-making has to be theirs. Execution is the responsibility of the military professional. But the preparation of plans and the long-term support for their execution is a mixed civilian-military responsibility, and that should take place in an integrated ministry of defence. In effect, relations between civilians and the military become more important as work on security matters moves from general to executive to administrative policy and then to action. As the saying goes, the 'devil is in the details' and, indeed, it is at this level that friction between military and civilian is most apparent. This points to the problem discovered by Eastern European civilian and military authorities that practising democratic civil–military relations involved a lot more than having a civilian minister of defence; it meant having a considerable number of civilian experts within the ministry as well. In the states in the study this was a grave problem because civilians were never trained in defence and security issues; this fact alone represented one of the main barriers to democratising civil–military relations.

The third area of concern was the institutional capacity of civilian agencies outside of the ministry of defence to provide effective oversight of the armed forces. In Eastern Europe these institutions were comparatively inexperienced and ineffective. Parliamentary control of the military budget and of its implementation, for example, is a function of government of which the post-communist states had no previous experience whatsoever. For such control to be effective, for members of parliamentary defence committees to be capable of making a balanced contribution to discussions on defence matters, parliaments needed to have access to defence and security expertise. Procedures of consultation had to be established between parliamentary committees, research institutions, departments of the ministries of defence and the government. All of this proved difficult indeed.

In short, parliamentary oversight was ineffective, with defence committees simply too overburdened with responsibilities to do their job effectively and often filled with politicians who had no experience with, or interest in, military issues. Moreover, in many cases they were actively shut out of any role in the exercise of oversight by a powerful presidency jealously guarding its prerogatives in defence.

Overall, it can be said that the problem of civil–military relations in Eastern Europe was not a matter of preventing direct military intervention in politics; rather it was a problem of how democratically-elected civilians could exercise efficient management, direction and oversight of their armed forces. In this respect, as Donnelly noted, '. . . there is not a single Central and East European country which has a civil–military relationship which it can consider satisfactory . . .'[16] Nevertheless, two broad patterns are evident in how civil–military reform progressed in Eastern Europe. In Poland and Hungary, there has been a slow, difficult and still incomplete process of adopting new norms of civil–military relations which culminated in their admission to NATO. In Ukraine and Russia there has been a stagnation of liberal-democratic reform and even a regression from the admittedly undemocratic, but stable, norm of civilian control which existed under the old system.

1 Approaches to civil–military relations

In the case of post-communist transition, where 'little or nothing in the theories of academic literature provides a guidebook for the re-making of military–civilian relations',[1] it pays to be wary of theory. Busy policy-makers, already wary of theory and impatient with it by nature, may wish to skip to the second half of this chapter, Indicators of civil–military reform, where I lay out the method and rationale of this book in a relatively accessible and jargon-free manner. Academics, however, tend to feel helpless and unable to assess the validity of a thesis without a theoretical basis. The first half of this chapter which summarises the main theories which inform the work is aimed mainly at them.

Armies in all societies exert political influence; they are the ultimate defenders and symbols of state sovereignty, they embody the virtues of discipline, honour and patriotism and, uniquely in most states, they possess arms and the means to employ them effectively. Given their monopoly over the use of force, armies have always represented a latent threat to the societies they are raised to preserve. Such is the civil–military dilemma: Who will guard the guardians? Or, as Samuel Finer put it in *The Man on Horseback*:

> Instead of asking why the military engage in politics, we ought surely to ask why they ever do otherwise. For at first sight the political advantages of the military vis-à-vis other civilian groupings are overwhelming. The military possess vastly superior organisation. And they possess arms.[2]

The great Chinese military philosopher Sun Tzu also spoke of this dilemma more than two millennia ago saying: 'Generals are assistants of the nation . . . when their assistance is complete, the country is strong. When their assistance is defective, the country is weak';[3] and 'the ordinary rule for use of military force is for the military command to receive the orders from the civilian authorities, then to gather and mass the troops, quartering them together'.[4] And Niccolo Machiavelli was the first to grasp the competitive nature of the emerging European state system and to underscore the relationship between political and military power in the state saying that 'the chief foundations of all states, new as well as old or composite, are good laws and good arms; and as there cannot be good laws where the state is not well armed, it follows that where they are well armed they have good laws'.[5]

By far the most important thinker on civil–military relations, however, was the nineteenth-century Prussian luminary Carl von Clausewitz. His dictum, 'War is nothing but a continuation of political intercourse, with a mixture of other means',[6] is the well-spring for most civil–military relations theory. Clausewitz explained that war was both *autonomous* (i.e., a unique activity with its own logic and methods) and *instrumental* (i.e., an activity subordinate to the policy which determines its ultimate ends): 'Is not War merely another kind of writing and language for political thoughts? It has certainly a grammar of its own, but its logic is not peculiar to itself.'[7] If war is both autonomous and instrumental, the same can be said of warriors: military officers must possess autonomy in the sense that they be permitted to perfect their martial expertise independently of civilian interference; but they remain instrumental in the sense that the determination of the ends to which their expertise is employed is not within their remit. On this point Clausewitz was clear:

> as Wars are in reality, they are, as we before said, only the expressions or manifestations of policy itself. The subordination of the political point of view to the military would be contrary to common sense, for policy has declared the War; it is the intelligent faculty, War only the instrument, and not the reverse. The subordination of the military point of view to the political is, therefore, the only thing which is possible.[8]

Clausewitz's thoughts on the nature of war, its duality and the role of the warrior in society are indispensable in later theories of civil–military relations. As Samuel Huntington wrote, given an understanding of these concepts 'all the other aspects of [military] professionalism must follow'.[9]

Although it has been over forty years since they were published, Huntington's *The Soldier and the State*, and Morris Janowitz' *The Professional Soldier* still represent the most theoretically exhaustive treatments of civil–military relations. At its core, Huntington's thesis is that civilian control boils down to one prime essential:

> the minimising of military power. Objective civilian control achieves this reduction by professionalising the military, by rendering them politically sterile and neutral. This produces the lowest possible level of military political power with respect to all civilian groups. At the same time it preserves that essential element of power which is necessary for the existence of a military profession. A highly professional officer corps stands ready to carry out the wishes of any civilian group which secures legitimate authority within the state. In effect, this sets definite limits to military political power without reference to the distribution of political power among the various civilian groups.[10]

Huntington claimed that there were two ways in which the civilian leadership could maintain control over the armed forces: *objective* or *subjective* control. 'The essence of objective civilian control is the recognition of autonomous military professionalism; the essence of subjective civilian control is the denial of an independent military sphere.'[11] Objective and subjective civilian control are thus antithetical to one another; the former achieves its objectives by 'militarising the military', making them the tool of the state; the latter achieves its objectives by 'civilianising the military', making them the mirror of the state.[12] Objective civilian control, it is argued, is the optimal model of civil–military relations because it simultaneously maximises military power and minimises military political involvement while subjective control, though it can also be quite effective, is sub-optimal because it impedes military efficiency, and it is characteristic of communist civil–military relations.[13]

Morris Janowitz's sociological portrait of the American officer corps in *The Professional Soldier* is often read as opposite to Huntington's thesis. He thought that war was so altered by the destructive capacity of nuclear weapons that armed forces had become more police-like than military. This radical adaptation of the military profession to what he called a 'constabulary force' was said to occur when 'it is continuously prepared to act, committed to the minimum use of force, and seeks viable international relations, rather than victory, because it has incorporated a protective military posture'.[14] A constabulary army, however, by definition, makes political decisions. Therefore, contrary to Huntington's view, Janowitz put forth that civilian control calls for the imposition of civilian oversight at various levels of military activities rather than the explicit recognition of an autonomous military sphere.[15] Ultimately, however, political control in Janowitz's model still hinged on the answer to the question why officers fight:

> The constabulary force is designed to be compatible with the traditional goals of democratic political control. The constabulary officer performs his duties, which include fighting, because he is a professional with a sense of self-esteem and moral worth.[16]

Thus Janowitz and Huntington were not that far apart; both saw professionalism as a main pillar of civilian control, though Janowitz added the element of common values between military and society to the liberal concept of civil–military relations.

The liberal model – or Huntington/Janowitz model, if you will – has come under much criticism, though never enough to necessitate its wholesale rejection. In the main, critics dispute that professionalism is the central force inhibiting military intervention in politics. Rebecca Schiff in elaborating her 'concordance' model of civil–military relations noted a longstanding criticism of the liberal model: the Huntingtonian standard of military professionalism assumed too much conflict and necessitated too much separation between civilian and military authorities. In her view, civil–military institutional separation was not the only possible form of stable civilian-dominated, civil–military relations which may involve institutional separation, integration of elites, or a variety of other forms.[17] Earlier, but in a similar vein, William Odom made a salient observation about the practical limitations of the professional ethic as an explanatory factor in the neutralisation of the military's political influence, noting that at the top level of military management the line between a political decision and a military one is ambiguous:

> In truth, almost any decision within the military has domestic political implications; deep commitment to the most admirable social ethic may at times soften or alter those implications, but it will not remove them. Thus, Huntington's concept of a professional military ethic tends to obscure the fact that an apolitical military establishment is a mythical convention concocted in the parochial minds of Europeans and later embraced in the United States.[18]

Samuel Finer was also a prominent skeptic. He pointed out three ways in which professionalism, in fact, could thrust the military into collision with civilian authorities:

1 The military may see themselves as the servant of the state rather than of the government in power 'which may lead them to contrast the national community as a continuing corporation with the temporary incumbents in office'.[19]
2 The armed forces may fall prey to 'military syndicalism', the idea that as specialists only they are qualified to make decisions about defence.[20]
3 The military may object to being used for the 'sordid' domestic purposes of the civilian leadership because it sees itself as the guarantor of the nation's external security, not as a body of heavily-armed policemen.[21]

In the 1980s a few analysts began to study the process of military withdrawal from politics as military regimes in Greece, Portugal, Spain, Latin and South America began slowly to give up rule to civilian politicians. The literature they generated contains some useful insights into how civilian control is consolidated in formerly authoritarian states which has some relevance to post-communism. An excellent example of this type of work was Alfred Stepan's study of civil–military relations in Latin America, *Rethinking Military Politics: Brazil and the Southern Cone*. He laid out a useful framework for how civil–military relations should work in a democratising state. Of central importance in this framework was the definition of three 'arenas' in which military politics takes place:

1 civil society, where 'manifold social movements . . . and civic organisations . . . attempt to constitute themselves in an ensemble of arrangements so that they can express themselves and advance their interests . . .';[22]
2 political society, where the 'polity specifically arranges itself for political contestation to gain control over public power and the state apparatus', which encompasses political parties, political leadership, intra-party alliances and legislatures, 'through which civil society can constitute itself politically to select and monitor democratic government . . .';[23] and
3 the state, the 'continuous administrative, legal, bureaucratic and coercive system that attempts not only to manage the state apparatus but to structure relations between civil and public power and to structure many crucial relationships within civil and political society'.[24]

Within the scope of civil society, he wrote, it is extremely important to forge new 'political institutions that have increased strength, autonomy, and legitimacy'.[25] Civil society must work toward building at least a few civilian institutes as repositories of capable, independent advice to government on defence matters so that there is

> a cadre of citizens who are masters in their knowledge of the force structure, organisational style, budgetary issues, doctrinal questions and the specific details of weapons systems . . . [they are] indispensable for the fulfilment of the military and intelligence oversight functions of political society, especially in the legislative branch.[26]

Political society must have a 'deliberate strategy for the empowerment of legislatures so that they are in a position to carry out their military and intelligence oversight functions in a mature, democratic fashion'.[27] Legislatures should have permanently standing committees devoted to the routine (not ad hoc) oversight of the army and these committees must be staffed by a permanent body of professional advisers. In this way mutual fears and ignorance of each other will be minimised (i.e., ad hoc commissions are inherently adversarial while standing committees are more collegial).[28]

The state must limit the scope of military decision-making to only the military sphere. If the military and the state disagree on their conception of democracy and the legitimate role of the military in it, then the new regime must either impose its view, or abdicate certain areas of government to the military. If it takes the latter option, it will have undermined its legitimacy and, therefore, its long-term viability.

Negotiation of the scope of the military's role in politics in a new democracy requires a careful, but forceful executive who plays the role of persuader and directs his attention to building 'professional, not personal, allies within the military'.[29]

> A passive executive who abdicates responsibility would probably mean that any effort to 're-professionalise' the military would be militarily led. A purely negative executive, who devotes all his efforts to eliminating military prerogatives but neglects to play a leadership role in attempting to formulate and implement an alternative model of civil-military relations would probably be locked in dangerous conflicts with the military. An executive who is positively involved in forging a new role for the military that narrows their involvement in state regulation of conflict, builds effective procedures for civilian control, seeks to increase military professional capacities and lessens the risks – for the polity and for the military – of further military intervention is what the theory and practice of democratisation would seem to indicate.[30]

Stepan also wrote that the leadership of the national security councils which serve as fora for high-level discussion of security and defence matters must be civilian: 'The very point is that such a council be democratically controlled by civilians, and that the military participate as advisers to the civilian leadership.'[31]

Building effective civilian control of the military entails efforts by the civil and political societies as well as the new state to empower themselves to increase their own capacity for control; it is not merely a matter of the military withdrawing from politics, civilians must step into leadership roles and equip themselves with the knowledge and expertise necessary to oversee and monitor the military establishment.

With relatively few exceptions, after Huntington and Janowitz the literature on civil–military relations was static. For the most part, debate tended to be concentrated so much on solving or preventing military coups that discourse on civil–military relations degenerated to a state which Bacevich characterised as 'No coup? No problem, and so no further discussion is required'.[32] This concentration on coups, admittedly an important problem, tended to overlook the other, more common, problems in civil–military relations which confronted all states, even democratic ones. In the 1990s, however, there was somewhat of a renaissance in the field caused in no small part by the perceived need in the West to assist the democratisation of post-communist Eastern Europe.

As Eastern European elites began to try to reform their civil–military relations they sought to answer some fundamental questions: How exactly is the military controlled by civil authorities in a democracy? What specific policies and structures lead to civilian control? What kind of civil–military relations best serve democracy in the long-run? What exactly is democratic civil–military relations?

There are two approaches to answering this question. First, there are the official versions of international organisations such as the OSCE and NATO which are rather general and vague. Second, there is a small but growing body of literature which is searching for a more detailed resolution of the problem.

All the countries under review are parties to the Organisation for Security and Cooperation in Europe (*OSCE*) *Code of Conduct on Politico-Military Aspects of Security* which states clearly that the participating nations bind themselves to an explicitly democratic regime of civil–military relations. The document calls for the participating states to: establish clear legal and constitutional lines of legitimate civilian authority over the armed forces; clearly define the responsibilities and authority of the main players in defence, to provide legislative oversight of the armed forces; ensure transparency in decision-making such that the public has access to information on the activities of the military; and, foster military political neutrality.[33]

NATO planners faced a difficult task in defining explicitly the specific pattern of civilian control which would form a fundamental part of the accession criteria because there is great variation among the member states in how *exactly* civilian control is instituted. Eventually, NATO did set out the kind of civil–military relationship which it expected from aspiring members.[34] States seeking to join the alliance were expected to implement both military and non-military reforms, while states not seeking membership at the time, as well as those to whom NATO membership would not be extended, were also encouraged to undertake similar reforms in the context of the Partnership for Peace Programme.

In terms of political criteria, NATO's accession requirements included: a demonstrated commitment to and respect for OSCE norms and principles, including the resolution of ethnic disputes, external territorial disputes including irredentist claims or internal jurisdictional disputes by peaceful means . . . ; a commitment to promoting stability and well-being by economic liberty, social justice and environmental responsibility; appropriate democratic and civilian control of the defence forces; and, a commitment to ensure that adequate resources are devoted to achieving the obligations described in section A [political expectations of new members] and C [military expectations of new members].[35]

In other words, new members were required not only to adopt the norms of NATO as a defensive politico-military alliance but, more importantly, they were expected to subscribe to Western political, social, and economic values – which entailed the implementation of democratic civil–military relations.

In the mid to late 1990s a few analysts began to tackle the issue of democratic civil–military relations more concretely. A general consensus emerged among specialists that certain features were distinctive of civil–military relations in democratic states. These features include:

1 *A civilian minister of defence.* 'It is the function of knowledgeable civilians to represent the military in political disputes.'[36] The role of the military is to *advise* civilians on defence issues and to voice the needs of the military in government, not to make policy – only elected civilians have that right. Society needs to be protected from overt military involvement in politics; the military, at the same time, needs to be protected from the efforts of politicians to employ them in partisan disputes. The minister of defence and the civilian staff of his department are a crucial buffer between the armed forces and society which works to the advantage of both sides.

2 *Clear and unambiguous lines of legitimate authority.* It is essential that the military should have no doubt as to what constitutes legal authority and to whom they are responsible. Civilian control requires 'a constitutional and legislative structure with clearly defined responsibilities and appropriate checks and balances among state institutions'.[37]

3 *Integrated civilian–military ministries of defence.* If there are no civilian experts with managerial roles in defence, then the military is able to dominate defence policy formulation because there is no other expert voice on military matters. Moreover, the ability of civilian authorities to effectively monitor the activities of the armed forces will be highly limited. 'If all advisers to defence policy-makers are military, and policy-makers are ignorant of military realities, then the army, not the government, is controlling defence policy.'[38]

4 *Parliamentary role in the oversight of defence.* Legislatures must exercise their authority over the armed forces through defence and budgetary committees at least. Moreover, parliamentary oversight of security policy and military spending must be 'substantive and detailed, not just perfunctory. A parliament which is limited, or which limits itself through lack of interest, to a rubber-stamp role in the oversight of defence is a clear indication of poor civilian control.'[39]

5 *Non-partisan armed forces*. That the military must be sheltered from political abuse is obvious. The army is the agent of the elected government, whatever party might form it. Nor should military officers be allowed to use their official position to support any particular party or to try to influence the votes of their subordinates. Optimally, according to one author 'the soldier should be a citizen wearing a uniform and, as such, an organic part of democratic political life'.[40]

6 *Public capacity for informed debate on defence matters*. A final and salient feature of democratic civilian control is the role played by civilian experts on defence in media, government, academia, political parties and by independent sources of advice such as research institutes. Without public awareness of defence issues effective civilian control is difficult to maintain. There is no interest for parliamentarians if the electorate is not interested in civilian oversight. 'Democratic control brings a responsibility for the military to educate civilians in the government, parliament and media on military affairs, and it is incumbent on civilian military officials to be prepared to learn, so that civilian and military can collaborate effectively.'[41]

On a more abstract level, theorists have started to look for a wholly new model of democratic civil–military relations. These theorists are all intellectually grounded in the liberal model of civil–military relations but seek to address the limitations noted above. The various approaches include: a model of civil–military relations based on the problem of political agency;[42] a model of shared military–civilian responsibility;[43] and, a 'civil army' model based on the civil societies literature.[44]

Peter Feaver argued that there are two fundamental and conflicting principles which underlie all problems in civil–military relations. The first principle is that nearly all societies need militaries in order to defend themselves against threats from the outside or to provide a deterrent against aggression, but armed forces can also threaten the society they were raised to protect. From this first principle, Feaver argued that a number of features of an ideal-type military could be deduced: 'it is tasked with defending the body politic; it is ready for extreme emergencies or for lesser tasks as required; and it is sufficiently strong and properly oriented to meet the peculiar threats facing that particular society'.[45]

The second basic principle which Feaver noted was that 'just as the military must protect the polity from enemies, so must it conduct its own affairs so as not to destroy the society it is intended to protect'.[46] From this second principle several other features of an ideal-type military were suggested: 'it is subordinate to the political authority of the state; while it should be large enough to protect against threats, its size and draw on society's resources must be bounded'.[47]

In democratic states the over-arching norm of civil–military relations is quite simple: the prerogatives of the civilian authority supercede those of the military in every case. As Feaver described it, the problem of civil–military relations is an extension of the problem of political agency. Society designates through the electoral process political agents who, in turn, control designated military agents.

It follows that regardless of how strong the military might be, civilians remain the political masters:

> In the civil-military context, this means that the military may be best able to identify the threat and the appropriate responses to that threat for a given level of risk, but only the civilian can set the acceptable level of risk for society . . . The military quantifies the risk, the civilian judges it. Regardless of how superior the military view of the situation may be, the civilian view trumps it.[48]

Douglas Bland's 'unified theory of civil-military relations' is somewhat more nuanced than Feaver's though the two are not incompatible. Bland suggested that there are four problems of civil–military relations. The first – because it is the most obvious – is the problem of praetorianism, or military coups. He proposed, however, that usually democracies need to concentrate on the problem of effective *management* of the military rather than on curbing its potential to intervene in politics. The second problem is ensuring that the armed forces behave in ways that safeguard the state without bringing harm – through indiscipline, misadventure, or the exaggeration of threats – to government or citizens.[49]

These two problems closely approximate Feaver's two principles, but Bland pointed out two other problems of civil–military relations. The third problem, which is particular to democracies, is that 'controlling the armed forces . . . means more than the simple, unquestioning obedience of the military to the government of the day because it entails protecting the military from politicians who would use their authority over it to enhance partisan interests and their own power'.[50] Finally, he posed the fourth problem as a question: 'How are ministers to control the armed forces when they (usually) lack the necessary knowledge and experience to do this effectively? Furthermore, what real control exists when ministers are dependent on the advice and council of the 'trade union of the generals'?'[51]

The key to controlling the armed forces in Bland's formulation is through the 'sharing of responsibility for control between civilian leaders and military officers. Specifically, civil authorities are responsible and accountable for some aspects of control and military officers are responsible and accountable for others.'[52] The theory rests on two assumptions. The first is that the term 'civil control' means that outside the defence establishment civilians are the only legitimate source for the direction of the military. This suggests that the forum for shared responsibilities is only *within* the defence establishment and hence it follows that the ministry of defence should be an integrated military–civilian one while political direction should be wholly civilian. The second assumption is that civil control is a dynamic process which is susceptible to 'changing ideas, values, circumstances, issues and personalities and to the stresses of crises and war'.[53]

Bland's model of civilian control puts a heavy burden on the existence of an integrated military–civilian ministry of defence. The central problem of civilian control is what Bland called 'managing the expert problem', the relationship between the military expert and the civilian minister.[54] In his view,

> The institution best suited to serve the minister's multifaceted duties is the integrated defence ministry. This type of ministry combines the minister's office, the civil service bureaucracy, and the military high command and their separate but linked responsibilities in one establishment. An effective integrated ministry facilitates the exchange of ideas and information between these branches and aids in consensus building.[55]

In his 'civil armies' model, Nelson pointed out that although armies can never be democratic – their hierarchies of rank and seniority predetermine a command system, without which armies cannot function – neither are they necessarily anti-democratic. He suggested that the 'democratic quotient of any army is judged by its institutional relationship with civil authority and the behavioural conformity of the armed forces to external norms'.[56] Nelson's proposition is fairly straightforward. It says, essentially, that armies in a democracy behave according to the rules and norms of the society of which it is a part, that is, 'civilly'. This means that:

> Senior officers or defence ministry civilians cannot merely speak the language of democracy. A *behavioural pattern* must develop in which key decisions are made through plural and open debate, adherence to broad constitutional patterns, responsiveness to public concerns and preferences, and obedience to elected civilian authorities.[57]

Nelson argued that in the post-communist states there are a number of key 'testing grounds' of democratic civil–military relations: the articulation of military doctrine, the allocation of resources within the army and when army needs are juxtaposed with those of society, the degree of criminal activity within the army, the treatment of minority ethnic, religious or cultural groups within the army, the treatment of conscripts, the criteria for promotion, dismissal and assignment of the army's officers. When there are problems in these areas over a long period of time, or transgressions of one or more aspects frequently, there is a clear indication that the country's military is not a 'civil army'.[58]

Indicators of civil–military reform

The study of civil–military relations, like the post-communist states themselves, is in a state of transition. The theoretical basis of the field – accepted largely without question throughout the Cold War – has been found wanting by scholars looking at the problems of civilian control in Eastern Europe. A few authors have begun steps towards a new formulation of civil–military relations. Nonetheless, the field remains in flux with the crucial concept of democratic civilian control still undefined and a matter of debate.

The book takes as a starting point the position that the problem in Eastern Europe is not how to prevent the direct intervention of the armed forces in civilian political life; rather, it is a question of how armed forces in a democratising state can be effectively *managed* in ways that do not undermine the wider on-going political, economic and social transition. That is to say, the problems of civil–military relations in Eastern Europe are largely problems of sound public administration and may be best approached from a public administration perspective focused on management structures and the role of civilians in them.

Another basic starting point is that, as Donnelly has written, 'democratic control is a two-way process between army and society, not one where politicians simply dictate to soldiers'.[59] Either directly or indirectly the literature on democratic civil–military relations points to the crucial role of civilians in this process. It cannot be said that civilian control exists simply because the state leadership is civilian. It is incumbent on the civilians to actually educate themselves in defence issues if they are to really have control of defence policy.

Richard Kohn wrote that 'there exists no set of standards by which to evaluate civilian control'.[60] We see, however, from the various theories and descriptions of democratic civil–military relations that this is not exactly true. The problem is that there are no *commonly accepted* standards from the multitude of approaches. The present work takes the view that the concept of civilian control can be disaggregated into three interrelated themes each concentrated on critical civilian responsibilities:

1 civilian control requires that civilians take responsibility for *directing* military policy decisions;
2 civilians must actively participate in the formulation of defence policy and *monitor* its implementation in the ministry of defence; and,
3 civilians must provide *substantial and detailed oversight* of the military through various legally-constituted bodies of civilian control including, strong civilian-led parliamentary committees on defence and the defence budget, national security councils bringing together the state leadership, the heads of key ministries and the military in a forum for the resolution of important defence issues, and other bodies depending on the national political context.

'The best way', wrote Kohn, 'to understand civilian control, to measure its existence and evaluate its effectiveness, is to weigh the relative influence of military officers and civilian officials in decisions of state concerning war, internal security, external defence, and military policy (that is, the shape, size, and operating procedures of the military establishment).'[61] These are precisely the issues that the Eastern European states have been tackling in the context of defence reform.

Feaver, Bland and Nelson all pointed out that as a first rule of good civil–military relations the armed forces, to paraphrase, must do no harm to its society. Harm, however, can be inflicted in various ways. The military could take direct control of the state, or more commonly, it could harm society through indiscipline, misadventure and the exaggeration of threats, or simply by consuming too much of the nation's finite economic resources. It could harm society by abusing conscripts, by involvement in crime or through repression of minorities within society.

The post-communist states of Eastern Europe inherited armed forces which were in all or some of these respects harmful to society. As a matter of first order then, all the countries under review have had to conduct fundamental defence reform.

Forty years ago, Janowitz emphasised the importance of civilian involvement at various levels of military activity to the maintenance of civilian control.[62] Nowadays, in most Western countries civilians are at the heart of the defence establishment. It is ever more difficult to draw a line between civilian and military: civilians perform tasks that previously were the preserve of the uniformed military and vice versa. Defence management in a democracy has come to be about integrating civilian and military decision-makers. As Donnelly wrote 'it does not matter how good in theory the democratic structures for control are if there are no competent civilians to man the ministry of defence or who can talk to the military on equal terms'.[63] The integrated ministry of defence is a crucial locus of civilian control. As Bland argued:

> Defence ministries are the instruments governments use to control the armed forces and the broader defence establishment. Weak or incomplete structures usually reflect poor control of civil-military relations. It is a mistake to think of defence ministries simply as necessary nuisances concerned with the 'outpouring of menial clerks'. The business of ministries is making choices about national defence and cannot be separated from the 'central business of government'. Therefore, the efficiency of their ministry as a controlling instrument should be a primary concern of ministers.[64]

Bland further contended that the real test of whether civilian control is exercised is when,

> civilians can require the military officers to account for their fidelity to the regime, for what they say they will do and for what they do. Therefore, the key to civilian direction of the military is an effective accountability mechanism that enables the civil authority to hold military officers to account and to scrutinise, interrogate, and, ultimately, to commend or sanction their behaviour against agreed-upon standards. Where the accountability mechanism is strong and effective, control is strong and effective.[65]

From one state to another the accountability mechanisms will vary in terms of institutions and their relative powers – depending on factors such as whether the political system is presidential, parliamentary or mixed – and can be quite complex. In essence though, the mechanisms of accountability in democratic systems are based on a simple premise, 'The army is accountable to the government, the government is accountable to the army and to parliament, and parliament is accountable to the people.'[66]

The present work looks at each of these issues in turn. Fundamentally, it seeks to answer three questions concerning civil–military relations in Poland and Hungary, Russia and Ukraine. Were their armed forces reformed to the point that the military was not too great a burden on the domestic economy, did not waste the human resources of society through abuse and misuse of the soldiery, did not undermine society through involvement in crime and other non-sanctioned activities, and was capable of performing its assigned tasks with *efficiency*? Did they manage to build an integrated military–civilian ministry of defence? And did they institute pro-active, civilian-led agencies for oversight of the defence establishment imbued with sufficient legal rights to investigate policy implementation and supported by expert civilian and military staff?

A key focus is the way external institutions like NATO influenced civil–military reform in Eastern Europe. Essentially, it is argued that the desire to enter NATO, the EU and the West generally, exerted a positive influence on civil–military reform in the Central European states. Whether or not the NATO aspirant states internalised the necessity and rationale for change in their systems of civil–military relations, institutions like NATO provided some objective requirements that could be fulfilled, at least formally if not always in substance. In the former Soviet Union states, by contrast, external influences were negative or ambiguous. Since NATO membership was not an open objective, meeting its criterion was not a major imperative. Moreover, particularly in Russia, Western blandishments about the desirability of civil–military reform were often seen as 'mentoring, patronising, and arrogant'[67] by many in military circles. Democratic civil–military relations were taken to mean *Western* civil–military relations, a notion that carried the unspoken meaning of *better* civil–military relations. In short, the terms themselves were value-laden, but interpreted in different ways in different countries.[68]

The full story, however, did not depend only, or even mainly, on external influences. The book also addresses the question of whether the state under review *wanted* to change – civil–military relations reform cannot be effected if elites do not want it to be. Central European elites were more open to reforming their civil–military relations systems to democratic norms than were elites in the former Soviet Union. In Russia especially, but also in Ukraine, it appears that neither military nor civilian elites were particularly committed to building a liberal-democratic civil–military relations regime. For civilian elites in an uncertain political environment it is sometimes preferable to have a partisan military – provided it is partisan in your favour. For military elites similarly, it is preferable to build personal relationships with civilian decision-makers as that is seen as a more effective way to guarantee budgetary allocations than going through formal channels.

Moreover, the quality of democratic functioning in the state is itself a limitation on the degree to which democratic civil–military relations can exist. To this fundamental restraint on reform can be added the restraints of finance and the willingness of society to shoulder the monetary and social costs of defence. Indeed, especially in the Eastern European context where financial constraints were very high, a conducive political atmosphere and a modicum of societal will and support were absolute requirements of reform. In short, the state of the economy, the nature of the political system and the mood of society all constituted potential restraints on reform. As Kohn stated:

> The first requirement for civilian control in democracy is democratic governance itself: the rule of law, civil liberty, a stable method for peaceful succession in power, workable practices for electing officials, and a government and governing process (perhaps spelled out in a written constitution) that are legitimate in the eyes of both key elites and the general public. Civilian control can reinforce democracy, but civilian control is only one aspect – necessary but not sufficient – of democratic rule. Without a stable and legitimate governmental system and process, the military may interfere in order to protect society from chaos, internal challenge, or external attack – even when intervention may itself perpetuate instability and destroy legitimacy in government. The tradition of legitimacy in government acts on the one hand to deter military interference in politics, and on the other hand to counteract intervention should it occur.[69]

There was a demonstrable need in Eastern Europe to reduce defence spending or at least to obtain more value for money in defence, mainly through downsizing and professionalising the armed forces. Obviously, if the condition of the economy did not allow for financial support for reform then the ability to implement reforms was highly limited. Poland and Hungary had more latitude in this respect than Ukraine and Russia. It is also clear that the political system had to be conducive to building democratic civilian control if there was to be success. If the state was incompletely or imperfectly 'democratised' then it stands to reason that civil– military relations would also be incompletely 'democratised'. One can see this most evidently in Russia and Ukraine where the divided political scene and an unsure commitment of elites to the rules of a 'democratic game' undermined democratic reforms in all spheres not excluding civil–military relations. Lastly, the element of societal will and support for reform is a factor in whether transformation can be achieved or not. Without pressure from society to reform there was less reason for elites to make the painful choices required. Indeed, in Donnelly's opinion, 'There is no doubt that neglect by political leaders is the single biggest obstacle to defence reform in Russia and several other Central and East European countries.'[70]

The countries in the study which had the greatest success in civil–military reform were those which had success in consolidating democracy itself, which had economies that allowed a reasonable level of defence spending, and which had consistent societal will and support for defence reform.

2 Security policy-making and defence reform

The aim of this chapter is two-fold. First, it acts as a background for the following chapters which are more narrowly focused on structures and personnel rather than policy. Second, it aims to gauge the effectiveness of civilian control and direction of the defence policy process (specifically in respect of defence reform) in Poland and Hungary, Russia and Ukraine.

The main objects of analysis are national security concepts, defence policies, military doctrines and reform plans. Briefly put, the differences between these key documents are as follows. The security concept lays out at the highest level the security concerns of the nation; all other documents are subsidiary to it. Defence policies and reform programmes address the force structures required to fulfil the assigned missions of the military and how to attain them. Military doctrine explains how those forces will be employed. At the conceptual level, the responsibility for decision-making is entirely civilian. However, in the process of policy formulation the integrated ministry of defence is usually the main workhorse preparing various proposals and policy options, working out logistical, financial and political details with other ministries and passing proposals on to higher civilian authorities for refinement and approval. In general, custom and law tend to ensure civilian control by placing matters of finance, politics and administration under the control of civilians in the ministry of defence; operational command and control of the armed forces under the military high command. In practice, military doctrine and defence planning is a shared responsibility.

With the end of the Cold War, the countries under review were faced with three main tasks in the security sphere. First, defence policies had to be altered in order to reflect the new security environment in Europe. Second, new doctrinal concepts had to be developed in accordance with altered notions of security. Third, very tough reforms had to be carried out in order to turn outdated, Soviet-type armies into more streamlined forces with new types of weapons, training and personnel. All of this had to be achieved with reduced defence budgets. Examining how the countries under review dealt with these tasks tells us a lot about the nature of their civil–military relations. For example, a security concept which is drafted without transparency suggests poor civil–military relations. Poor civil–military relations would also be indicated if the security concept lacked internal consistency, or if the objectives it set out were not reflected in other policies. In other words, was the concept really an effective policy guideline?

Moreover, a reform programme that goes unfunded is worthless. The failure of civilians to develop realistic reform plans (in consultation with their military advisers) based on rational political and economic calculation and to carry them out is a strong indicator of poor civil–military relations. Finally, problems of lack of reform such as squalid living conditions for military families, burgeoning crime in the armed forces, military pay arrears, hazing of conscripts, and so on, are also symptoms of inadequate civil–military relations. Notwithstanding that Russia and Ukraine, from the beginning, faced a bigger job than Poland and Hungary with regard to the reform of their defence establishments, all of the states under review encountered similar dilemmas in re-examining their security needs and creating or adapting structures to manage them, of finding sufficient financial means to build their armed forces, and of figuring out how to go from a Soviet-type army to a more flexible, deployable, professional one. At an even more fundamental level, all the countries under review have had to come to terms with the fact that there is no point having armed forces if they are not effective. As Donnelly pointed out, a country without effective armed forces cannot either assure its sovereignty or make the necessary contribution to an alliance.[1]

None of the countries under review had totally solved this problem by the end of the 1990s. However, the Central European states had made more progress than those in the former Soviet Union.

The Soviet-type defence establishment

To appreciate the difficulties of reform in the former Soviet bloc countries it is useful to understand first how defence policy was made under the old system as well as the type of armed forces that obtained in the Soviet-bloc. Governance in the Soviet Union was based on a dual Communist Party-government structure, consisting of two parallel hierarchies linked in a multiplicity of institutions. Policy was formulated in these institutions which could be government-based, party-based or mixed. Overwhelmingly, however, the authority to formulate policy and to oversee its execution was preserved by the central organs of the Communist Party.

At the top of the Soviet decision-making chain, for defence as for all other areas of policy, was the Politburo of the CPSU Central Committee, which contained only party functionaries. For the determination of Soviet defence policy, however, the Defence Council was probably the most important state body. Whereas the Politburo included members from a wide variety of backgrounds, the Defence Council was composed only of the leaders of the power ministries, plus selected members of the military. In effect, the Defence Council worked as a sub-committee of the Politburo, which tended to confine itself to confirming propositions of the council on military matters.[2]

The General Secretary of the CPSU was the most powerful individual in the system as he headed both the council and the Politburo and was commander-in-chief of the army. But the general staff of the Soviet army was the main defence policy-planning organ of the ministry of defence and for the state in general. In theory, the chief of the general staff was the subordinate of the minister of defence. In practice, the minister of defence and the chief of the general staff were broadly equal in power; in fact, a strong minister of defence was only marginally stronger than was the chief of general staff and a weak minister could be easily overwhelmed. The major levers of the general staff's power were its control of policy-planning and its strong hand in setting the agenda for Defence Council meetings. As they had few other reliable sources of defence expertise outside of the military, the Defence Council essentially reviewed the policy options provided to them by the general staff, and chose the preferred course.[3]

The structure of the Soviet-type defence establishment gave rise to two distinctive areas of defence policy in which different players were dominant. In matters of military-technical policy and strategy, 'it was the general staff that designed policy options and pre-decided issues, relying on its military science and main operations departments . . .'[4] In matters of military preparation and weapons procurement, on the other hand, the design of policy options was a long, drawn-out process to which both the military and military–industrialists contributed. This structure was full of latent conflicts. For example, the general staff had a monopoly of military expertise that allowed it to advocate its preferred direction of armaments procurement, but it lacked strong leverage over the military–industrial complex.[5] The crucial point, for the purposes at hand, however, is that although the general staff had to collaborate with some other institutions with which it had overlapping interests, the Politburo lacked alternate sources of policy option formulation. Therefore, the political leadership could 'only set the military-political and economic confines and had to leave more detailed policy design to the military'.[6]

There was an additional twist to this system in the non-Soviet Warsaw Pact states because their security policy was decided by Moscow and dictated to them through the Warsaw Pact which, until Gorbachev renounced the Brezhnev doctrine, was prepared to use force to prevent its members straying from the Soviet line. The impact of this situation on the Central European states after the collapse of the Warsaw Pact was that neither their political nor military elites had much experience with strategic issues and, as a result of the backlash of the new elite against anything smacking of the old ways, their strategies came to be largely inspired by Western ideas. This is in contrast to the former Soviet Union states which had much more experience in strategic thinking and had less desire to adopt Western ideas in preference to their own, homegrown military traditions.

Comparing defence reform in former non-Soviet Warsaw Pact states with the successor states of the Soviet Union one must bear in mind that the USSR was far more militarised than any of the satellite states. As a consequence, the difficulties of reforming the armed forces were more substantial in Ukraine and Russia than they were in Poland and Hungary. For our purposes it is not necessary to revisit the controversial issue of estimating Soviet defence expenditure in great detail as a broad brush comparison is sufficient to illustrate the disparity of defence burden between the Soviet Union and the satellite states of Central Europe. Estimates of the share of defence expenditure as a percentage of Soviet GNP in the 1980s range from a low of 10 per cent to a high of 17 per cent.[7] By contrast, defence spending in Hungary in the 1980s averaged only 3.5 per cent of GDP[8] – relatively high by Western standards but still a fraction of the Soviet outlay.

The problem, according to a former planner in the general staff, was that the Soviet economy was not simply militarised, as was the US economy which had a large defence industry inside a much larger and generally more efficient civilian economy. The Soviet economy was *structurally militarised*. Defence industry was the core and substance of the economy, to which the civilian sector was merely an adjunct, inefficient both in a free-market comparison and relative to the domestic defence sector. To be sure, in the aftermath of the Cold War, Poland and Hungary found themselves in possession of over-manned, over-equipped armies that were largely obsolescent. The problem, however, was much greater in Russia and Ukraine.

Central Europe

The non-Soviet Warsaw Pact armies were not meant to be used for *national* purposes; they were simply agglomerations of basic units trained, equipped and employed according to Soviet doctrine, ready to be slotted into the Soviet order of battle, under Soviet operational command. That is, 'they were bone and muscle, without heart or brain and without the capacity for independent action'.[9] Notwithstanding the powerful homogenising and de-nationalising influence of the Warsaw Pact, however, it would be a mistake to neglect the differences between member states because national traits were still observable – differences between Poland and Hungary that bear on the present research. Let us examine their impact before moving on to the detailed analyses of security policy-making in the 1990s.

During the Communist era, the Polish armed forces were not only insulated from civilian influence, after the imposition of martial law in 1981 Polish military officers began more and more to take over prominent positions in the state leadership, including General Wojciech Jaruzelski as first secretary of the Polish communist party. Arguably, the military's prominent role in politics, its long history of independence, and conception of itself as the defender of national integrity, pre-disposed the armed forces leadership to resist what they perceived as unwarranted civilian meddling in their internal affairs. According to one Western analyst, the prevailing attitude of the Polish officer corps in the aftermath of the revolutions of 1989 was that civilian control in the new regime need only amount to the armed forces answering 'to its own internal chain of command and, ultimately, to the president as commander-in-chief'.[10] The experience of Hungary was markedly different. To be sure, some Hungarian military leaders probably shared the proclivities of the Polish military toward a more independent role than would be acceptable in a truly democratic system. However, the historical basis of such an attitude was less strong, and the support of the Hungarian people for the military was less pronounced in Hungary than it was in Poland. It is reasonable to suggest, therefore, that the attitudinal barriers to civil–military reforms that involved diminishing the stature of the military in policy matters were probably less significant in Hungary than Poland.

According to Cold War stereotypes Poland was a 'Red Eagle' more or less ready and willing to engage in offensive operations against NATO forces in conjunction with the Soviet army, especially if they had been targeted against German troops;[11] the Hungarian army, on the other hand, was a 'problematical performer'[12] whose reliability in the event of a confrontation with the West was considered minimal – in other words, Poland was more militarised. In and of themselves, these stereotypes of Poland and Hungary's potential reaction to an event that never occurred, based as they are on the limited information available to scholars twenty years ago, are of passing interest. That said, they are reflective of deeper differences between Poland and Hungary during the Warsaw Pact era that had effect into the 1990s.

In all the non-Soviet Warsaw Pact states the prestige of the military profession was in decline through the 1980s, but, according to Zoltan Barany, that decline was more pronounced in Hungary than in Poland. One symptom of this decline was the low quality and quantity of the arsenals of southern-tier Warsaw Pact states like Hungary which received less and more obsolete equipment from the Soviet Union than more strategically located northern-tier states like Poland.[13] To some degree this state of affairs was one created by the Hungarians themselves who in the 1980s deliberately tried to reduce the demands imposed by defence spending on the economy. A Hungarian participant in a RAND conference in 1990 remarked: 'Whenever Marshal Kulikov came to Hungary there was always a fear that he would demand something more. It was not a question of refusing altogether, but rather of how much we could bargain him down.'[14] In some respects, however, the experiences of Poland and Hungary were more similar. Both armies sought, with limited success, a modicum of independence from the Warsaw Pact. In Poland this involved the development by military theorists of a concept of 'defence of national territory' that had a distinctly national flavour.[15] Hungary, uniquely among the Warsaw Pact states, in the mid-1980s began to downsize its army, moving from the Soviet-style divisional structure to a Western-style brigade structure.

Moreover, the differences between Poland and Hungary should not be overemphasised because in most respects their experiences have been quite similar. While it is true that the Hungarian and Polish militaries had quite different relations with political authorities in the 1980s, it is also true that in both cases their transitions were 'gradual and elongated'[16] and were characterised by the least direct involvement of military power. The absence of a dramatic, swift and complete turnover of power from the old regime to the new regime had both positive and negative effects on civil–military reform. On the one hand, it gave the armed forces more time to acclimatise to the ongoing democratic changes in society which probably enhanced the stability of the new regimes. On the other hand, the gradual handover of power generated political compromises between the old and the new elites which would continue to resonate into the mid-1990s at least. In civil–military reform in particular, it meant that reform tended to take the form of tinkering with the functions of old structures rather than wholly re-organising them or creating totally new structures.

From the revolutions of 1989 to the Partnership for Peace: rapid demilitarisation, limited reform

The Warsaw Pact warped the national strategic orientation of its member states according to the desires of the *Soviet* general staff and the Kremlin in Moscow. In practical terms, this meant that Warsaw Pact armies were large, conscript-based and tank-heavy, had logistics systems designed to support offensive operations on foreign territory, and were deployed in areas close to the West. The task of defence reform in Poland and Hungary has been to shift their military infrastructure from this denationalised, offensive, implicitly anti-NATO orientation, to a more defensive, deployable (particularly for multinational peace-support operations) orientation. Without doubt, the substance of the Polish and Hungarian armed forces required changing, but to what, how, and by what means exactly was the question that reveals the salience of effective civilian management and guidance of the military.

On 1 July 1991, after nearly two years of increasing irrelevance, the Warsaw Pact was officially disbanded. On 6 October 1991, in Krakow, Poland, the presidents of Czechoslovakia, Hungary and Poland collectively announced their desire to accede to NATO. At a basic level then, the main problem of defence reform was plain: how to become compatible with NATO forces in the minimum time and at the minimum cost? For analytical purposes, however, this problem needs to be broken down. Tremendous changes were required across the board: in the way the armed forces were manned, in the type and sophistication of the weapons and equipment they employed, in the way they were trained and where they were deployed. Complicating matters was the enormity of the changes required in each area, especially when juxtaposed with the limited fiscal resources available. All these changes generated insecurity in the military. As a result, dissatisfaction and low morale, quitting the military service, and to a certain extent crime and corruption grew more prominent.

A major problem for the Central European states was that prior to the Partnership for Peace and the *NATO Study on Enlargement*, the intentions of the West towards the region were not clear and neither were the concrete requirements of NATO membership. This meant that the Central European states had no clear idea of what they should do, let alone how to do it. In the words of one Hungarian analyst: 'Before 1994, we spent a lot of time and money creating a new military structure and a lot of effort was wasted because we did not know what type of structure to build and without a national security concept the army did not know what to do.'[17] Not knowing the ultimate political end, changes in the military structure initiated by the military leadership were often misguided.

The first public announcement of a new approach to defence doctrine in Poland came before the collapse of the Warsaw Pact, in February 1990, in the form of defence policy guidelines issued by the National Defence Committee, headed by President Wojciech Jaruzelski, which still included communists at that time. These new guidelines included only one sentence reiterating loyalty to the Warsaw Pact amongst a number of other propositions emphasising Polish sovereignty over its defence affairs. Nonetheless, the National Defence Committee's guidelines were criticised in the Sejm (which was not controlled by communists) as insufficient guidance for a full defence reform and also because they implied the continuance of the Warsaw Pact. A year later, the total collapse of the Warsaw Pact necessitated a more complete revision of military doctrine and a new programme called *Armed Forces 1990* was initiated. According to a well-placed Polish observer, however, these early attempts at formulating new policies amounted to very little.[18]

The first serious look at reforming the defence sector was the *Zabinski Report* presented to parliament in October 1992 by the Commission for Reforming the Organisation of National Defence. The aspect of the *Zabinski Report* that most merits highlighting was its recommendation that the Polish defence establishment be divided up between a civilian-military side responsible for administrative tasks and a strictly military side responsible for purely military tasks (the general staff). Duly enacted in April 1993, this division effectively endorsed the proposition that military expertise was exclusive to the military profession. According to Jerzy Milewski, one of the highest-ranking civilians in the defence establishment from 1991 to 1996, the approved model was faulty:

> The civil–military part of the ministry of defence was supposed to manage the armed forces, provide for them, oversee them, take care of the defence policy, social affairs, education, etc. The military part of the ministry is a general staff to which the whole of the army has been subordinated. Those two structures were supposed to cooperate. But this model, in spite of the good will of the subsequent ministers could not function properly and with time it has led to the increasing alienation of the civilian part of the ministry. Ministerial departments which do not have an independent access to the army must work through the respective directorates (which are parallels of ministerial departments) in the general staff. Necessarily the general staff has grown, the respective directorates have duplicated the ministerial structures and became independent. So they no longer need the cooperation from the partner civilian departments.[19]

In the early 1990s the topic of defence reform was discussed fairly extensively in Poland but really effective action was stymied by political conflicts. Nevertheless, some basic policy points were agreed and formalised in two documents: *The Principles of Polish Security Policy* and *The Security Policy and the Defence Strategy of the Republic of Poland*, both of which were signed into law on 2 November 1992. The policy line outlined in these documents boiled down to a relatively few core propositions:

1 The mission of the Polish armed forces was the protection of the sovereignty and integrity of the Republic of Poland, not the preservation of the rule of a particular party or ideology;
2 Poland saw no immediate threat to its security in the traditional sense. However, though it was not specifically named, Russia clearly remained a *potential* hard security concern;

3 In the meantime, the most immediate concerns were domestic security and possible soft security threats which might be posed by the outbreak of regional conflict in the former Soviet Union states;
4 Poland attached great importance to European integration and to future membership of NATO as a key strategic goal.[20]

The logical consequence of these goals was that the Polish army would require modernisation if it were to qualify for NATO; while if it was going to protect the territorial integrity of the state there should be a balanced distribution of military forces throughout the country. The means to accomplish this, however, was more problematic. Various proposals were made from various quarters but very little was actually accomplished. One of the main constraints on a pro-active defence reform was the state of the military budget which declined from 1986 until 1994–1995. From 1991 to 1994 the military budget dropped from US$2.6 billion to a low of US$2.1 billion.[21] Over the same time period, the size of the military was also cut drastically. Basically, reacting to the unstructured, spontaneous cuts was almost more than the military managers could handle:

> We cut our armed forces from 450,000 in 1989 to 200,000 troops by 1999. A lot of our problems are a direct result of this cutting process. The first is pensions. We have to pay those. The second is retraining officers for the civilian market. We have a high unemployment rate in general, but in the West and the North where the major military bases are located unemployment is even higher than the national average. There are a lot of problems employing former soldiers . . . Many other sectors of reform also require money: administrative reform, pension reform, health reform and insurance. A lot of things require government investment and they take precedence over the military . . . The public's awareness of why more money should be spent on defence is very general but uncommitted; they want money spent in a lot of areas.[22]

Another major cause of the failure to reform was the ambiguity and confusion about means and ends that prevailed at the time, combined with the fact that defence reform was not a priority of government. Poland's post-Cold War defence policy began its evolution in an atmosphere defined on the one hand by the ending of the paradigm of East–West confrontation and the diminution of traditional security concerns; and, on the other hand, a feeling of uncertainty about its return to and eventual place in the new Europe, accompanied by continued apprehension about potential security threats from Russia, a traditional bête noire. Foreign Minister Krzysztof Skubiszewski in 1991 argued in a speech to the Sejm:

> The whole of Europe should be treated as a homogeneous area of security . . . From the point of view of security, Central Europe in particular cannot become a gray, buffer, or neutral zone. The area in such a situation, because of its geographical situation, will easily become the object of rivalry of stronger states.[23]

Therefore, building connections to European institutions was considered important – the more the better. Yet, concerns that Russia would see their accession to NATO as a hostile step meant that they could not move too far or too fast toward the West. What emerged was a policy of pragmatic neutrality: Poland would be an independent, armed, Western-orientated country, but not a member of the Atlantic Alliance. In the words of defence minister Piotr Kolodziejczyk, Poland's defence posture 'for today and for the next few years is armed neutrality in the middle of Europe'.[24]

A final problem was the lack of consensus on the direction of reform between military and civilian officials which was undermined by the faulty institutional design of the defence establishment, the power-grabbing tactics of President Walesa, and the determined independence of the chief of general staff, General Wilecki. The separation of the general staff and the ministry of defence had effectively preserved the monopoly of the military on military issues. This system allowed an anti-democratic relationship to develop between the president and the chief of general staff that excluded the civilian minister of defence from a major decision-making role. According to one interlocutor,

> The worst period was in the early 1990s when there was a strong conflict between the politicians and the military under a strong chief of defence staff [Wilecki]. The chief of defence was very jealous about having information and not sharing it. The military wanted money but did not want to have to explain what they wanted it for.[25]

The problem, however, was not only on the military side. Among the civilian elite there was, and to some extent remains, a tendency toward a declarative approach to defence reform: demanding that changes take place but providing neither the resources nor guidance to make them happen. 'It is a problem with our elites,' reported the head of the NATO integration department. 'There is a weak understanding of the fact that we must not only ratify NATO standards, but implement them.'[26]

Hungarian post-Cold War security policy evolved in much the same atmosphere as Poland's. The added twist in Hungary was the rise in insecurity stemming from the appearance on its borders of five new states, in many of which resided a Hungarian diaspora. This brought Hungary a less stable security environment than it had before, though one with both positive and negative features since the appearance of Ukraine placed a buffer between it and Russia. The Yugoslav crisis, on the other hand, generated both a genuine military threat as well as a threat of refugees.

As with Poland, Hungary's security policy prior to the Partnership for Peace was also based on pragmatic neutrality. The general policy line on security issues was set down a little later than in Poland in spring 1993 in two main documents: the *National Security Principles of the Republic of Hungary* and the *Basic Principles of National Defence of the Republic of Hungary*.[27] According to the *National Security Principles*, adopted on 2 March 1993, the aims of Hungarian security policy converged on a few key issues: protecting the state's sovereignty and territorial integrity, maintaining its internal stability, preserving the undisturbed functioning of the market economy, and contributing to international peace and European stability. It took as a starting point that security could not be guaranteed in isolation but only in conjunction with other European states. There was no preconceived notion of major military threat from any direction. At the same time, real and potential conflicts in bordering nations posed credible security threats. Thus, the document concluded that despite the favourable international security situation created by the end of the Cold War, new threats had arisen that necessitated the preservation of reliable armed forces. The *Basic Principles of National Defence of the Republic of Hungary* was adopted on 23 April 1993. It reflected the perception that Hungary bordered on a zone of insecurity and instability. In the short term, Hungary had to rely on its own resources to defend itself on all azimuths. In the long term, Hungarian elites placed high priority on achieving integration in NATO as the only credible guarantor of their security. Given this threat analysis and a consideration of available resources, the reform efforts focused on creating smaller but more modern armed forces.[28]

Defence reform in Hungary began early under the transitional government of Miklos Nemeth which passed a reform programme in December 1989. This programme, however, created more problems than it solved, notably by creating an institutional division between the ministry of defence and the general staff, and between presidential and governmental authority over the defence establishment. The reform separated the command of the armed forces from the defence minister and placed it within the authority of the president – who the communists originally thought would be their reform leader Imre Poszgay. As a result, when Hungary's first post-communist civilian defence minister was appointed in May 1990, the commander of the army was not subordinate to him, but to the president. By 1994, the size of the army had been slashed from 91,000 to 51,100 conscripts, and from 30,500 to 22,900 officers and NCOs, while civilian employees fell from 33,300 to 26,000. The length of conscript service was reduced to twelve months.[29] The army was getting smaller, but was it getting more modern and more prepared? The answer must be no. As one Hungarian planner recollected,

> I remember the first time I worked for the ministry of defence between 1990 and 1993. In 1992 there was a plan for restructuring and reforming the armed forces. It cost a huge amount of money. I do not remember how much, but it was very expensive and also unreal. Of course that plan went nowhere.[30]

It is clear that Hungary's new leadership was not interested in long-term security issues. Despite all the changes in the military, detailed analyses of how, why and what was being done to reform the military were lacking:

> The biggest problem of the last ten years is that many times we have changed the structure without any long- or mid-term plans. Every year we would receive from the parliament different orders – cut this and cut that. But you

> know if you are reducing the army you cannot just cut this unit or that unit without an idea of how to manage this very complex process. You need to keep those units which are very important and get rid of or change those which are not. You cannot just cut everything here and there and expect good results. So, we have not had any idea what we were doing.[31]

This reluctance of civilians to take a long-term view of what they wanted to achieve in the defence sphere was a grave problem. Consider, for example, the *National Security Principles* and the *Basic Principles of National Defence*. Logically, as the conceptual document the *National Security Principles* was drawn up by civilians, in this case the main workhorse being the ministry of foreign affairs. As the subsidiary document, the *Basic Principles of National Defence* was drawn up mainly by military experts in the general staff. However, although parliament approved the *National Security Principles* first, the *Basic Principles of National Defence* was actually drafted well before that in 1992. That is, the military doctrine guided the formulation of the security concept, not the reverse as would be expected had the civilian elite worked out their preferred approach to national defence.

The problems of the Hungarian peacekeeping training centre illustrate the ways in which the dichotomy of power between the general staff and the ministry of defence thwarted some basic reform steps in the period prior to Partnership for Peace. In 1993, in order to enhance its prospects of NATO membership it was decided that Hungary would develop a peacekeeping training centre. Two plans were developed. The first was prepared by the department of multilateral relations of the ministry of defence. According to which, a small centre would play a coordinating role in the military, organising special training for officers and soldiers who had volunteered for peacekeeping duty. Ultimately, this would result in a pool of trained peacekeepers, some of them reservists, who could be mobilised in short order in units of varying size and type depending on the mission. The second plan was prepared by the general staff. Their approach was to create a dedicated, battalion-sized training centre which would train a new company of mechanised infantry for peacekeeping duties every six months. The overworked and understaffed department of multilateral relations was only able to present a general concept at cabinet meetings where the plans were discussed, while the general staff was able to work up its plan in considerable detail. With the announcement of the Partnership for Peace in January 1994, the establishment of the centre became an urgent political priority and it was finally decided to go with the more detailed plan. Unfortunately, the weaknesses of the general staff's plan grew apparent. By 1996, when Hungary was tasked with providing an engineering battalion for IFOR in Bosnia, the number of personnel at the training centre was insufficient, and they lacked engineering training because the centre only trained mechanised infantry. The army had to call for reservists (which the general staff had not planned for). Eventually, under financial pressure and with the deficiencies of the centre become manifest, it was disbanded in spring 1996. In short, the lack of an effective system of civilian management, complicated by the separation and rivalry of the planning functions of the ministry of defence and the general staff, resulted in wasteful, ineffective policy choices.[32]

Partnership for Peace to NATO: a more pro-active approach to defining priorities

The year 1994–1995 marked a turning point for Central Europe in defence and security issues. At the January 1994 Brussels summit meeting of the North Atlantic Council the Partnership for Peace programme was initiated. However generally, the *Partnership for Peace Framework Document*[33] and chapter 5 of the *Study on NATO Enlargement* set out the requirements of membership. With respect to the current analysis, the most salient of these requirements were:

1 transparency in national defence planning and budgetary processes;
2 democratic and civilian control of the armed forces; and
3 armed forces interoperable with NATO forces.

According to the *NATO Handbook*, the Partnership for Peace is focused on 'defence related cooperation but goes beyond dialogue and cooperation to forge a real partnership'.[34] For Poland and Hungary, whether or not this was NATO's original intention, Partnership for Peace was seen as the first step towards full membership. As such, according to a Hungarian analyst, Partnership for Peace was perceived as a series of three waiting rooms: the first was for countries waiting to join NATO as soon as the first expansion was agreed by its member states; the second was for those preparing to join at a later stage; the third was for permanent Partnership for Peace states who would never join the Alliance.[35] Thus the object of reform in Poland and Hungary became more concrete: make sure of being in the first waiting room.

Staying in the first waiting room for eventual NATO membership necessitated certain reform steps be taken in the Central European states. In the words of an interlocutor in the National Security Bureau of the Office of the President of Poland:

> NATO imposed a kind of discipline on us. We had to answer a lot of questions, to adapt our force structure, to prepare annual reports for NATO and to implement NATO's Strategic Concept. We had to adopt civilian democratic control of the armed forces if we wanted to be a member of the alliance.[36]

The desire to enter NATO imposed on politicians the obligation to undertake specific normative changes in their defence establishment. At the same time, NATO and its member states offered specific assistance for reforms. The same interlocutor in Poland continued,

> You can say that they offered us much more help than we could accept. We received a lot of support from our NATO allies. We think it is our

> responsibility to take what we have learned and pass it on to our neighbours. We must export these lessons and take on a regional leadership role.[37]

These words, however, reflect the upside of the NATO coin; there was a downside as well. The desire to enter NATO forced politicians in Central Europe to pay more attention to questions of military significance. Yet, while they became focused on NATO, politicians

> recognised only the advantages of membership not the responsibilities. Civilians tended to look to NATO and EU to the detriment of national institutions. To be honest, Hungarian politicians just neglected the military most of the time. They were not interested or they had other things to do.[38]

In effect, there was a strong tendency amongst Central European reformers to try and simply adopt the forms of democratic civil–military relations without seeking to understand the logic behind them. As a result, reforms were designed without understanding, and they were implemented because NATO required them, not because they were seen as intrinsically necessary. Even worse, there emerged a 'right answer culture' whereby officials learned to declare that all the proper reforms had been undertaken.[39] To a certain extent, the West was complicit in this phenomenon. NATO's Central European adviser wrote,

> We in the West have not actually been very good at analysing the situation, either in our own countries or in Central and Eastern Europe. Therefore we have found it difficult to cross the cultural divide and lend a hand to the new democracies in their task of transformation. A lot of our well-meant effort has been wasted because it was inappropriate, inapplicable or just plain wrong. We overestimated the competence of Central and Eastern European governments to draw up and implement plans in this sphere. We underestimated the impact of corruption and vested self-interest as an obstacle to change.[40]

The result was a process of imperfect copying of liberal-democratic norms of civil–military relations for a variety of non-exclusive reasons (as a form of reductionism, as an abstraction from the original, as a falsification of reality, and/or as a means of formalising relations with other states). This resulted in systems of civil–military relations which were liberal-democratic in form but idiosyncratic and sui generis in practice. This is not to deny the positive impact of NATO on defence reform, which was considerable. Poland and Hungary wanted to join the Alliance and, therefore, they had to agree to its rules and take steps to harmonise their systems with it. At the same time, the approach to NATO was conditioned by the experience of the Warsaw Pact where policy was simply dictated by the alliance's hegemon.

> It was not a question in Hungary whether to have democratic civilian control of the military or not: military commanders wanted control more than the

> civilians did – we needed to know what kind of army the government wanted. That was the problem, the politicians did not have any idea and it is still the problem today. The idea was that NATO would tell us what we needed to do – but NATO is not the Warsaw Pact.[41]

Learning that NATO was not simply a Western version of the Warsaw Pact, that Brussels was not going to hand down policy decisions cooked up in the Pentagon to be faithfully implemented as Moscow once did, and coming up with national solutions was the main task of the period from Partnership for Peace to the invitation to join the Alliance.

As president, Lech Walesa set out for the military leadership the task to build an army that could,

> act as a deterrent and as an encouragement at the same time. It must deter potential aggressors . . . and it must encourage potential allies, who must be made to realise that it is worth cooperating with us, that we are a responsible partner with whom it is worth developing close ties, and that we are strong and stable enough to consolidate international security.[42]

By the time of the NATO Madrid Summit in July 1997, despite budgetary pressures, faults in the design of its institutional structure and political conflicts over its fate, the army had made some modest steps towards accomplishing Walesa's tasks. By no means was the transformation of the military complete, but there was a willingness to adapt the military and its management structures in order to bring it into line with NATO norms. A major contributing factor to this success was that 1994–1995 proved a watershed year for the Polish military budget. After eight years of decline the defence budget rose from US$2.1 billion to US$2.6 billion.[43] Also, in February 1995 the Sejm passed legislation that placed defence spending on five-year planning cycles and committed the government to increasing defence spending to 3 per cent of GDP by 1997. These acts marked the end of uncontrolled military decline in Poland and the modest beginning of military reinvestment.

If the main thrust of reforms up to 1995 was the separation of the administrative functions of the ministry of defence from the command functions of the general staff, the aim after 1995 was to reverse that trend. Given that the civilian bureaucracy in the ministry of defence was highly politicised and subject to a very high rate of turnover, the general staff was reluctant through most of the 1990s to relinquish its prerogatives in the policy-planning sphere and its operational control of the troops to the officials of the ministry of defence. Until Walesa's defeat in the presidential elections of 1995, the general staff proved very successful in playing the president and the parliament off against each other, and thus managed to retain considerable independence from the ministry of defence.

With regard to specific changes in the armed forces, efforts continued to improve the structure and quality of the forces, to redeploy units more evenly throughout the country and to modernise the arsenal of the military. Poland's long-term plan to reform its armed forces, called *Army 2012*, appeared in July 1997. The plan envisaged dramatic cuts in the size of the military from approximately 240,000 to 180,000 troops by 2004. Conscription was to be retained as the main mode of recruitment, but the number of soldiers serving on contracts was to be gradually increased and the length of obligatory military service reduced from eighteen months to a year. The percentage of officers in the military was to be reduced to 30 per cent of total manpower; at the same time, the percentage of professional NCOs would rise to 40 per cent.[44] Overall, by the time they were invited to join NATO the Polish armed forces had achieved some success in transforming the army it inherited from the communist era. NATO's basic military requirements amounted to five conditions:

1 an effective internal security system capable of protecting the Alliance's secret information;
2 integration with NATO's air defence network;
3 infrastructure, such as ports, airstrips and bases for landing and deployment of troops and equipment;
4 a minimum contribution of forces to Alliance operations; and
5 compatible command, communications and information systems.

According to NATO, these basic standards were met.[45]

Despite its generally obsolescent equipment the army put intense effort into achieving a minimal level of interoperability with NATO.[46] A more even distribution of troops from their previous heavy concentration in the West to a more balanced deployment throughout the country was also executed. These successes, however, have to be considered alongside some persisting problems. A report of the Supreme Audit Chamber conducted in 1997–1998 showed that the full reform of the army was still a long way off. Shortcomings in the ratio of officers to soldiers, the quality and sophistication of armaments, the generally low level of expenditure on defence, and even hygiene (some units were held together 'only by dirt', said the report), were pointed out.[47] To a certain extent the persistence of these problems can be attributed to inadequate financing. Changing the system of manning the armed forces from a conscript to a mixed conscript-contract system is an expensive project, as is modernising the military arsenal. The lack of money, however, cannot *fully* explain the problem. In the words of the director of the NATO integration department of the ministry of defence, 'Of course, we have money, money, money problems. Well, mainly it is true we need more funds, but sometimes this is just an excuse.'[48] In fact, although the military budget was on the rise after 1995 in dollar terms, as a percentage of GDP it declined slightly from 2.3 per cent in 1994 to 2.1 per cent in 1998 (despite the 1995 commitment to raise the budget to 3.0 per cent of GDP by 1997).[49] On the other hand, though the budget was tight it was also relatively stable. The problem, therefore, was not the level of resources per se; rather it was the discontinuity between the level of resources and the type of force structure it was supposed to sustain.[50]

This discontinuity becomes evident when the military budget is broken down to reveal the ways in which fiscal priorities were profoundly skewed by Western standards. For example, the Western norm for expenditure on procurement and personnel is approximately 30 per cent for each; in Poland, however, personnel expenditures averaged 65 per cent of spending from 1995 to 1997, while procurement averaged only 15 per cent. Military research and development averaged less than 1 per cent of the budget and investment in infrastructure 3.6 per cent.[51] Procurement of modern weaponry has been the most politically sensitive issue. Officials found themselves subject to conflicting pressures. On the one hand, they had limited funds for procurement. On the other hand, the military and a large domestic defence industry with strong labour unions were desperate for contracts on new weapons. At the same time, 'in the minds of freedom fighters and democratic revolutionaries elected after 1989, there was still a nagging doubt that maybe the West in its heart of hearts really cared more about its financial interests than shared values'. The result was that defence officials came to 'exaggerate both the size of their pocketbook and the immediacy of their need for advanced military equipment' – particularly big ticket items like combat aircraft.[52]

The *Army 2012* reform programme assumed further changes in the organisational structure of the army: reducing manpower to 150,000 troops, changing the personnel structure to 25 per cent officers, 25–30 per cent professional NCOs, the remainder conscripts; personnel costs to be reduced from over 50 per cent of the budget to 34 per cent in 2010; maintenance costs reduced; and procurement raised to 30 per cent.[53] The procurement section of the plan was given positive reviews in a confidential report of the Supreme Allied Command Europe (SACEUR).[54] This is not to say that such changes had actually been accomplished; they had not, and how exactly they would be was not yet clear. Nonetheless, there was a shift in mentality among planners away from simply demanding more money to support a largely unchanged military structure to a more reasoned approach based on a calculation of desired ends and available means. 'NATO does not want these countries to start a process of spending lots of money on re-equipment,' said a NATO spokesman in 1999. 'What is more important is that the equipment they have represents investment which is bearable for their weak economies – let's be frank, they are in transition, their economies are weak – so that we can work together.'[55] During a visit to Poland in March 1998, NATO SACEUR General Wesley Clark allegedly made the point that 'I have no need for modern fighters with pilots having only 40 hours of flying time.'[56] On the eve of its accession to NATO, more and more Polish defence officials were beginning to grasp the wisdom of this statement.

Like Poland, Hungary's joining up to Partnership for Peace coincided with the first increase in the military budget since 1988 from US$556 million in 1994 to US$641 million in 1995. In contrast with Poland, however, the budget increase was not sustained, falling both in absolute terms to US$520 million in 1996 and US$511 million in 1997, and as a percentage of GDP from 1.6 per cent in 1994 to 1.3 per cent in 1998 (the lowest of the three new NATO members). Only in 1998 did the budget begin to rise again to US$648 million after the government committed itself to raising the defence budget by 0.01 per cent of GDP annually until reaching a level of 1.8 per cent of GDP.[57] The Hungarian budget exhibited dysfunction in the way it allocated resources among spending categories. Personnel costs from 1995 to 1997 averaged 49.9 per cent of total spending; 37 per cent was devoted to operations and maintenance; and only 4.9 per cent to procurement (only 2 per cent by 1997).[58] To make matters worse, the ministry of defence was required to generate up to 20 per cent of its budget for itself (through a variety of commercial ventures and sale of surplus equipment) in what were called 'predesignated expenses'. If the military failed to generate the required money no new funds from the state budget would be applied to make up the difference.[59] In short, the defence budget was as skewed as the Polish budget in terms of its allocation of resources, but it was even more unstable.

With procurement spending so low, military modernisation was proving to be a fantasy. In 1993, 113 units of an American-made identification-friend-or-foe (IFF) system and a small number of French-made Mistral and Atlas missiles were purchased. Otherwise, most procurement was of used equipment, mainly from Russia, Belarus and GDR stocks.[60] The military was, in essence, being de-modernised. All in all, the defence budget between 1994 and 1998 was insufficient and produced a crisis in the military. The ministry of defence could only keep its equipment operable through the cannibalisation of assets freed up by the execution of its CFE Treaty obligations. Stocks of fuel, spare parts and so on grew smaller. At the same time, the renovation of barracks and other installations on military bases had to be put off which, in turn, made the recruitment of professional soldiers even more complicated. New systems were not being created, while existing ones were allowed to disintegrate. Even the relatively modern MIG-29s acquired from Russia proved a double-edged sword since the cost of one flight hour in a MIG-29 was five times the cost of that in the old MIG-21.[61]

As with Poland, however, the state of the budget explains only part of the problem. At a more basic level, the problem was that politicians had not decided on a concept of security; because of that they had no clear ideas about the resolution of the problems of the military and could not provide real guidance. What emerged was a conflict of military vs civilian psychology:

> the military mind wants to be *doing* something, to be active, to make plans and to put them into action. But in Hungary, civilians did not know what to do. They had so many problems that giving guidance to the military was not a priority. So, the military did things for itself without seriously checking in with political or societal opinions. Some units were relocated (which cost a lot of money) only to be cut the next year. There were lots of examples like that, a lot of money was wasted.[62]

The politicians lacked experience in the defence sphere and failed to recognise their responsibilities. On the other side, the thinking of the military was very narrow, focusing on the problems of the military, not on the troubles in the country that limited the capacity of the state to modernise the armed forces:

> It was a really big problem that the civilian side did not have enough experience to say how to reform and modernise the military structure, how to

> modify the system and make it work better and so on. And they did not want to believe the suggestions of the military.[63]

Things began to improve with the second large military reform in Hungary in 1996–1997 under the MSZMP government which was straightforward: 'to create smaller and modern armed forces with deterrence value and capable of integration into the military organisations of NATO'.[64] The defence command was converted to a NATO-type joint staff structure in September 1997. The numerical strength of the army was reduced between 1994 and 1998 by 45 per cent from 97,800 troops in 1994 to 53,150 in 1998. The percentage of officers rose from 16 per cent of personnel to 18 per cent, while NCOs rose from 11 to 18 per cent over the same period.[65] The length of obligatory military service was also cut back to 10 months in February 1996.

On the eve of its accession to NATO, Hungary was lagging somewhat behind Poland in coming to grips with the problems in its defence establishment and designing solutions from first principles. The budgetary crisis was deeper and longer than in Poland; while elites allowed the situation to drift without direction for longer. As a result, defence reform made less progress from 1994 to 1998. To its credit, the ministry of defence had made efficient use of the meagre resources allotted to it in trying circumstances, but estimable crisis management skills could not mask the obvious decline of the armed forces. That said, the pressure of looming accession was beginning to have an effect on Hungarian policy-makers:

> Until last year [1998] the government never paid any attention to the military. But when it was clear we were getting into NATO it changed things. Before, because the civilians had no experience and no interest in defence issues they did not want to spend any money or to plan anything. And the military could not push them. They could not say 'hey guys, look at the future!' Every new government had a different policy. Now with NATO, the military can say 'OK gentlemen you wrote this and this in your document, so what about the practice?' Its harder for the politicians to say they have no money for that now. There is a common interest now, the civilians realise they have to do something in the military because otherwise within two years there will be nothing.[66]

The first year in NATO: implementing reforms, persisting problems

After the NATO summit in Madrid in July 1997 there were reports in some Western media that one or another of the new members were militarily not fit for NATO.[67] Such reports were true in a sense and, at the same time, quite unfair. The fact is that almost no member states' armed forces were ready for the future roles and missions envisaged in the latest NATO *Strategic Concept*. Nonetheless, the deficiencies of the Polish and Hungarian armies were quite evident:

1 Major changes in the personnel structure of the armed forces were required. Crucially, they lacked a corps of professional NCOs – the essential linchpin

of Western-style armed forces. Within the officer corps there were far too many senior officers and not enough junior officers.

2 Attracting high quality recruits for the military profession and retaining them required improving barracks and housing for servicemen and their families, raising salaries, and increasing the prestige of military service.
3 Efforts to improve interoperability with NATO forces, especially in the area of command, control and communications systems had to be intensified.
4 Education and training had to be improved, not only in the technical sense such as increasing the flying hours of pilots, but also in language and military professionalism.
5 Modernisation of military equipment had to be undertaken, especially systems required for more flexible and deployable forces such as support, transport and logistics systems.

It was clear from the beginning that the transformation of the armed forces would not be easy. Considering the position from which they started, the progress achieved by the new members by March 1999 was considerable. In the words of a Hungarian analyst speaking in late 1999:

> We know very well that the technical level of the Hungarian military is not good enough for NATO. That is no secret to anyone. In many respects it does not meet basic requirements and there are some basic policy documents which are still not ready. But the way of thinking in the military from the sergeants to the generals is changing. In this way, joining up to NATO has definitely been beneficial.[68]

A more reasonable concern was that having achieved the goal of acceding to NATO, elites would be tempted to ignore defence reform and that a new period of stagnation would set in as the pressure for change lessened. The fact that defence spending in Poland, for example, began to fall again in 1999 prompted a Polish interlocutor to remonstrate:

> Everybody understands that we have some difficulties with the military budget and some of the politicians try to say, 'OK, now we are in NATO so it is not our problem anymore. It is the problem of the army to figure it out.' But if our military has certain obligations, standards, or requirements stemming from the Alliance then it has financial requirements. That is the problem of the Polish parliament. Unfortunately, some Polish politicians do not understand this and they do not want to take responsibility.[69]

However, such indicators need to be put in the context of the August 1998 economic crisis which hit hard in Eastern Europe. Membership of NATO inevitably produced stress and confusion in the Polish and Hungarian armed forces to which they showed signs of adapting, learning by doing. But were their politicians following along? In the first year of membership there were contradictory signs of both progress and persisting problems. On the one hand, a complex understanding of NATO and the responsibilities of membership was not common in political circles:

> the majority of people in politics and in society think of NATO in the old terms – like a pre-1991 alliance. In the media that is the way it is discussed. But NATO is quite different now and that is not widely recognised. The common view of NATO is as if it were a superstate. You know in the papers we see articles talking about cooperation with NATO but there is no realisation that we *are* NATO.[70]

On the other hand, there were signs of progress. Poland managed to work out a new *Security Strategy, National Defence Strategy* and armed forces development programme while Hungary updated its 1993 *Basic Principles of Security Policy* and launched a *Strategic Defence Review*. These steps marked the beginning of serious steps in both countries to define their defence goals rigorously and to work out reasoned policies for their realisation.

On 4 January 2000, a new *Security Strategy of the Republic of Poland*[71] was adopted by the Council of Ministers and a *National Defence Strategy of the Republic of Poland* was adopted on 23 May 2000.[72] The first document described in some detail Poland's strategic goals, the perceived threats to its security, the various national security instruments and the types of activity they would engage in, the impact of Poland's alliance commitments on its defence, the fundamentals of the defence strategy and the roles and organisation of the armed forces. The second document reiterated the general propositions of the first and then elaborated in more detail the concept of national defence, the organisation of the defence establishment and plans for defence preparation. Basically, the *Security Strategy* described the dangers for the country and, roughly, what would be done to meet them. The *National Defence Strategy* contained the mobilisation plan for the army and described how the army would be manned, deployed, equipped and so on. The ministry of foreign affairs was mainly responsible for drafting the *Security Strategy*, while the ministry of defence handled the drafting of the *National Defence Strategy*.[73] The differences between the 1992 and 2000 versions of the *Security Strategy* and *National Defence Strategy* stemmed from membership in NATO. The new *Security Strategy* began:

> Membership in the Atlantic Alliance in a significant way has changed Poland's geopolitical and geostrategic position. Poland has become a part of an effective allied defence system guaranteeing security and providing conditions for stable development.[74]

At the same time, the *Security Strategy* reiterated the threat to peace and stability posed by non-traditional factors, such as: ethnic conflicts, economic crises, political instability, human rights violations, proliferation of weapons of mass destruction, terrorism and organised crime.[75] One of the most interesting aspects of the *Security*

Strategy is the declared aspiration of Poland to play a 'significant role – commensurate with its potential and needs – in shaping and implementing NATO's politico-defensive strategy towards Eastern Europe'. In particular, it noted Poland's interest in NATO-Ukrainian cooperation, strengthening its independence, democratic institutions and links with European structures.[76] Generally speaking, the *Security Strategy* and *National Defence Strategy* are considerably more refined and detailed than the 1992 versions they replaced, revealing a more mature analytical approach to defence in Polish military and political circles.[77] Nonetheless, not all was well with the process of their formulation. The 1992 documents were drafted under and approved by the president as the head of the National Security Committee. The 2000 policies were drafted under the direction of, and approved by, the Cabinet of Ministers. According to the cabinet, the *Security Strategy* and *National Defence Strategy* were state policy. According to the president, who had not signed them by June 2000, they were not.[78] In 1999, also, there were continuing signs of difficulty meeting obligations to NATO. The *Army 2012* reform programme was under severe criticism from Bronislaw Komorowski, then chairman of the parliamentary national defence committee, who told Polish Radio on 27 December that the plan was based 'on financial hopes rather than realities' and that owing to low defence spending efforts to modernise and adapt the armed forces to NATO standards would have to be cut back.[79]

Hungary's 1993 *National Security Principles* and the *Basic Principles of National Defence* were updated in 1998. The principal motivation for reworking the documents was to bring policy into line with the implications of NATO membership. The preamble to the *Basic Principles of Security and Defence Policy of the Hungarian Republic*[80] reads much the same as the Polish *Security Strategy*, noting that the attainment of full NATO membership drastically changed the security environment of Hungary for the better while also pointing out a broad range of non-traditional threats to security. The problem with the Basic Principles is that it was only meant to provide a framework for the development of a much more detailed *National Security Strategy* and *National Military Strategy* which were supposed to have been approved in the summer of 1999 but have not yet been approved as of April 2001. Without a security strategy, however, there can be no reasoned basis for the development of the armed forces; without a military strategy, force requirements and unit designs cannot be worked out properly. Detailed work in any functional area runs the risk of being misdirected if it is not based on the objectives and tasks set out in these crucial documents.

Nonetheless, in July 1999 the government ordered that a steering group led by the administrative state secretary of defence and made up of senior civilians and military leaders conduct a *Strategic Defence Review* with the purpose of creating modern, NATO-compatible armed forces. Specific weaknesses of the Hungarian defence forces that were highlighted in the *Strategic Defence Review* included: force structure and doctrine, force design, military pay, personnel management, recruitment, leadership training, base infrastructure, equipment and training. Inter alia, the table of organisation and equipment of units were judged to be in quite poor shape, being essentially based on Soviet models with inappropriate authorisations of officers, NCOs and men. The pay system was found to favour position over rank and to reward officers serving in higher headquarters more than officers in command of operational forces. The facilities found on military bases were in extremely poor shape since most were built in the 1950s and had suffered from a decade of essentially no maintenance throughout the 1990s.[81] The *Strategic Defence Review* was hardly an unqualified success. It identified many of the problems of the military, but how *exactly* the ministry of defence was going to address specific problems such as the creation of a corps of NCOs, the unbalanced structure of the officer corps, or the essential unattractiveness of the military profession in society was not spelled out. Moreover, as soon as the review was announced it came under fire from opposition politicians, military officers and academics. In the opinion of a senior Hungarian officer, the government was misguided in conducting the review 'in a strictly top-down manner with the involvement of very few senior military personnel. Not only was the involvement of the military missing during the review but opposition members of the parliamentary defence committee were also not included.'[82]

Nonetheless, at the end of their first year in NATO there were tentative signs that the Hungarian government was taking stock of its desired ends and available means in the defence sphere. Heretofore, defence reform had been driven mainly by unstructured cuts. Shortly after the *Strategic Defence Review*, the government committed itself to raising defence spending to 1.61 per cent of GDP by 2001. It also eliminated the 'pre-designated expenses' which had reduced the military budget throughout the 1990s. The ministry of defence was permitted to transfer obsolete military equipment to the State Privatisation Corporation which meant that it would not have to waste time and resources storing and guarding redundant equipment. Additionally, in 1999 the ministry received a one time financial injection from the government in order to pay debts to banks that had been accumulating since the purchase of the Mistral/Atlas rocket system in the early 1990s.[83]

Former Soviet Union

In the normative sense of deliberate, orderly, change for the better it is reasonable to say that neither Ukraine nor Russia accomplished *much* reform of their defence establishments in the period under review. To be sure the armed forces of both countries experienced profound changes, but changes for the *better* were few and far between in a time characterised by crises and looming disasters. Before we look at the reasons behind this failure to reform, however, it is worthwhile noting in some detail the unique factors in Russia and Ukraine that figure into the analysis.

From January 1654, when the Ukrainian Hetman Bohdan Khmelnitsky swore allegiance to the Russian Tsar Alexis I at Pereyeslavl, until the Ukrainian Declaration of Independence in August 1991, Ukraine and Russia existed as separate states for only a few short years (1918–1921). Given this history it is no surprise that the similarities between Russia and Ukraine outweigh the differences by a large margin. Nonetheless, as with Poland and Hungary there are crucial differences which bear examination.

Ten years after the collapse of the USSR it is easy to forget that the huge arsenal of the Soviet forces based in Ukraine made the nascent Ukrainian army, on paper, one of the strongest in the world. Yet the raw numbers belie a deeper reality: what Ukraine inherited was not an army as such; rather, it simply laid claim to the parts of the dismembered Soviet army that happened to have been based on its territory, minus the bureaucratic structures needed for its management and control which existed only in Moscow. It had no ministry of defence, no general staff, no central command structure nor any other administrative apparatus for its defence establishment in 1991. By contrast, in the early 1990s, Russia's military existed in a different kind of administrative limbo. Initially, it was intended that the Soviet armed forces would be preserved in some form by the creation of the Commonwealth of Independent States (CIS) Joint Forces to which the armed forces of the successor states would be subordinated. This implied that much of the bureaucratic structures of the Soviet ministry of defence would remain at the supra-national CIS level. However, as it became obvious that most of the newly independent states, notably Ukraine, were unenthusiastic about belonging to a unified CIS armed forces headquartered in Moscow and directed by the Kremlin, a Russian Federation ministry of defence was created in May 1992.[84] With this act, most of the bureaucratic structures of the CIS (effectively Soviet) ministry of defence and general staff were appropriated by the Russian ministry of defence.[85]

The main differences between Russia and Ukraine lie in the contrasting attitudes of their political elites to the West in general and to NATO in particular. In Russia, the spectrum of foreign policy views have been seen by some as including 'liberal westernizers' at one extreme, opposed by 'fundamentalist nationalists' on the other, with 'pragmatic nationalists' occupying the middle ground. Liberal westernisers, broadly speaking, were democrats in favour of the free market and believed in maintaining friendly relations with the West. Pragmatic nationalists also professed admiration for democratic principles and capitalism, but stressed the necessity that they be adapted to Russian conditions. They favoured good relations with the West, yet they also did not shy from putting Russian national interests ahead of any international agenda. Fundamentalist nationalists believed in a unique Russian (or Eurasian) approach to economic and political development which entailed preservation of many elements of authoritarianism. They tended to view the West as implacably hostile and favoured restoring Russia's regional hegemony.[86]

In the early 1990s, particularly when Andrei Kozyrev headed the foreign ministry, Russian policy tended to reflect the liberal westernising view. In 1994 Russia joined Partnership for Peace (though amidst heavy domestic opposition). In the mid- and late-1990s, however, attitudes toward the West began to harden. The *NATO-Russia Founding Act* of 27 May 1997 did not assuage Russian fears of increasing exclusion from the centre of European security decision-making.[87] A few Russian analysts voiced cautious support for the Act, suggesting that the NATO–Russia Permanent Joint Council which it established might allow Russia a voice in European security issues.[88] But the majority of analysts and political figures saw it as symbolising Russia's powerlessness to resist the advancement of

NATO.[89] By 1999, under Vladimir Putin pragmatic nationalism had become the order of the day in foreign and defence policy.

As in Russia, a variety of Ukrainian foreign policy camps with opposing views have been pointed out. Light and Löwenhardt noted the diverging views of those favouring a 'Slavic choice' or a 'European choice' as significant.[90] The 'Slavic choice' camp called for deepening links with Russia and Belarus with the end goal of creating a federation of the Slavic successor states of the USSR. In general, their views were similar to Russian fundamentalist nationalists about the essential malice of the West toward the Slavic nations. By contrast, those in favour of a 'European choice' believed strongly in defending Ukrainian sovereignty. To this group, Ukraine's future as a democratic state lay in strengthening links with the West, and in particular NATO, as this would help guarantee Ukrainian independence from Russia while at the same time stimulating the economy and stabilising democratic transformation. On the other hand, they recognised the imperatives of having good relations with Russia which necessitated maintaining a tactful policy of official non-alignment.[91]

Whereas in Russia liberal westernisers, pragmatic and fundamentalist nationalists alike were united in opposition to the enlargement of NATO, Ukrainian authorities did not consider NATO a threat. Indeed, Ukraine eagerly joined Partnership for Peace and has been by far its most active CIS participant. The July 1997 *Ukraine-NATO Charter on a Distinctive Partnership* was highly esteemed by many Ukrainian analysts who saw it as a potentially effective mechanism for counterbalancing the influence of Russia.[92]

In addition to its participation in Partnership for Peace activities abroad, Ukraine hosted a number of joint exercises on its territory.[93] Since 7 May 1997 Kiev has hosted a NATO Information and Documentation Centre actively disseminating materials on the Alliance to the public and press. As of May 1998, NATO has permanently staffed a formal Liaison Office in Kiev in order to facilitate Ukraine's participation in Partnership for Peace. And in November 1998 a *State Programme for Cooperation Between Ukraine and NATO Up to 2000* was presented at NATO headquarters which included provision for joint defence planning and operations. In short, political and military elites in Kiev were much more open to NATO than those in Moscow. In 2000 there were more than 500 bilateral and multilateral activities between Ukraine and NATO and its member states. In particular, the Ukrainian ministry of defence sought to put defence reform under the Partnership for Peace planning and review process (PARP). And a NATO–Ukraine Joint Working Group on Defence Reform was established in 1999.[94]

Unlike Ukraine, Russia made only limited use of training assistance programmes offered by NATO or by its member states individually. Military to military contacts were hesitant, politically-charged and characterised by considerable mistrust on both sides.[95] No officers from the ministry of defence were permitted to attend programmes at the US Army Marshall Centre in Southern Germany, for example. The ambivalence of the ministry of defence towards participation in Western outreach activities turned to open distrust in 1999 during the Kosovo conflict. All Russian military personnel training in NATO countries were recalled. At the same time, the newly opened NATO Documentation Centre on European Security Issues in Moscow was closed down.

From the collapse of the Soviet Union to the war in Chechnya: reform by declaration

Under the terms of the Conventional Forces in Europe (CFE) Treaty, between them Russia and Ukraine were entitled to maintain in the European part of the former USSR up to 79 per cent of the tanks, 85 per cent of the artillery, 88 per cent of the combat aircraft and 71 per cent of the combat helicopters of the Soviet armed forces. In terms of manpower, Russia had an army of 2.72 million men and Ukraine had an army of 726,000 in 1992.[96] This legacy was both a blessing and a curse. On the one hand, the vast stockpiles of Soviet military materiel enabled both armies to endure the collapse of procurement in the 1990s without having their forces fall into complete ruin for much longer than might have been expected. To these advantages must be added the benefit of having inherited a large number of well-trained professional officers accustomed to strategic planning in a way that officers in the non-Soviet Warsaw Pact states were not. On the other hand, what the division of the Soviet army's personnel and equipment left Russia and Ukraine with were disoriented, skewed, embittered and essentially rudderless militaries facing a myriad of crippling and inextricably linked problems.[97]

Many of the forces Russia took over, for example, were third-rate cadre units manned at low levels and equipped with older equipment.[98] The best units were the more than 600,000 serving abroad. Unfortunately, repatriation of these forces represented a logistical nightmare for the general staff. Often depleted or fragmented – and with their dependents amounting to more than a million people – these military formations had to be absorbed into formerly second or third echelon military districts where no adequate facilities for their housing, training or upkeep existed. Moreover, inheriting the Soviet officer corps was also a double-edged sword. On the one hand, the Ukrainian and Russian officer corps possessed a wealth of military expertise and experience in strategic planning. But this came at a price: the preservation of the old-thinking, prejudiced and blinkered conservatism of the old Soviet officer corps.

A key feature of the Soviet military mindset which is still prevalent in the Russian and Ukrainian defence establishments is the distinction between the concepts of 'military reform' and 'reform of the armed forces'. This difference was clearly demarcated by Russia's second minister of defence, Igor Rodionov, who argued that 'military reform is the process of bringing the entire defence activity of the state into conformity with the new political, economic and social changes in the society . . . [It] is not quantitative change in the armed forces but a fundamental qualitative reorganisation of the essence of the state's military system.' As he saw it, this was the responsibility of the political leadership of the state. It was they who must determine the objectives of military reform and see that they were put into effect. 'Reform of the armed forces', on the other hand, 'is but a component of [i.e., dependent on] military reform.' It is the responsibility of the ministry of defence under the guidance and supervision of the civilian government.[99] There is a certain logic to this intellectual approach to reform and the firm belief of the army that it should be the instrument of the state and not its master is admirable. Nonetheless, it is also true that this attitude prompted the Russian and Ukrainian military elite to adopt a dilatory approach to reform; without clear cut guidelines or leadership from their civilian masters the training and gut instinct of the military leadership in both countries was to see their duty as being not so much to build a new system as it was to *preserve* as much as possible of the old until the arrival of better times permitted more investment.

For Russia the main strategic reality to be confronted in the 1990s was the loss of its allies in the Warsaw Pact as well as the fourteen other former republics of the USSR. In the past, Russia faced potential conflicts to the east with China and to the west with NATO. While conflict on these frontiers was potentially dangerous to the point of nuclear confrontation, it was also stable and, to a large extent, predictable. By contrast, the 1990s was a time of open or latent conflict on almost every frontier. To the south Russian strategic planners perceived a growing threat from Islamic fundamentalism aimed at them from outside the borders of the USSR, from some of the CIS states, and from some areas of the Federation itself. From the east economically and militarily ascendant China posed a threat to the underpopulated, resource-rich far eastern regions of Russia. While from the West NATO bent on expanding eastward, perhaps even so far as to taking on former Soviet republics, was a gnawing concern to Russians of nearly every political stripe. By contrast, Ukraine had never had a ‘strategic context’ of its own. It had none of Russia’s aspirations to great power status nor did it harbour designs on the territory of any of its neighbours. Nevertheless, as the westernmost (Slavic) successor state of the USSR, situated at the crossroads between Europe and the mineral and oil resources of south Russia and the Caucasus, and occupying the northern coast of the Black Sea, post-Soviet Ukraine was also a country of exceptional strategic importance.[100]

Like Poland and Hungary, reform of the armed forces in Russia and Ukraine was driven by the need to adjust the size, composition and structure of the armed forces to reflect the new political and military situation as well as the economic potential of the state. To a much greater extent than in Central Europe, however, the problems of the armed forces in the former Soviet Union states grew to crisis proportions as military and political elites failed to reach any workable consensus on the ends and means of reform. In both Ukraine and Russia a clear institutional preference for mass armies was evident among the military leadership. Thus the desire in both armies was to preserve the organisational structure of the mass Soviet army despite the obvious lack of money which made such preservation practically impossible. The results of this disjuncture between the size of the military and its level of funding were made clear by Shlykov in 1997:

> If we were to begin to supply and pay and, most importantly, train Russian soldiers as the countries of NATO and China do we could afford an army of the following size: 100,000 men according to the American model, 120,000

> according to the English model, 180,000 according to the German model, 170,000 according to the French model, and 360,000 according to the Chinese model.[101]

By 1998, however, the Russian army still had about 1.2 million men organised into 52 divisions (active and reserve) and numerous independent brigades, as compared to the 22 US army and marine divisions for a slightly larger force of 1.45 million men. In short, the army insisted on maintaining more divisions than it could effectively man and more troops than it could effectively train and equip. The basic problem facing both armies was that they absolutely lacked the financial wherewithal to maintain a professional military. In both countries financial obligations to retiring servicemen made disbanding units more expensive than manning them.[102] For example, it was estimated in 1996 that it cost 14 billion rubles to maintain a motorised rifle regiment as opposed to 48 billion to disband it.[103] Thus the military leadership was faced with a dilemma: without the political will to make an extra-budgetary financial investment in downsizing, the ministry of defence could not release personnel. In both Ukraine and Russia the upshot of the situation was that service in the ranks of the armed forces quickly became applicable only to the lumpenised strata of socicty who either lacked the means to avoid service or who were so poor that military service still looked like an avenue for social mobility.

Increasing the effectiveness of the armed forces was another broad and frequently stated main goal of reform.[104] The reality, however, was that in the 1990s both militaries slipped into deep decay. Effective training essentially ceased with exercises above battalion size growing exceedingly rare. Pilots logged flight hours less than a fifth of those considered by NATO forces as the minimum necessary to maintain proficiency. Ships ceased putting to sea for lack of fuel and parts. Equipment became unserviceable for lack of regular maintenance. And procurement of new equipment fell almost to zero.[105]

In July 1992, shortly after his appointment, Russian defence minister Pavel Grachev announced his plans for reforming the armed forces. He suggested that the military be reformed in three stages over a period of six to eight years. In the first stage (one to two years), a ministry of defence would be set up, plans for the numerical strength and structure of the armed forces would be made, and a system for controlling the sequence and time frame for defence reform would be established. In the second stage (two to three years), the total strength of the armed forces would be reduced to 2.1 million (by 1995), and a mixed manning system would be introduced. During the third stage (three to four years), the force reductions mandated by the CFE would be implemented, structural and organisational reforms would also be launched and the numerical strength of the armed forces further reduced to as low as 1.5 million troops. The only really novel element in Grachev's plan was its emphasis on the creation of 'mobile forces'. These mobile forces equipped with high-tech weapons would be based mainly on the five airborne divisions and three independent brigades Russia inherited from the Soviet Union.[106]

As their former commander, Grachev's favouring of the airborne forces was predictable. However, the logic of having smaller, more mobile forces equipped with high-tech weaponry was not unsound.[107] Nonetheless, in view of the fiscal straitjacket placed on the state the plan was unmistakably utopian. How the ministry of defence was going to pay to keep a large fraction of the massive military structure of the Soviet Union going while at the same time adding on high-tech mobile forces of a new type was never explained. In fact, no serious and organised discussion of military reform was really possible in the ministry of defence under Grachev.[108] It is not surprising then that the mobile force plan was never developed into a concrete state programme for reform backed by real political and financial means. In fact, according to one analyst, the general staff under General Mikhail Kolesnikov disagreed with Grachev's 'high-quality/low quantity' army and quietly sabotaged the mobile force plans.[109]

Nonetheless, throughout the early 1990s, Yeltsin periodically proclaimed military reform to be on track. Speaking to the collegium of the ministry of defence in Moscow on 14 November 1994 Yeltsin stated that the creation of the mobile forces was being completed, that a new concept for the development of the armed forces was drawing to a close and that Grachev was the best defence minister of the past decade.[110] But the overt military campaign to reassert federal control over Chechnya which commenced on 11 December 1994 brought an end to the charade. During this time, the Russian government did take some formal steps to reform the military, to place it within a new legal and administrative framework, and to modify the military doctrine. But the new state was too disorganised to pursue a consistent and effective course in any area, and the president's attention was focused not on creating a viable system of civil–military relations, but rather on assuring the army's loyalty in the bitter struggles for power – at a time when the military budget was being drastically slashed. Yeltsin's solution to the problem was to put the army under the command of people he trusted – and to grant the military a considerable autonomy in coping with the hard times from its own means as it saw fit; as in so many other areas of Russia's transition, Yeltsin's success was primarily in the destruction of the old system, rather than in the creation of a new one.

Russia pronounced its first *Military Doctrine* on 2 November 1993.[111] At the time the doctrine was issued the political power of the pro-Western elite in Russia was already beginning to wane. That said, the doctrine did not mark a complete about face to an anti-Western stance; rather, there was a more subtle shift in emphasis and nuance. On the one hand, the doctrine was explicitly defensive in nature. Moreover, non-military means of conflict resolution were preferred over the use of force. It also assumed no threat from the West or imminence of a global war. On the other hand, neither was the *possibility* of conflict between Russia and the West ruled out. According to the doctrine, while the threat of armed aggression against the Russian Federation had diminished, it had not disappeared. The main danger was seen in local wars and regional conflicts exacerbated by 'social, political, economic, territorial, religious, national-ethnic and other contradictions . . .'. But the 'expansion of military blocs and alliances . . .' was also noted as a threat to security.[112]

The most significant aspects of the 1993 *Military Doctrine* were, first, its subtle differences from a draft doctrine published in May 1992 which was thought to have been the product of the general staff while the 1993 doctrine was reputedly the work of the ministry of defence.[113] The 1993 *Military Doctrine* muted the prospect of confrontation with the West. By contrast, the 1992 draft strongly implied the hostility of the United States and NATO. This suggests that the general staff and the ministry of defence did not see eye to eye on the threats to Russia's security but that the view of the ministry of defence had more backing in political circles at the time. Second, the 1993 *Military Doctrine* had only the most tenuous connection to an overarching security concept. Presumably, there was some connection to the *Basic Provisions of a Foreign Policy Concept* which was adopted by the Security Council around the same time.[114] Nonetheless, at that time Russia had no formal security concept as such. As a result, both the 1992 draft and the approved doctrine of 1993 read very much as expositions of the army's preferences for military development and reflected their world view of potential threats rather than the considered foreign and security policy plans of the state as a whole. In short, there was little sign in either document of a civilian influence. This suggests that the 1993 *Military Doctrine* was written by the military leadership in an attempt to lock their priorities into state policy before those of the politicians had clarified.

The formal approval of the 1993 *Military Doctrine* despite its disconnection from any overarching foreign policy concept, its absence of any obvious civilian input and its calls for greater investment in the armed forces can only be understood in the context of the October Crisis of that year. Yeltsin's strong political instincts warned him early on in 1992–1993 that the military might be the decisive player in the rapidly escalating confrontation between him and the parliament. Accordingly, he took care that the generals were on his side by promising to give the army a higher priority in financing than the economic situation warranted. In essence, the *Military Doctrine* of 1993, which was enacted by presidential decree (No. 1833) just a few days after the bombardment of the White House by army tanks brought the parliamentary revolt of Rutskoi and Khasbulatov to an end, was part of the price Yeltsin paid for the army's support. Shortly afterwards, in answer to a reporter's question of what the army would do if the Duma amended his new military doctrine, Grachev replied 'we shall amend the parliament'.[115] In a normal country such a joke from the top military officer would have been his last official statement. In Russia at the time it simply reflected the reality of the balance of political power: the military had protected the president in return for which the president promised to protect the military's budget; the parliament could say nothing about it. In short, the 1993 *Military Doctrine* was not written with the purpose of defining the military crises with which Russia might be faced; rather, it was designed to justify the goals of the military leadership.

It is easy to claim that essentially nothing was accomplished in terms of reforming the Russian military in the first few years of the 1990s. However, the general staff should be credited with carrying out determinedly and relatively efficiently four major tasks: the withdrawal of former Soviet troops from the non-Soviet Warsaw Pact states; the withdrawal of tactical and strategic nuclear weapons from Belarus, Kazakhstan and Ukraine; the distribution of CFE quotas of conventional armaments between Azerbaijan, Armenia, Belarus, Georgia, Moldova and Ukraine; and, the consolidation of control over forces in a number of conflict areas (Azerbaijan, Chechnya, Georgia, Moldova and Tajikistan).[116] Nonetheless, little *else* was accomplished and the war in Chechnya effectively brought to an end the implicit bargain between Yeltsin and the military – loyalty in return for priority in funding. Indeed, the war in Chechnya convinced many military officers of the essential malfeasance of the Yeltsin regime which sent an unprepared army into battle against its own citizens only to withdraw support and deny responsibility for the campaign when things went bad, leaving the army to 'hold the bag'.[117]

The breakdown of the compact between Yelstin and the ministry of defence was evident in the fall in defence spending. From 1992 to 1994 the defence budget had been relatively stable. According to estimates of the International Institute of Strategic Studies (IISS) the budget even rose slightly from US$74.6 billion in 1992 to US$79.0 billion in 1994. More conservative estimates from SIPRI point to a decline in that period from US$47.5 billion in 1992 to US$40.5 billion in 1994. Both institutes, however, point to a sharp decline in the defence budget in 1995, to US$62 billion according to the IISS, or to US$25.7 billion according to SIPRI – a plunge of 22 or 27.5 per cent respectively in one year. In short, Yeltsin thoroughly cowed the parliament with the help of the military. But he and Grachev did little to actually reform the armed forces. Neither could he nor the military force the Duma to spend money it did not have on ill-defined schemes for military development in whose development it had been allowed no input.

Ukraine's 24 August 1991 *Declaration of Sovereignty* announced the nationalisation of all conventional military forces on Ukrainian territory and the determination of the Ukrainian SSR to be a neutral, non-nuclear state. On 11 October 1991, the *Concept for the Defence and the Formation of the Armed Forces of Ukraine* was adopted, providing for a national security structure which included a ministry of defence, a Defence Council, and a general staff of the armed forces. On 22 November 1991 the Supreme Soviet of Ukraine declared its intention to create a national armed forces and a law on the armed forces was passed in December 1991. A presidential decree of 5 April 1992 directed that all military formations and troops on Ukrainian soil (except strategic nuclear forces) be put under national command and authorised the formation of a navy. Finally, in July 1992, a three-year plan to introduce a new military uniform and insignia was announced.[118] The boldness of Ukrainian authorities in building their own armed forces reflected their desire to extricate themselves from the Soviet Union and to avoid any military entanglements with Russia either bilaterally or through the CIS. For the most part, however, beyond changes on paper and changes in uniform and insignia, very little reform of the armed forces took place in the early 1990s.

In hindsight, the reasons why are clear. Two prominent Ukrainian defence analysts highlighted a number of economic, political and organisational reasons. They noted that even if the military had enjoyed political and funding priority in the first two years of independence, by 1994 in the face of GDP figures showing a nearly 50 per cent decline since 1991, the condition of the military was at the bottom of the public agenda. According to figures of the IISS the defence budget plummeted from US$3.9 billion in 1993 to just US$881 million in 1994.[119] The multitude of legal acts adopted concerning defence were all declarative, politicised and naive. What constituted the armed forces and its distinction from other military formations were not even defined in principle, while their functions were only vaguely specified in the *Concept for the Defence and the Formation of the Armed Forces of Ukraine*, the *Law on Defence* and the *Law on the Armed Forces*. The result was the narrow-minded reduction of the discussion of national security issues to little more than turf wars between various security agencies each claiming a share of defence spending.[120]

Moreover, there was a battle for political power between the presidency and the parliament. Much as it was in Russia, in this struggle for power the issue of consuming importance to politicians was to whom the armed forces would be subordinated, not the planning and direction of its reform. Ukraine found itself in a contradictory situation wherein the authority to direct reform in the military and the responsibility to fund and support it were possessed by different implacably opposed political players: the president had sole authority to direct the armed forces, but his responsibility for the state of the army was limited since he was not empowered to resolve financial issues; the Rada controlled the budget but it was excluded from the planning of military reform and, consequently, it felt no responsibility for its execution; while the Cabinet of Ministers also had no role in the resolution of strategic matters and so it too assumed no obligation to see that defence policy was wisely designed and faithfully enacted. Thus a paradox emerged: the military was under control but no one bore responsibility for its critical condition.[121]

With surprising rapidity the Ukrainian ministry of defence prepared a draft military doctrine in early 1992. However, the draft was twice rejected by the Verkhovna Rada before being adopted formally on 19 October 1993. The Rada's initial rejections of the draft hinged on two factors. One was that the first draft, in line with the July 1990 *Declaration of Sovereignty*,[122], included a unilateral renunciation of nuclear weapons which many Ukrainian policy-makers were unwilling to support. The non-nuclear provisions of the *Declaration of Sovereignty* were meant as a gambit to achieving independence from the USSR and Russia. After independence, however, many of Ukraine's leaders began to have second thoughts about de-nuclearisation. Ukraine was being forced to renounce its nuclear defence at a time when it did not have any credible conventional alternative. Some members of the Rada felt that Ukraine was also not receiving from the West or from Russia just compensation for the loss of its nuclear assets. As a result, the military doctrine which was finally approved, while maintaining a long-term commitment to nuclear disarmament, laid down Ukraine's outright claim to the nuclear forces on its territory:

> Having become the owner of nuclear weapons through historical circumstance, Ukraine will never sanction their use and excludes the threat to use nuclear weapons from its foreign policy arsenal. In the future, Ukraine intends to

> become a non-nuclear state and links the reduction and destruction of nuclear weapons with appropriate actions by other nuclear states and by granting them and the world community of reliable security guarantees.[123]

The doctrine's provisions on nuclear weapons were 'confused (and confusing)';[124] and there were many good political and practical reasons for Ukraine to de-nuclearise. On the other hand, balanced against these arguments there was a feeling that, as the defence minister pointed out to NATO colleagues in March 1993, 'the West will take heed of what Ukraine says only as long as there are nuclear weapons on its soil'.[125] Eventually, Ukraine's leaders were forced to accept the logic of denuclearisation which was completed in 1996. But it was a difficult decision which at the time the military doctrine was written in 1993 was still unacceptable to much of the Ukrainian elite.[126]

The second sticking point of the initial draft was its failure to specify what was meant by the 'probable enemy' and also that it did not ban the basing of foreign troops on Ukrainian territory – both measures being aimed at Russia. The Verkhovna Rada, dominated by nationalists at that time, viewed Russia as an enemy – at least in potential – and wanted that made more plain. Ultimately, the approved doctrine stated that, 'Ukraine will regard as a potential enemy any state whose policy consistently threatens its military security, interferes in its internal affairs, or aspires to control its territory or infringe its national interests.'[127] In other words, the unspoken but unmistakable background to the doctrine was fear of Russia.

Aside from the influence of the Rada on the wording concerning nuclear weapons and the identification of the main threat, the impact of civilians on the drafting of the doctrine was minimal. The draft was prepared by the general staff and reflected their interests and priorities. In the military economic section of the doctrine a few words were said about the need to create a reliable defence capability in the context of 'reasonable' defence expenditure. But then the doctrine presented a shopping list including precision weaponry, advanced reconnaissance capabilities, air and space defence, electronic warfare equipment, missile forces and aviation, air mobile units and future oriented ocean-going ships and submarines.[128] For what purposes such armaments were required or how they could be paid for was not explained. Indeed, independent Ukrainian analysts estimated that satisfying the army's demands for high-tech weaponry would have cost between US$80 billion and $200 billion, at a time when the defence budget stood at less than a US$1 billion![129] In other words, the 1993 Ukrainian *Military Doctrine* was hopelessly unrealistic – 'Ukraine needs to be more modest; it shouldn't make the world laugh at such documents . . .'[130] – as such, it could not form any coherent basis for a military reform programme.

In the early 1990s there was a tremendous amount of activity in the Ukrainian defence sphere which showed that the building of national armed forces was seen as being integral to the building of an independent state – first in the assertion of Ukraine's de facto independence from the USSR and later in the maintenance of its distance from the CIS. The possession of strong armed forces was key to

President Kravchuk's nation-building strategy: 'Ukraine needs an army as a guarantor of democracy and independence,' he stated.[131] Indeed some scholars have argued that in the early 1990s Ukraine prioritised the construction of its military forces at the expense of much needed efforts at social reconstruction, economic reform, and political institution building.[132] Nonetheless, despite the powerful political rhetoric about the building of capable national armed forces, Ukraine's leaders did not launch a comprehensive reform of the armed forces in the early 1990s. Rather than creating effective armed forces that might embody Ukrainian national pride and independence they allowed the army to degenerate to a point that it came to symbolise all that was wrong in the country.

From the war in Chechnya to the reforms of 1996–1997: holding on to everything, saving nothing

By 1994 the extreme debasement of the Russian and Ukrainian armies was manifest. The abysmal state of morale in both armies found reflection in numerous ways, notably in the explosion of crime and indiscipline in the ranks, the inability of the ministry of defence to recruit new junior officers of high calibre or retain the old ones, and the disintegration of the conscription system. Derisory references to the criminality of the security services – e.g., 'mafia in shoulder boards' – were commonplace. Of course corruption was not a new phenomenon. Nepotism, theft of state property, abuse of one's rank and so on, were all part of Soviet military life.[133] Nonetheless, the scale of criminal activity as well as the implication that corruption in the higher ranks was to some extent sanctioned by the authorities in order to keep the upper echelons of the military loyal was alarming. In 1995, while the overall crime rate in Russia was said to have risen by 5.6 per cent, in the military the crime rate rose by 30 per cent.[134] The range of illegal activity of Russian army officers was extremely broad, much of it being rather minor and brought on simply by economic exigency. Yet large scale corruption at the highest ranks was also evident. By the end of 1997, 21 Russian generals, including the former deputy minister of defence and head of the main military inspectorate, General Konstantin Kobets, were under investigation for corruption.[135] As Graham Turbiville noted:

> Endless variations of business ventures involving the sale of miscellaneous military property abound. The incident in which senior officers of a unit engaged in developing 'new military technologies' melted down and sold the silver, gold and other precious metals in their equipment is one innovative, but by no means unique case, of selling anything that might bring a good price. Overall, the range of military business intended for personal profit – irregular, semi-legal, patently criminal – is integral to the domestic operations of the Russian Armed Forces . . .[136]

Crime in the Ukrainian military was similar in extent. Socioeconomic conditions resulted in a serious decrease in military discipline. In 1994 breaches of service regulations increased by 47 per cent over the previous year while the increase in criminal proceedings rose by more than 50 per cent.[137] The theft of military equipment, exploitation of conscripts' labour, moonlighting and so on, all grew in prevalence. Regulations for two new penal battalions, one in Kiev and one in Crimea, were published in June 1994 in an attempt to deal with the growing problem.[138] The 'Main Control Inspectorate' was also created in March 1993 to look into corruption in the armed forces while the commercial centre of the ministry of defence was ordered shut for 'serious violations of economic and financial discipline'.[139] Over the course of 1992–1993 a total of five generals were dismissed for corruption, including the head of the personnel directorate of the ministry of defence.[140] In a 1997 memo the acting Prosecutor General Oleg Litvak noted that the number of petty crimes committed in the army had soared by as much as 100 per cent, while the number of 'grave' crimes committed by officers had increased by 200 per cent since independence. Reportedly the most common crimes were: abuse of power (77 cases in 1997 compared to 33 registered in 1992), embezzlement of state property (72 compared to 24) and bribery (17 compared to 3). The memo went on to specify the rather obvious causes: delayed salaries, the cost of housing (65,000 officers lacked living accommodation of their own), and job shortages (almost 70 per cent of all officers' wives were unemployed). In other words, by reducing the military budget year by year the state was ensuring that 'non-budget financial sources' would be employed – and officers employed them indeed, using all the assets and property to which they had access in order to generate income.[141]

Due to the appalling conditions of military service both the Ukrainian and Russian armies faced extreme difficulty in recruiting and retaining officers. By 1995, the Russian army was reported to be facing a shortfall of officers as high as 25 per cent with the biggest troubles at junior officer levels where the shortfall was as high as 45 per cent.[142] Whereas in the Soviet system high rates of pay, social prestige and special housing ensured a steady supply of top-quality officer candidates, the situation was utterly reversed by the mid-1990s. By 1995 Moscow bus drivers were earning more than trained fighter pilots.[143] Such examples of the degradation of service conditions might be cited ad nauseam. Equally galling for army officers was the knowledge that their pay was considerably less than that of their peers in both the border and interior ministry troops. The military-sociological and legal research department of the ministry of defence reported in 1997 that 95 per cent of officers felt it was impossible to live on their pay.[144]

The situation was no better in Ukraine. In December 1997 it was reported that nearly 70,000 Ukrainian military officers and their families lacked housing, while over 30,000 retired officers were on waiting lists for apartments.[145] Ninety-three per cent of officers were unsatisfied with their financial position with many claiming that their pay was sufficient only to buy food and that they had to rely on family and friends for financial support.[146] According to figures published by the Ukrainian Centre for Economic and Political Studies in 1998 only 20 per cent of officers felt satisfied with their service, 66 per cent felt no reason to expect positive changes in the near future, and 66 per cent would oppose their own children pursuing careers in the armed forces.[147] The upshot of this situation was that the best young officers began leaving military service as quickly as they could. In turn, the movement of young officers into the civilian sector lead to the skewing of the officer corps. Both armies came to possess large numbers of officers with fifteen or more years in service at one end of their personnel profiles, a fluid cadre of officers with less than three years service on the other, but a yawning gap among the middle ranks.

Obtaining draft deferments or evading the draft became far less difficult than it had been under the Soviet system. In late 1998 only 20 per cent of those eligible for military service ended up getting drafted as there were over twenty legally accepted reasons for deferment or exemption including higher education, medical unfitness (most common), and family status.[148] Exemption certificates could also be purchased or draft boards bribed. Finally, if all else failed, potential draft evaders could simply not show up since very few criminal proceedings were instituted against draft dodgers: in Russia in 1996, for example, of 31,000 potential conscripts who evaded the draft only 394 had criminal proceedings brought against them and only 87 were convicted.[149] In essence, society was not willing to punish young men too harshly for avoiding service in an army where the living conditions were so spartan and the (in)discipline so brutal that potentially thousands of them were dying from non-combat causes every year. To make matters worse, the quality of the draftees who failed to avoid induction was very poor: from a quarter to one third of conscripts had not finished high school, as many as half were regular drinkers, a smaller but still significant proportion were drug and alcohol addicts, many had criminal records, and their overall level of health and fitness was very poor.[150]

In both countries – but most obviously in Russia where the army was astonishing outsiders with its wretched combat performance, loathsome brutality, and complete inability to defeat the lightly armed Chechen resistance – what was happening to the armed forces was not reform but *collapse*. By the time of the parliamentary elections in December 1995, political conflict over the moribund defence reform had begun to grow as a result of the continuing debacle in Chechnya. On 16 February 1995 in his annual address to the Russian parliament President Yeltsin declared the situation in the armed forces 'unsatisfactory' and demanded that urgent measures be taken for its reform. Then on 23 February 1995 at a wreath-laying ceremony on Defenders of the Fatherland Day he reinforced that point saying that 'the army is slowly beginning to get out of hand – the conflict in Chechnya convinced us once more that we are late with reform of the army'.[151] The reaction of the military to Yeltsin's urging on the course of defence reform was lukewarm at best. Questioned by journalists about reform Grachev pronounced blithely: 'If there is money, there will be reform' – with the rather obvious implication that absent more funds there would be no reform.[152] And indeed for another year virtually nothing more was said about reforming the armed forces.

In fact, after simmering since the early 1990s, the military's pay crisis came to a head in 1995 after the government finally announced that it would index officers' pay to the inflation rate. The plan, however, quickly broke down when the ministry of finance offered a 28 per cent pay rise while the ministry of defence argued that a 208 per cent rise was the minimum necessary to bring pay back into line with pre-inflationary levels. In the end, the ministry of finance released only 10.5 trillion rubles for military pay for the whole year and by the middle of 1995 the army had spent 80 per cent of its salary budget. The funds provided by the state treasury proved insufficient to cover even un-indexed salaries for the whole year.[153] At first, the ministry of defence ceased paying officers' special allowances for children, rations, travel and miscellaneous items, then it began to default on basic pay as well. By January of 1996, 80 per cent of officers had gone without pay for five months or more, and it was estimated that on average officers were owed the equivalent of US$750 each in back pay.[154] This was the context in which in February 1996 Yeltsin demanded that Prime Minister Viktor Chernomyrdin present a comprehensive proposal for the reform of the armed forces within ten days. When ten days passed and no military reform plan materialised the president simply announced that he would create a new commission on military reform. Both the government and the military had long since learned to ignore the president's bluster about 'imminent military reform'.[155] In any event it seems unlikely that Yeltsin in an election year was really serious about launching a comprehensive reform of the armed forces as that would have entailed painful decisions such as closing military bases and discharging hundreds of thousands of officers which would have cost votes among the military electorate.[156]

On 16 May 1996 at the height of the presidential campaign, Yeltsin decreed that the Russian military would be manned entirely on a professional basis by April 2000. On the one hand, the decree was absurd – as Lebed put it 'It is a purely populist decree and nothing will be achieved . . .'[157] While General Igor Rodionov, called it 'dangerous and irresponsible electioneering rhetoric that at best would never really be implemented and at worst could cause the final downfall of the Russian army'.[158] These were trenchant criticisms, since in truth the decree was based on no financial or military analysis. On the other hand it was a masterful political sneak attack that caught Yeltsin's opponents off-guard. It is a measure of how weary the Russian public had grown with the waste of young lives in military service that a patently hollow promise to end the draft could still be thought to generate votes. A few analysts like Dmitri Trenin at the Carnegie Foundation and the popular general Boris Gromov even endorsed the decree, though it seems theirs was a more general support for the *concept* of professional armed forces rather than any confirmed belief in the practicality of the decree in question.[159] In June 1996 Yeltsin also ousted the deeply unpopular Pavel Grachev from his position as minister of defence, as part of a bargain with Alexander Lebed who threw his support behind Yeltsin in the second round of the presidential elections in return for being named secretary of the Security Council and for the appointment of his ally General Igor Rodionov as minister of defence.[160]

No doubt these tactical manoeuvres contributed to Yeltsin's reelection but they did nothing to further the cause of reforming the armed forces. In fact, Lebed's tenure as defence 'supremo' was short-lived. He and Rodionov had only a brief time in which they floated a few ideas for changing the armed forces which boiled down to more or less what had been proposed before: consolidating the manpower of the multitude of undermanned divisions into fewer full-strength units and creating powerful, mobile rapid reaction forces.[161] There was general agreement on the desirability of professionalising the armed forces but again no plan or timetable for how this would be done. Lebed, however, was soon consumed with negotiating an end to the conflict in Chechnya and embroiled in a battle with members of Yeltsin's entourage which finally culminated in his dismissal in October 1996.[162]

With Lebed gone Rodionov was without allies. 'I stand on the sidelines as a spectator to the process of destruction of the army, and am unable to do anything about it,' he lamented in January 1997.[163] He was entangled in a conflict with Yuri Baturin, head of the newly created Defence Council which was tasked with overseeing the reform of the armed forces.[164] Contrary to popular belief, the conflict was not over competing visions of reform. In fact, neither Baturin nor Rodionov ever produced anything but the sketchiest outline of a reform agenda. The gist of their conflict was more basic than that: Rodionov maintained that without money, there could be no reform of the armed forces, while Baturin argued that the military had to utilise as yet untapped reserves from the Soviet era to survive, make less demands on the federal budget and reform at the same time.[165] In his efforts to pressure the state for funds, Rodionov made dramatic pronouncements about the disastrous state of the army which embarrassed the government, such as when he told reporters that 'if the military has been reduced to a desperate state, this is primarily the fault of the country's political leadership which has completely removed itself from the management of military reform.'[166]

Then in spring 1997, despairing at the rapidly worsening state of the armed forces and his inability to get the authorities to pay any attention to it, Rodionov stated boldly that without proper funding 'after a certain period of time, Russia could near a threshold beyond which its missiles and nuclear systems would become uncontrollable'.[167] In hindsight an importunate gambit, Rodionov's voicing concern over the control of nuclear weapons was to no avail. Having generated some public sympathy he was not immediately fired but the writing was on the wall. In March 1997 he and Baturin held a joint press conference in order to quell reports of a serious falling out between the ministry of defence and the Defence Council and to outline yet another three stage reform programme for the armed forces. However, the tension between the two men was clearly evident. Each was trying to secure the support of the media – with Baturin the more successful performer. Ultimately, Rodionov and Chief of the General Staff Viktor Samsonov were publicly humiliated and fired by Yeltsin who judged their efforts at reform in a televised meeting of the Defence Council saying, 'I am not simply dissatisfied. I am indignant over the state of reforms in the army and the general state of the armed forces . . . The soldier is losing weight while the general is getting fatter.'[168] In essence, given a choice between spending more money on the potentially elaborate reforms likely to come from Rodionov or the minimalist, cheap approach championed by Baturin, Yeltsin chose the latter and with it a more tractable and carefully-spoken minister, General Igor Sergeyev.

By July 1994 when Leonid Kuchma defeated Leonid Kravchuk in presidential elections in Ukraine, the case for a comprehensive reform of the armed forces was clear to virtually everyone – except to the new state leadership which proved as tardy in getting down to seriously planning reform as its predecessor. On 2 December 1994 Kuchma authorised the preparation by an inter-agency commission of the *State Programme of Armed Forces Development to 2005*.[169] Two years later he evaluated the progress of development as follows:

> This is not work. It is the worst type of imitation . . . Today we can only speak in future tense about the state programme for the buildup and development of the armed forces.[170]

Yet the *State Programme of Armed Forces Development to 2005* was adopted by the National Security and Defence Council only thirteen days later on 28 December 1996. It was approved by the president on 18 January 1997. The programme outlined the reform agenda for several main areas of national defence: the roles and missions of the armed forces; the organisation of the military; the defence budget; the plan for modernisation of weapons and equipment; the organisation and functions of the ministry of defence and the general staff; and, the organisation of the ground forces with priority placed on developing a rapid reaction (highly mobile) force. The major limitation of the programme was that much of it was prepared before the constitution was finished and in the absence of any overarching national security concept. Thus the programme put the cart before the horse, setting out what sort of armed forces the state would have before it had even been decided what the state wanted its military to do. In short, it was based on insufficient and inappropriate data concerning the politico-military situation as well as the economic limitations on defence spending.[171] More generally, the main weakness of the military restructuring process was the consistent way in which long-term goals were sacrificed to short-term political or economic exigencies. The emphasis was on implementing limited reforms such as downsizing, or cosmetic ones like changing uniforms and insignia, but hardly any attention was paid to conducting a thorough review of the geo-strategic, socio-economic, scientific-technical and legal implications of restructuring the whole of the defence establishment.

A number of factors lay behind the poor quality of the 1996 reform programme. However, the continuous squabbling between the president and the Verkhovna Rada was a main problem. By law it was parliament which had the sole authority to set out the structure, function and manpower limits on the armed forces. Moreover, parliament was responsible for the military budget. But, fearing that the parliament would obstruct the reform of the armed forces, the Rada was excluded from preparation of the programme which was eventually passed by presidential decree. Given their exclusion from the process of its design it was no surprise that the parliament felt no responsibility for its implementation. A second problem was the continued failure of the authorities to take responsibility for the process. The interdepartmental committee for military reform which drew up the programme was headed not by the prime minister or the secretary of the National Security and Defence Council (as one would expect of an inter-departmental reform programme), but by the minister of defence. 'Nobody else was willing to assume responsibility for the solution of complex military problems.'[172]

From the national security concepts of 1997 to the reform plans of 1998–1999: the crises deepen

By 1997, observers of the Russian and Ukrainian militaries were reminding themselves of an old truism: 'The Soviet army is never as strong, or as weak, as it seems.' The fact was, however, that both armies had become very, very weak indeed. Still reeling from its humiliating defeat at the hands of the Chechens the Russian army seemed to be redefining the meaning of 'bottom of the barrel' falling ever deeper into degradation with no end in sight. The view that defence reform thus far had been a sham was ubiquitous in Russia. According to one interviewee:

> The military reform in Russia is a big hoax. All military reforms in other countries have amounted to the demobilisation of the old army and the creation of a new one which is based on a different recruitment mode, doctrine, etc. This has not been done in Russia. The old army has not been disbanded, no new one has been built, and meanwhile the military are decaying somewhere in between . . .[173]

Or as a serving military officer put it: 'There is talk of military reform but no real military reform is being carried out.'[174] By 1997 the urgency of beginning serious reform of the armed forces was undeniable. The Council on Foreign and Defence Policy gave this bleak assessment of the situation:

> The current state of the Russian armed forces can be described only as an accomplished catastrophe, which will develop into a national catastrophe very soon, unless the society and the state at long last put forth responsible efforts to ward off this impending threat.[175]

A range of opinion existed on what form the 'catastrophe' might take. In the main, however, the quiet disintegration of the army was considered the most likely outcome. One interviewee spoke of a continued convergence of a sick and wasting military with a similarly sick and wasting society:

> Our army is becoming a bunch of gangsters just like the rest of our society . . . The fact that soldiers have weapons and ammunition does not make them too distinct from civilians, since huge numbers of young Russians today have machine-guns – it is an open question whether the army has more machine-guns than the society. In other words, the army is fully merging with society; they are two parts of the same body afflicted with the same diseases.[176]

In Russia in response to the growing awareness of the crisis a public campaign to 'save' the armed forces was launched in June 1997 by General Lev Rokhlin – a hero of the Chechen war who had become chairman of the Duma Defence Committee.[177] Ever sensitive to the winds of political change, Yeltsin promptly signed a decree *On Priority Measures to Reform the Armed Forces of the Russian Federation and Improve their Structure* in July 1997 that was meant to provide the basis of a meaningful military reform.[178] Following from this decree Russia's new minister of defence, General Igor Sergeyev, in time honoured fashion announced a new plan for the reform of the armed forces that differed only in a few minor details from the ideas of his predecessor. His reform plan entailed:

1 From 1997–1999 – reductions in the total size of the armed forces to 1.2 million men.
2 From 1999–2001 – the first stage of reorganisation in which the branches of service would be consolidated into Ground Forces, Air and Missile Space Forces, and the Navy.
3 From 2001–2005 – Completion of manpower reductions and further consolidation of the services into three arms: Air Space forces, Air Defence Forces and Operational Forces (which would include ground and naval elements).[179]

The main innovation of the plan was the favouring of the nuclear forces which would be integrated under a single command. Given Sergeyev's background in the strategic rocket forces the ascendancy of the nuclear forces was not surprising – just like Grachev's favouritism towards the airborne forces. In December 1997 Sergeyev gave an optimistic update on the first five months of his reform programme claiming that the first practical results had been achieved and that the transformation to 'small, fully-manned and combat-ready armed forces with effective deterrence capabilities, a rational structure and number of personnel' was on track.[180] In fact he spoke too soon. The political battles in Moscow that followed in the wake of the August 1998 financial meltdown meant that the reform package was badly neglected.

Experts in Ukraine were hardly less scathing in their estimations of the deepening crisis of their armed forces. While thankful that their army, unlike Russia's, was at least spared the ravages of an interminable war, Ukrainian analysts could generate little optimism for their own situation. In some ways their problems were even more severe. In the words of an interviewee:

> We have come to a situation where the parliament adopts a budget with only enough money to pay for the salaries of the number of personnel they authorise which is not the same as the actual size of the military. The problem is they do not give any money for combat training, for the organisation and administration of the army, and they give only a tiny amount for procurement. At the same time, they do not give enough money for the retirement of servicemen. We calculate that they give seventeen times less per man than is

> the Western standard. If you are going to fund the army as it is now, in terms of size, what you need to pay is 5 to 7 billion US dollars. But what they get is 300 million. This is just stupid, ridiculous. It is not even enough to sustain decent living standards for military servicepeople. Active military officers who have not received their salary are not able to sustain their families. NCOs have the same problem – maybe worse. Talk of reform is just irrelevant until this gap between what is needed and what is provided gets much smaller.[181]

It had also become obvious that the1996 *State Programme of Armed Forces Development to 2005* – weak as it was – would never be implemented. Ukraine had tried to do the undoable: reform the military while having no agreement on objectives, key assumptions and their ramifications. Moreover, the continuing struggle for political power between the president and the parliament 'intruded into every domain and trumped every other policy consideration.'[182] As a result, neither the president nor government was in a position to provide support or direction to defence reform. The March 1998 parliamentary elections which saw the left wing majority in the Rada increased and the anti-NATO outcry caused by the Kosovo conflict provided further cause for delay.

Nonetheless, despite the continuing degradation of the armed forces, the period 1997–1999 did see some further conceptual work that merits examining, notably both Russia's and Ukraine's national security concepts which are interesting not only in their national contexts but in contrast with one another. Like Ukraine, a main problem for reformers in Russia was the lack of any overarching perspective on what kind of armed forces were required and how they could be paid for. Both countries approved military doctrines long before setting out an overarching concept of national security – with the result that the military doctrines were inappropriate to the new situation. The national security concepts of 1997 were meant to rectify this problem.

In May 1996 Yeltsin ordered the Security Council to draft a new *National Security Concept*. A draft was completed under the leadership of the council's secretary on 7 May 1997 and after some months of debate was enacted by presidential decree on 17 December 1997.[183] The purpose of the *National Security Concept* was defined in the preamble:

> The *Concept of the Russian Federation's National Security* is a political document, which reflects a total combination of officially accepted views as regards specific goals and the appropriate state strategy aimed at ensuring individual, public and state security against political, economic, social, military, man-made, environmental, information and other internal and external threats (with due account taken of available resources and possibilities). The concept formulates the most important state-policy guidelines and principles, constituting a foundation for the elaboration of concrete programmes and organizational documents in the field of ensuring the Russian Federation's national security.

In the four sub-chapters which followed, Russia's place in the world, its national interests, the main internal and external threats to its security, and the ways of coping with them were all discussed. Some specific developments were noted as having a direct and negative bearing on Russia's national security:

1 the lack of success in creating a comprehensive security regime for Europe;
2 the imminent enlargement of NATO which 'threatens national security'; and
3 the ineffectiveness of existing peacekeeping and international security mechanisms.

It also stated that Russia's interests 'are based on the national heritage and national values of the Russian Federation's peoples' and are ensured by Russia's 'economic potential, that of the state's political and military organisation, as well as by the spiritual-moral and intellectual potential of Russia's multi-ethnic society'. The main goals of the foreign policy of the state were said to be 'consolidation of Russia's position as a great power and as one of the influential centres of the emergent multipolar world'. Russia's strategic goals included: further integration of the CIS member states; expanding relations with other great powers; promoting international cooperation in fighting trans-national crime and terrorism; and strengthening mechanisms for international collective security, particularly the UN Security Council where Russia plays an important role. 'The main task of the armed forces of the Russian Federation is to ensure nuclear deterrence, which is to prevent both a nuclear and conventional large-scale or regional war, and also to meet its commitments towards allies.' Nuclear forces should be sufficient that 'planned damage will be caused to any aggressor state or a coalition of states'. The document stated that Russia should have some capacity to project force abroad but noted realistically that the state 'has a less impressive potential for ensuring the Russian Federation's security'.

Notwithstanding the concerns raised by a few Western analysts about the concept's apparent emphasis on restoring Russia's influence in the newly-independent states and the attention on nuclear forces as the ultimate guarantee of security, the really significant aspect of the concept was how vague and platitudinous it was.[184] The military needed a specific blueprint for reform; what it got was only a broad discursion on national security interests, priorities and responsibilities.

Ukraine also needed to define its national security needs and objectives and a strategy for their resolution. By contrast with Russia, however, the *National Security Concept* of 1997 (in combination with the *Constitution* of 1996) answered these questions to an extent sufficient to guide reform of the armed forces. The significance of the 1996 *Constitution* should not be underrated. Perhaps most importantly in the reform context was the enshrinement in the *Constitution* of the National Security and Defence Council which was tasked with coordinating and controlling the activities of different executive bodies in the sphere of national security and defence. This gave the president a high-level advisory body – comprised of all the relevant departmental heads and the chairman of the parliamentary commission on 'Questions of Security and Defence' – which could coordinate and oversee the implementation of defence policy not only in the ministry of defence but in the full range of power ministries. Crucially, the National Security and Defence Council was also supported by a solid military–civilian professional staff. Indeed it was experts of the National Security and Defence Council who wrote the *National Security Concept* which was adopted by parliament on 16 January 1997. The document impressed many analysts with its 'clarity and realism'.[185] It set out Ukraine's national interests which, though written in rather broad terms, represented a reasonable compromise between the competing agendas of the parliament and president. Essentially these interests consisted of creating a strong civil society and effective economy, increasing the effectiveness of state institutions, guaranteeing sovereignty and independence, and pursuing integration in Europe. The concept also mapped out a wide range of security threats. On the military side it noted the following as significant:

1 encroachment on the state sovereignty and territorial integrity of Ukraine;
2 the buildup of foreign military forces on Ukraine's borders which might upset the existing balance of forces;
3 the military and political instability of neighbouring states;
4 the potential use of weapons of mass destruction against Ukraine;
5 the distinct fall in the military capabilities of Ukraine's armed forces;
6 the politicisation of its state military structures; and
7 the existence of illegal paramilitary formations.[186]

It went on to note another rich inventory of main threats to security in other fields ranging from the political to the economic, social, and ecological which might provoke a military conflict. The concept stressed that the main danger to Ukraine stemmed from the weakness and underdevelopment of its society, political institutions and economy which might be exploited by a foreign actor.[187] Accordingly it called for the creation of effective mechanisms to prevent outbreaks of conflict, to localise them internally, to liquidate their consequences and prevent their exploitation from abroad.[188] This, in turn, required the cost-effective coordination of action between law-enforcement agencies, internal security forces and those of the ministry of defence. Moreover, it required transparency and trust if politicians, society, the military and police forces were to cooperate in resolving a wide range of traditional and non-traditional threats. Thus the provision of democratic control of the military was made an explicit part of the state's approach to ensuring its security.

Undoubtedly the Ukrainian national security concept contained bromides not unlike those found in the Russian concept. Nonetheless, it is also clear that unlike the Russian concept it did contain more than platitudes. It showed that the Ukrainian defence establishment was at least beginning to think at the level of first principles. Moreover, it represented a welcome challenge to the Ukrainian military mindset which, like the Russian, was still reluctant to think of the army's involvement in resolving security matters within anything other than the context of general war.

Comparative conclusions

Most objective observers would agree that the former Soviet Union states had bigger problems in terms of defence reform than did the Central European states. Unlike Poland and Hungary, or even Ukraine, Russia's geography requires that military forces be spread over a very large area with long land frontiers, low population density and a multitude of border conflicts and potential flash-points both internal and external. At the same time, the Russian economy in the 1990s declined more steeply than Poland and Hungary's, though perhaps less than the Ukrainian, and began to recover later. Therefore, despite the fact that Russia's defence budget represented a large percentage of measurable GDP, it was in decline year after year throughout the 1990s and was always quite small in absolute terms relative to the size of the armed forces. The same downward tendency in the budget was observable in Ukraine but the percentage of GDP spent on defence was lower than in Russia. By contrast, defence spending in both Poland and Hungary after a steep decline in the first half of the 1990s began to rise again in the latter half.

In this context of extreme financial constraint, the accomplishments of the former Soviet Union states should not be underestimated. Russia's completion of the withdrawal of Soviet forces from abroad and the division of CFE quotas amongst the Soviet successor states were major tasks, as was Ukraine's unilateral nuclear disarmament. Indeed, Ukraine's difficulties in respect to military reform must be understood in light of the fact that they were not simply *restructuring* their armed forces but *creating* new, national armed forces based on a fragment of the Soviet military which lacked any developed administrative or command structures. Furthermore, though it is fair to say that the former Soviet Union states accomplished *less* reform than those in Central Europe, the main accomplishment of Poland and Hungary was more in avoiding the extreme examples of degradation in the armed forces that plagued Russia and Ukraine than in actualising a profound change in their armies to a new level of effectiveness. That is to say, they avoided a negative result more than they achieved a positive one.

In other words, it is important not to overstate the successes achieved by Poland and Hungary in terms of defence reform relative to those of Russia and Ukraine. The fact is that a year after their accession to NATO neither country possessed reorganised armed forces that could be considered satisfactorily effective. Still, it is also true that many Western countries also faced complex problems of reorganising their armed forces to meet a greatly changed international security environment. At the same time, Poland and Hungary made significant contributions of soldiers, logistics and intelligence assets to UN operations and to NATO's operations in the Balkans. Thus, we can say that there were signs of progress intermixed with signs of persisting problems.

The profound impact of NATO on this process had positive and negative consequences. On the positive side, NATO offered examples of good practice as well as advice and assistance at a crucial time. The importance of having a positive relationship with NATO – working toward eventual membership – as a motivator for Poland and Hungary to undertake reforms becomes obvious when compared to Ukraine and Russia. That said, the impact of NATO on reform planning in Ukraine was also growing toward the end of the 1990s. On the negative side, however, for most of the 1990s NATO was understood by the aspirant states and, to an extent by Ukraine, as an end in itself rather than as a *means* to an end. As a consequence of this, too often it seemed as if the real reform of the armed forces as a whole was being sacrificed in favour of investing in showcase exercises and special units in order to impress NATO. Unrealistic declarations of imminent purchase of big ticket weapons systems like fighter aircraft also fit in this category of unreasoned reform.

When they were invited to begin NATO accession talks in 1997 there was a well founded fear that Polish and Hungarian elites would regard the NATO problem as solved and so their commitment to further reform would be diminished. While some diminution of intensity was observed, particularly in the level of spending, the worst-case scenario did not materialise. Indeed, there were signs of a new more thoughtful approach to defence reform based on an examination of first principles emerging. In this respect Poland appeared to be making more progress than Hungary. Polish defence spending was more stable than in Hungary and planning cycles were longer. Moreover, Poland worked out in more detail its concept of national security and military doctrine, as a result of which defence planners had more effective policy guidelines for the development of the armed forces. The problems encountered by the Hungarian *Strategic Defence Review* had a lot to do with the dilatory approach of its political elite towards passage of the *National Security Strategy* and *National Military Strategy*.

Both Russia and Ukraine ended the twentieth century with essentially unreformed armed forces in disarray. The processes of their reform had been driven more by the logic of disintegration of the old system rather than the creation of a new one. Both states encountered a vicious circle: it was hard to expect reforms to be generated by an army in a shambles, but the longer it remained in such a state the more urgent was the need for reform. In August 1999, however, the situation in Russia began to show signs that both the internal political and economic constraints as well as the attitude of the elite towards reform was improving. The appointment of Vladimir Putin as prime minister, the start of the second military campaign to restore federal control over Chechnya, parliamentary elections resulting in a victory for Putin's supporters, Yeltsin's resignation and Putin's subsequent election-confirmation as president resulted in an unusual degree of consolidation of the political class, and of a significant majority of Russian citizens, around the new leader. As one of Putin's main political tools and strongest partisans in the crucial first months of the transition of power in the Kremlin, the military played a major role in assuring his success. In turn, the new president began to show more resolve about addressing the problems afflicting the armed forces than did his predecessor.

In January 2000 a new *National Security Concept*[189] was adopted, followed in April 2000 by a new *Military Doctrine*.[190] These documents were meant to provide guidance to the reform of the armed forces but essentially failed to do so, being still rather broad declarations of intentions based 'on the lowest common denominators between several bureaucracies'.[191] A new security mindset also emerged which in some respects was the exact opposite of the relative optimism of the early 1990s. Even though Russia was smaller than the Soviet Union, it still needed a strong army in the face of external and internal challenges to its geopolitical and economic interests. The security threats Russia needed to respond to include international terrorism inspired and supported by Islamic radicalism, NATO's eastward expansion, American challenges to Russia's influence in the other post-Soviet states, and overall US attempts at enforcing its hegemony in international relations. Russia should use its defence–industrial potential as an important engine of economic growth. The role and status of the armed forces in post-Soviet Russia needed to be upgraded. And the overwhelming need to restore Russia's external and internal security put the military and the security services at the centre of state-building.

After his reelection in 1999 President Leonid Kuchma also began some positive steps in Ukraine. He established an inter-agency working group to draw up a new *State Programme on Armed Forces Reform and Development Until 2005*[192] which was markedly superior to its 1996 predecessor in realism and practicality. First, it set out in decisive language the 'urgent need' for reform created by the geopolitical situation as well as the decade long degradation of the army. Second, unlike its predecessor it was truly a *state* programme, drawn up not just by the ministry of defence but in consultation with the ministry of finance and in accordance with a 'Long-Term Defence-Related Funds Allocation Forecast to 2015'.[193] He also decreed the demobilisation of the National Guard transferring its units to the ministry of the interior and the armed forces. And he appointed an experienced and responsible reformer, Viktor Yushchenko, as prime minister. Yet the new reform programme was still no panacea and came under severe criticism:

> In our society we never talked about what type of army we needed to have. This led us to this situation we have now where the idea of what sort of army to have is formulated by the army itself. Whether it's necessary to have such a huge army as we have now is not discussed. On the other hand, we don't even have the capacity to provide basic social protection for the army as it is now. But the decision of the latest reform plan to the year 2005 is to increase the army by 10,000! This is crazy. How do we feed these people let alone provide them with some sort of training? Our pilots only fly two or three hours a year. We have no fuel for trucks. The only time we have for training is when NATO or defence attaches are involved. Otherwise nothing real happens.[194]

Moreover, the dismissal of Yushchenko in 2001 in the wake of the political conflict caused by the 'Kuchmagate' allegations that the president had ordered the murder of a troublesome investigative journalist, Georgii Gongadze, also fed pessimism about the prospects of reform.

Security policy-making and defence reform as a test of civil–military relations

Chris Donnelly wrote that there are four principles which could serve as the start for addressing the core of the problem of defence reform.[195]

1 'A country which has no problems of civil–military relations and democratic control is a country which has no democracy.'

By the time of their accession to NATO there is little doubt that Poland and Hungary were democratic states and their problems of civil–military relations were of a democratic nature.[196] Although problems remained in both countries – for example, in the continuing division of the Hungarian general staff and ministry of defence – the centre of gravity of defence policy-making had shifted to the civilian political realm. The *quality* of defence policy could be questioned but not, for the most part, the legitimacy of the way in which it was formulated. The same cannot be said of Russia and Ukraine. In both countries the quality of their defence policy products was not the *main* question; rather, it was the quality of the democratic functioning of the state *in general*. In some cases, notably the Ukrainian 1997 *National Security Concept* and the *State Program on Armed Forces Reform and Development Until 2005*, in fact, the sophistication of policy was high. What was lacking was evidence of strong civilian direction of the formulation of said policies outside of the narrow and non-transparent confines of the presidential administrations.

2 'Every country will have a different solution to the problem which they will have to work out for themselves.'

Both Poland and Hungary encountered considerable difficulties in this respect. Their military and political elite expected – and most likely would have welcomed – NATO solving their problems for them. It took most of the 1990s for them to get over this expectation and begin to design their own solutions. Ukraine too showed a similar desire at times for NATO to simply tell them what they should be doing. A NATO official in Kiev, however, stressed that though they had tried hard to get the Ukrainian defence reform process put under the Partnership for Peace planning and review process, 'ultimately, it is the Ukrainians' plan. We can assist here and there, offer advice and so on but they have to come up with it themselves.'[197]

Russia's military has a longstanding tradition of solving its own problems in its own way. That said, judging from the *National Security Concept* and *Military Doctrine* of 2000 it was not at all clear that Russia's leadership had learned much from ten years of transition: they were still resistant to looking at their defence needs and potentials from a first-principles perspective; preferring, it seemed, to continue trying to preserve – or restore – the Soviet military system in a reduced form. Though a few military leaders accepted that the state of the economy would be a deciding factor in the type of armed forces the nation should have – a refreshing change from the traditional military view that the state's defence needs were a fixed constant that could be calculated only by experts in the general staff and that the responsibility of the state was to provide the necessary resources[198] – even by the end of the decade few of its military leaders had internalised this fact. In other words, the army at the end of the 1990s still looked like a poor, shrunken, and angry version of the Soviet army and the prospects for change looked uncertain. In this respect, in comparison with Russian attitudes toward reform, the changes in Ukraine's approach at the end of the 1990s were impressive.

3 'Defence transformation, good civil–military relations and democratic control are problems which must be solved. They cannot be ignored or they will destabilize society.'

Despite fears that Polish and Hungarian elites would, with membership of NATO achieved, regard democratic control as being solved, the pressure to reform was not lessened so much as it shifted focus. As one Polish interlocutor pointed out, there is a big difference between having a relationship *with* NATO and being *in* NATO. The shift in both Poland and Hungary toward more realistic reform plans of ten- and twelve-year duration suggests that defence reform was being taken seriously. That said, there was still a possibility of a return to stagnation. In Hungary, in particular, an American advisory team felt it necessary to strenuously underline in their recommendations to the government: 'What is most important is to develop a carefully thought-through and time-phased plan, AND WITH GREAT DISCIPLINE IMPLEMENT THE PLAN.'[199] The need to reform in Ukraine and Russia was both more acute than in Poland and Hungary and delayed for longer. Only at the end of the 1990s were there signs of real steps to halt and reverse the ten-year decline of the armed forces, but even those signs were equivocal. In the end, the crises in the Ukrainian and Russian armed forces throughout the 1990s reflected the crises of society at large. Similarly, the prospects for their reform depended ultimately on the course of reform more generally. It is possible that the new millennium might finally see a post-Soviet economic and political renaissance occur in Ukraine and Russia but the road is not yet clear.

4 'Democratic control is a two-way process between army and society, not one where politicians simply dictate to soldiers.'

In Poland, while General Wilecki was chief of the general staff, it seems fair to say that there was no two-way street between the army and society. The general staff jealously guarded its prerogatives in the defence sphere, a task in which it was actively abetted by the president himself. By all accounts Wilecki's successor, General Szumski, was a different type of officer more open to two-way dialogue and the dominance of the president in the defence sphere has given way to the increasing authority of the Cabinet of Ministers. Hungary showed more worrying signs of its political elite maintaining a suspicious – even punitive – attitude toward its military commanders. In Ukraine and Russia by the end of the period under review it was still not possible to speak in terms of a two-way process between army and society. In both countries, to the extent that there was dialogue on reform it was between the armed forces and the presidency – a dialogue in which other political players such as parliament, let alone society at large, had essentially no voice. A Ukrainian interlocutor explained the problem as follows:

> This is a post-communist society with a tendency to totalitarianism; with oligarchic clans having the real power in practically all spheres of political, economic and social life. And we have strong remnants of the former Soviet thinking within the force structures. So we cannot speak about democratisation of the force structures – not real democratisation . . . Our level of civilian control is the same as the level of our democracy. In this country we can see, hear and read practically everywhere that we are building a new country. But it sounds in Ukrainian like a new *state*. Nobody even talks about *society*. For the citizen the state is still a monster which stands above the people.[200]

At a somewhat less abstract level, however, one of the main limiting factors on effective two-way dialogue between army and society in states under review was the deficiency of civilian expertise in defence. But that is the subject of the next chapter.

3 Civilian integration in the ministry of defence

In a democratic system elected politicians are *ultimately* the controllers of all policy decisions in the state, including those of the military. Their problem is to maintain and demonstrate the reality of that control, bearing in mind the vastness of the state bureaucracy and the necessity of 'managing the expert problem'. However, the concern of the politician with *control* sometimes conflicts with the concern of the administrator, and perhaps even more so the soldier in an operational context, with *effectiveness*. Most policy-implementers, military or civilian, are open to effective policy-guidance; what they object to are rigid procedures designed to realise the desire of politicians to control without knowing how to exercise their power.[1] These kinds of questions are highly germane to civil–military relations in the states under review; they are questions of management and effectiveness and how to properly handle the delegation of authority and responsibility. As such, they are not much different from questions asked throughout the public sector.[2] However, to understand the concept of civilian control better it is useful to disaggregate the notion of policy:

1 *General policy* is the policy by which the government of the day is guided. It is the policy of the party in power, to which the people have given their approval through the power of the ballot box. It is an exclusively civilian matter.

2 *Executive policy* is the form in which the government puts general policy into practical operation. As such, it must be based on something more than opinion and political rhetoric. That is, it must be based on rational analysis and for this purpose the government must consult with experts. With regard to defence policy this would naturally include experts from the ministry of defence, including the military leadership, but in order to mitigate the problem of political agency would also include outside experts.

3 Further down the policy chain is *administrative policy* whereby the minister puts into effect the will of the government. In working out a plan of action the minister will need to consult experts both within and outside the ministry and advisory committees may be organised. Nevertheless, the main workhorse providing advice and assistance to the minister will be his professional staffs, both military and civilian.

No civilian minister of defence, however bright and well-informed, could hope to control all the activities of the armed forces without support. The institution best suited to supporting the minister in the performance of his duties is the *integrated* defence ministry. According to Bland,

> This type of ministry combines the minister's office, the civil service bureaucracy, and the military high command and their separate but linked responsibilities in one establishment. An effective integrated ministry facilitates the exchange of ideas and information between these branches and aids in consensus building . . . The effect is to provide the minister and the government with a coordinated source of contested advice and a single locus of administration where authority, responsibility and accountability are sharply defined.[3]

In this chapter we are interested in the way ministries of defence function as the institutional setting for the working out of *administrative policy* in the states under review. All of them faced considerable difficulty creating integrated ministries approximating that described above. More often than not, defence establishments built on the Soviet model proved inflexible to change. The delegation of tasks from higher levels to lower ones did not work well because of an institutional culture of avoiding responsibility for decisions. Internal cooperation was stymied by formal and informal divisions between general staffs and ministries of defence, and by attitudinal differences between civilian and military officials. The Central European states had somewhat more success than the former Soviet Union states in civilianising their ministries of defence, but the problems were similar in all the countries under review and were by no means solved by the end of the 1990s.

Before moving on, however, it is worthwhile examining briefly the types of ministry which obtained in the Soviet-bloc.

The Soviet-type ministry of defence

Soviet-type ministries had essentially no civilians in responsible decision-making positions; the Soviet-type ministry was an almost wholly military institution. The socialist regimes in Eastern Europe were not concerned with questions of *democratic* legitimacy or accountability, in civil–military relations or in political life more generally. The legitimacy to make policy, for example, was a function not of a democratic process but of ideology. Since the senior leadership of the military was explicitly communist in political orientation (no other position, including political neutrality, was acceptable), there was no obvious superiority in legitimacy between a civilian Party apparatchik and a military man as minister of defence; either would do, but Soviet-type ministries of defence tended to be headed by men in uniform. Similarly, the issue of accountability was manifested in an utterly different political context. The armed forces were accountable to the government only superficially. The real focus of accountability was to the ruling Party. There was no need for a buffer between the armed forces and the Party; in the extreme view, the two achieved a kind of organic symbiosis and systemic interdependence that virtually precluded the existence of a division between the senior officer corps and the Party elite.[4]

The Soviet-type ministry of defence did not have a distinctive three branch structure – minister's office, civilian bureaucracy, armed forces command – meant to combine in one establishment the inter-related players in civil–military relations. It was instead a wholly military organisation made up of various separate services, directorates and administrations, as well as the general staff.[5] Although civilians never deeply penetrated the structure of the Soviet ministry of defence, an avenue of civilian influence on defence policy began to open in the mid- to late-1980s. As part of his efforts to wrest control of defence policy from its traditional repository in the general staff,[6] Gorbachev permitted intellectuals from the Academy of Sciences (*institutchiki*: mainly from the Institute of USA and Canada and the Institute of World Economics and International Relations), and experts of the ministry of foreign affairs research department (*mezhdunarodniki*) to offer an alternate view on defence and security policy than that offered by the military. Because they were not part of the defence bureaucracy it is debatable exactly how much influence these civilians enjoyed, but their relationship with the military is worth examining.

The intrusion of civilian analysts into the defence policy debate was fiercely resisted by the military. In the military's view, these civilian analysts were self-promoting academic dilettantes who lacked the judgement and professional competence to make policy recommendations. Civilians were equally as scathing about the military. The army, wrote Aleksandr Prokhanov, was a 'threatening, awesome force that has led to the militarisation of the world, to the militarisation of history, to the militarisation of life . . . the source of all that is stagnant and conservative, of everything that rejects the new thinking, *perestroika*, and experimental models of behaviour for the nation and the state'.[7] The military had a point about the competence of civilian defence analysts in the Soviet Union. The defence expertise of civilian analysts in Eastern Europe was generally low in comparison to their counterparts in uniform. Stephen Meyer suggested in 1985 that civilian analysts in the USSR should not be taken seriously because they lacked inside information and were mainly propagandists.[8]

It needs to be emphasised, however, that the rise of civilian involvement in defence policy debates in the Gorbachev era was much more a political than an institutional phenomenon. Civilian defence analysts gave Gorbachev a supportive voice in internal policy debates over the unilateral draw-down of Soviet force levels. According to one analyst, they played a prominent role in Gorbachev's assertion of authority in doctrine and force posture which had been the exclusive purview of the military.[9] But this never equated to a formal role for civilians in the defence establishment.

Structurally, the ministries of defence in the non-Soviet Warsaw Pact states followed the Soviet pattern. About the Polish case, Michta concluded that 'the communist-era system produced a consensus that matters of national defence were best left to the military'.[10] Similarly, Pecze wrote about Hungary:

> The ministry of defence was staffed completely by military personnel. Those civilian politicians who were assigned to top positions in the ministry of defence were awarded a military rank commensurate with their new position regardless of their lack of any military education.[11]

The main difference between the Soviet ministry of defence and the ministries in Central Europe stemmed from the lack of state sovereignty in the latter.[12] As a Hungarian observer, pointed out:

> Most experts agree that the armies of Central Europe as all the former Warsaw Pact armies were the *limbs* of a body called the Warsaw Pact, the trunk of which was the Soviet army and the brain of which was the Soviet general staff. These Central European armies with not too large differences, were not designed to carry out national security, but to carry out the Soviet will.[13]

With respect to the role of civilians in the ministry of defence the external domination of the Central European states also had concrete effects. Whereas in the USSR perestroika allowed *some* civilian analysts to enter the debate on defence policy, the same did not occur in Central Europe. In the Warsaw Pact, strategic decisions were made in Moscow, not in the national capital. Similarly, doctrinal debates took place in the *Soviet* general staff. There was, therefore, even less call for civilian strategists in Poland and Hungary than there was in the Soviet Union. In fact, the domination of defence decision-making by the Soviet general staff also impeded the development of Central European military skills in this area: 'The lack of strategic planning capacity of the Hungarian ministry of defence and the general staff were only revealed when the country regained its independence in 1990.'[14] The same was true of the Polish general staff which 'did not engage in strategic planning at all' under the old system.[15]

Central Europe

The problem of 'civilianising' the ministry of defence in the post-communist context had three main aspects. First, there was the problem of finding a suitable civilian candidate for minister of defence. As Szemerkenyi pointed out: 'The lack of civilian expertise in defence matters created a serious dilemma for the newly elected governments. They could appoint a minister of defence with democratic credentials, or one with knowledge of military issues' – but not both.[16] In 1990, the Hungarian government opted for the appointment of a civilian, Lajos Fur, with democratic credentials at the expense of a military man with real expertise. The Poles, on the other hand, took the opposite route, appointing a career military officer, Admiral Piotr Kolodziejczyk – who was acceptable to the military and considered reliable by the politicians – to head the ministry of defence. By 1994, however, after experimenting with civilian ministers both countries reverted to appointing retired military men as minister of defence – Kolodziejczyk (for the third time) in Poland and retired army Colonel Gyorgy Keleti in Hungary. This process of 're-militarisation' of the ministry of defence prevailed until 1998, by which time civilian ministers were again in place in both countries.

The second aspect of integration was the task of introducing civilian bureaucrats into the ministry of defence at lower levels. This was a more pernicious problem than finding a suitable civilian minister. The underlying reasons for the rather limited success of integration boil down to two main problems: a narrow (mis)-understanding of civilian control by civilian and military elites; and, a dire shortage of civilians with expertise in the defence sphere. Political elites tended to interpret civilian control in the literal sense that civilians should be in *control* of the army (in an often vindictive way that was dismissive of the military's genuine and legitimate concerns). In Hungary, for example, Sherr quoting various politicians, characterised the attitude of political elites as follows: 'We need to break the back of the general staff . . . they need to know there is a strong master in the saddle . . . they need to understand that even if politicians give stupid orders they must shut up and obey because politicians are elected . . .' These types of comments, he concluded, were characteristic of a political establishment whose instinctual military policy was demilitarisation, not reform of the armed forces per se.[17]

For their part, the military also tended to see civilian control through the filter of past communist indoctrination. This perception was aggravated in both countries by the practice of appointing civilians to staff positions in the ministry of defence merely for the sake of having civilians perform certain roles. Civilian officials' lack of training and experience made them noticeably less capable than their military counterparts. To the military, this caused considerable resentment and suspicion.[18] The outcome of these developments was to provoke the development by the military of more sophisticated smoke screens against civilian authorities, to create an atmosphere of uncertainty which impeded substantive civil–military cooperation, and to foster the building in the officer corps of a besieged fortress psychology.

The third aspect of the problem of integration was the relationship of the general staff to the ministry of defence. Under the old system the general staff was the 'brain' of the army while the ministry of defence had fairly limited functions. Certain functions like policy planning, logistics, military education, international cooperation, and so on were traditionally concentrated in the general staff. In a democratic system, since these are matters of public policy, they should be under the supervision of an integrated military–civilian ministry of defence. Transferring these functions from the general staff to the ministry of defence was quite a problem. The underlying reasons why are complex but centre on two main issues. First, the general staff resisted the diminution of its role. In a time of economic distress and given the low market value for military officers in the civilian world, members of the general staff tended to see civilianisation as a personal threat to their well-being. Second, the manner in which the reforms played out both motivated the military to resist civilianisation while providing them with the means to do so. The motivation to resist stemmed from the often antipathetic attitudes which military and civilian elites harboured towards each other:

> Defence reforms in Central Europe were hampered by the opposite political backgrounds of the military and the new political elites. Since the military personnel had inevitably been trained and educated under the Warsaw Pact system, the civilian elite detected political reasons behind the military's slowness in implementing the reforms.[19]

Military officers, for their part, saw the inordinate suspicion of civilian elites as questioning their loyalty to the nation. The introduction into the defence establishment of untrained civilians prompted them to see their duty as being to preserve the army from 'degradation due to incompetent civilians' and avoiding having the military fall 'subject to a knife wielded by someone ignorant of military realities'.[20] In addition to motivating the armed forces to resist the integration of civilians, the way in which reforms were conducted provided many avenues to do so. In Poland, the conflict between Walesa and the Sejm allowed the general staff to scuttle reforms they did not like into the mid-1990s. A 1995 article in the newspaper *Wrpost* concluded that 'The manner in which the general staff has played off the president and the prime minister has effectively brought the military an independence not found anywhere else in Central Europe.'[21]

Political elites did not anticipate these problems. As Szemerkenyi put it, 'intra-ministerial and bureaucratic intrigues proved more intense than expected. Public administration represented a somewhat unexpected challenge to civil–military reform.'[22] Civilians in Central European defence establishments were perceived as too transitory to have real influence or to develop substantial expertise in their duties. Therefore, they were considered in military circles to be an unavoidable burden that must be endured, and whose negative influence on the armed forces must be mitigated. The attitude was that while civilians in the ministry of defence might, at best, be trained in general strategic studies and the broad aspects of security, they lacked the specific knowledge of military structures that would have enabled them to engage constructively in dialogue with the military.[23] The upshot of the situation was that neither Hungary nor Poland had adequately integrated their ministries of defence by the end of the 1990s. Some progress has been made, but ten years after the fall of the Berlin Wall the situation had not changed substantially in the deep structures.

A civilian minister of defence

Finding a suitable civilian minister of defence in Poland and Hungary was a real problem for the new regimes. The problem had two aspects. First, the marked deficit of civilian expertise in defence matters meant that there were few politicians suited for the role by training and background. Second, the political divide between presidents and parliaments perpetuated an ambiguous chain of command and delayed the passage of crucial legislation defining the balance of powers of the various players in civilian control of the military, especially the minister of defence.

In Hungary after the elections of 1990 a centre-right coalition government made up of the Hungarian Democratic Forum, the Independent Small-holders' Party and the Christian Democratic Peoples' Party took power. Both the prime minister and the new civilian defence minister were from the Hungarian Democratic Forum. The president, on the other hand, was a member of the strongest opposition party, the Alliance of Free Democrats. One might have expected that a system of cohabitation with a president and prime minister from different parties would have lead to greater political conflict and instability than it actually did. In fact, Hungary's first post-communist government under Prime Minister Joszef Antall was, overall, one of the most stable in Central Europe and managed to serve out its full four-year mandate (1990–1994). Lajos Fur served as minister of defence for the duration of the Hungarian Democratic Forum's coalition government. On one level then, Hungary's transition to a civilian minister of defence could be called a success. A closer look at Fur's tenure, however, reveals a number of problems which prompt a rather serious caveat to the proposition that civilianisation was on track. First, the institutional separation of the defence ministry and the Hungarian Defence Force Command (general staff) in 1989, posed a major obstacle to the minister's effective supervision of the military.

The rationale of the bifurcated Hungarian system was explained to a British ministry of defence management consultancy team in 1995 in the following way. First, the defence ministry functions as a sort of impact point between the parliament and the general staff on the one hand, and the Hungarian Defence Force on the other hand; thus it separates the military from the politicians. Second, the ministry of defence has an overview on the general staff and the Defence Force and it supervises them by continuously watching them.[24] The British team expressed doubts that the ministry of defence could really carry out these tasks 'as it has only a limited role in the development of the defence policy and the Hungarian Defence Force can be made responsible only by the minister of defence'. In conclusion, they argued that while government supervision of the military was legally supposed to be carried out by the defence minister, the structure did not always make it possible for him to carry out that task.[25] Szenes described this as a problem of a 'strong military commander contrasted with a weak civilian defence minister', arguing that it was a perennial problem in Hungary's civil–military relations.[26] The crux of the issue was that the 1993 *Defence Act*[27] ascribed to the chief of the defence staff many key tasks and responsibilities; the minister of defence, on the other hand, was limited to exercising control only through the chief of defence.

The second problem was that according to the 1989 *Constitution*, control over the Hungarian armed forces was shared by the minister of defence and the president. This arrangement of command authority was, in the opinion of many analysts, a tactic of the departing Hungarian Socialist Workers Party to keep as much power as possible out of the hands of the prime minister and minister of defence as both posts were expected to be taken by non-communists after the free elections in 1990. In this way, substantial powers would be retained by the president who it was expected would be a reformed communist.[28]

An additional reform in December 1989 saw the ministry of defence divided into a small ministry which would report to the minister, and a large defence staff which would report to the president. The weakness of the civilian minister was clearly evident in the way this separation was carried out. Before the move, the ministry of defence consisted of 1,348 personnel. By 1992, the ministry of defence consisted of only 135 personnel.[29] That is to say, only ten per cent of the pre-1989 ministry of defence personnel remained under the immediate authority of the civilian minister, the rest having been transferred to the defence staff.

The conflict inherent in the divided authority over the military rapidly came to a head in October 1990 with the 'taxi blockade' protest over rising fuel prices. Essentially, the Antall government wanted to use the military to break up the taxi strike and restore transportation; the president, on the other hand, opposed any use of the military. Thus a situation arose whereby the intentions of the minister of defence were in direct conflict with the orders of the president as commander-in-chief. This was an untenable situation for the military command: in deciding to follow the orders of one side and not the other, the military would have effectively been making policy. The immediate crisis was resolved by the decision of the prime minister not to order the military into action against the strikers, but the problem continued to simmer through the next year. The commander of the armed forces, Lieutenant General Kalman Lorincz, eventually threatened to resign over the fact that the military had been turned into a battlefield between political authorities.[30]

In August 1991, the defence minister made an attempt to break the deadlock by submitting a request to the Constitutional Court asking it to clarify the limits of presidential powers to command the armed forces. The decision of the court was in favour of the minister: the president had the right only to 'direct' the armed forces and could not provide 'leadership' except under specific crisis conditions; 'leadership' of the armed forces was deemed to be the prerogative of the government.[31] In short, although Hungary moved quickly to appoint a civilian minister of defence who managed to last for four years in that position, peculiarities of the structure of the ministry of defence, the institutional separation of the ministry and the defence staff, and the competing authority of the president and government over the military, all combined to undermine the real authority of the minister.

Poland also adopted a mixed presidential–parliamentary system which led to a conflict arising between the president and the legislature over who would control the military. However, the greater strength of the reformed Polish communist party, the military's tradition of independence and political activism, and the fact that the president had a direct and popular mandate, caused this conflict to be longer and more contentious than was the case in Hungary. To a great extent, the weaknesses of Polish civilian control were attributable to the political compromises enshrined in the 1992 *Little Constitution*,[32] which was not superseded until 1997. The *Little Constitution* reflected the weakness of the 1989 parliament – elected under provisions which guaranteed control of the Sejm to the communists and their supporters – and the strength of the first democratically elected president, Lech Walesa. As such, it gave the president a decisive voice in matters of national security, including the selection of the minister of national defence, the chief of the general staff and most other high posts within the military services. According to Michta,

> these constitutional prerogatives became a powerful incentive for Walesa and the senior officers to bypass the institutions of the ministry of defence and often ignore the defence minister altogether. The 1992 *Constitution* in effect made the Polish military a player in Polish domestic politics.[33]

A further legislative complication to civilianising the Polish ministry of defence was that until the passage of the 1996 *Law on the Duties of the Office of the Minister of National Defence*,[34] the ministry of defence was governed by the many times amended 1967 *Law on National Defence*. Under the latter law the minister controlled the armed forces through the chief of the general staff, the commanders of the military districts, and the service chiefs. Implicit in the 1967 law was the assumption that the minister would be a high-ranking military officer.[35]

In the early days of transition, the preference of the president to keep the military in his own camp and outside the orbit of the legislature, the constitutional and legislative regulations on the ministry of defence and a desire to 'encourage widespread military involvement in the restructuring process',[36] led to the appointment of a military man, Admiral Piotr Kolodziejczyk, as minister of defence in July 1990. By January 1992, however, under Poland's third government in as many years, Jan Parys became the first civilian minister of defence. Parys' five-month tenure as minister of defence cannot be rated as much of a success. Indeed, the so-called 'Parys Affair' of 1992 contributed greatly to the highly conflictual civil–military relationship that would prevail in Poland until at least the mid-1990s. Parys seems to have been especially unsuited to the role of minister of defence:

> Staunchly nationalist and anti-Soviet in his outlook, Parys took over the office with the anticipation that he was entering an institution riddled with former communists and possibly intelligence agents spying for Moscow. From the start he appeared to have assumed that there was no one in the Polish military that he could trust. By setting a hostile tone for civil-military relations, Parys became the focal point of a struggle for power between the president and the prime minister.[37]

The 'Parys Affair' was part of a larger struggle between the government of prime minister Jan Olszeski and Walesa over the real extent of the president's powers in the sphere of defence. With regard to the minister of defence specifically, the conflict was over who would appoint the chief of the general staff. What set off the crisis was a meeting in April 1992 between Jerzy Milewski (a member of the Presidential Chancellery responsible for state security affairs), and General Tadeusz Wilecki. Allegedly, Milewski informed Wilecki that he was Walesa's favourite for the new chief of the general staff. Parys then accused Walesa of both usurping his authority as minister of defence, and of bribing Wilecki with the post of chief of the general staff if he, in turn, would back the idea of a strong presidency.[38]

Ultimately, a special legislative commission was convened to look into the matter. It concluded that Parys' allegations were 'unfounded and detrimental to the state's interests' and he was forced to resign.[39] Wilecki was subsequently appointed chief of the general staff under the government of Hanna Suchocka in August 1992. According to Michta, the 'Parys Affair' helped to strengthen the position of the general staff (as the president's men) vis-à-vis the structures of the ministry of defence, thus making the allegiance of the general staff a political prise. More importantly, the affair strengthened the perception among officers that the army faced a concerted onslaught from the civilians against which, Wilecki observed later on, the army had the 'right to defend itself'.[40]

Poland's next minister of defence, Janusz Onyszkiewicz, was also a civilian. However, his dismissal in October 1993 after 17 months in power marked the beginning of the remilitarisation of the ministry of defence.[41] As minister of defence, Onyszkiewicz appeared to recognise that without clearly defined lines of authority Poland's constitutional framework lent itself to abuse by the president as he sought to exert control over the armed forces and to make the chief of the general staff his personal confidant. The fear was that continued conflict in civil–military relations might worsen Poland's chances for admission to NATO; according to a senior official of the ministry of defence: 'The sole condition which will determine the accession of Poland to NATO is her willingness to accept and implement all the obligations which this entails, including civilian control over the Polish armed forces.'[42] Michta argued that Onyszkiewicz viewed the attempts to subordinate the general staff to the president's office as 'a coup against Poland's vital national interest' – i.e. accession to NATO.[43]

Onyszkiewicz' response to the crisis was to launch a comprehensive reform of the organisational structure of the ministry of defence in mid-1993. His other initiative was to oversee the drafting of the new 'Organisational Regulations of the Ministry of Defence in Peacetime' which were introduced in September 1993. The gist of Onyszkiewicz' reforms was to put the general staff firmly under the authority of the minister of defence, and to create a three-part integrated ministry of defence made up of the minister's executive office, an integrated military–civilian administrative bureaucracy, and the general staff. Unfortunately, the issuing of the new regulations coincided with the fall of Hanna Suchocka's coalition government. In the September 1993 parliamentary elections, the reformed communist party together with the Polish Peasant Party, came to power. One of their first acts was to announce sweeping changes in the senior leadership of the ministry of defence including the appointment of Admiral Kolodziejczyk as minister of defence for the third time in four years in October 1993.

In November 1993, Koldziejczyk suspended implementation of Onyszkiewicz' regulations. Another sign of the re-militarisation process was the transfer of responsibility for military education from the ministry of defence back to the general staff. Military education had been seen as one of the important ways in which the attitudes of the military could be transformed over time; the control of military education was one of the first things transferred to the ministry of defence in the early stages of reform and losing control was a setback for the institutionalisation of civilian control.[44]

The rift between civilian and military personnel in the ministry of defence widened under Kolodziejczyk. The new minister, however, did not have an easier relationship with the president than any of his predecessors. In fact, it was around Kolodziejczyk that the most infamous scandal in Polish civil–military relations, the so-called 'Drawsko Affair', centred. A one-time ally of the president, Kolodziejczyk eventually had a bitter falling out with Walesa which broke into the open at a luncheon for the senior military and ministry of defence leadership at the Drawsko Pomorski Training facility on 30 September 1994. At the luncheon Walesa expressed his opinion that the military command had lost confidence in the minister of defence. With Kolodziejczyk present, Walesa polled all the officers there, including Chief of the General Staff Wilecki, as to whether Kolodziejczyk should be removed and expressed his intention of appointing a new minister who would be prepared to assist in the exercise of the president's prerogatives in the defence sphere.[45] Essentially, the military were encouraged by the president to pass judgement on a minister of defence who had been elected. That the president incited this anti-democratic move is demonstrative of how strained civil–military relations had become as a result of the divided authority between the president and the Sejm. Ultimately, a special Sejm committee which criticised everyone at the luncheon recommended that the generals involved be disciplined, and that civilian control of the military be reasserted.[46] Instead, Walesa fired Kolodziejczyk.

Hungary's experience of re-militarisation was similar to Poland's in its root causes, but less dramatic. Civilianisation of the ministry of defence, for all the problems of its practical implementation, had been a stated goal of the Antall Government from 1990 to 1994. The attitude of Hungary's second government, led by the reformed communist MSZP, was markedly different. Under this government the process of civilianisation was halted and then reversed. The appointment of retired army Colonel Gyorgy Keleti as minister of defence in May 1994 was only the most obvious aspect of the re-introduction of military officers to the top decision-making posts in the ministry. According to Szemerkenyi, this was a demonstration of what happens 'when the executive's commitment to civilianise the ministry of defence disappears'.[47] Similarly, the British ministry of defence study also concluded that 'if civilianisation of senior ministry of defence posts is to take place and succeed, it will require the endorsement of the government and the commitment of the minister of defence and the defence collegium' – a commitment that the research was unable to detect.[48]

There are several reasons for the new government's retreat from the process of civilianisation. Logically, the serious problems of the federal budget at that time and the substantial cuts this imposed on defence spending were a motivating factor. More important, however, seems to have been the essential lack of interest of MSZP politicians in the issue of defence reform. An independent review of security policy in the 1990s claimed that the MSZP government simply could not conceive what kind of security challenges were facing the state, nor what kind of armed forces were needed.[49] More succinctly, Janos Matus, a civilian bureaucrat in the ministry from 1995 to 1997 who was head of the department of Security Studies at the National Defence University when interviewed, suggested that 'the [MSZP] politicians simply neglected the military. They were focused on NATO, but they recognised only the advantages of membership, not the responsibilities.'[50]

Hungary's return to a civilian minister of defence came in June 1998 with the appointment of Janos Szabo after parliamentary elections in May brought the FIDESZ-MPP party to power under the leadership of Prime Minister Victor Orban. As opposed to the MSZP, FIDESZ had a much better developed governmental programme on defence and security policy which was set out in the policy document *At the Threshold of the New Millennium: Governmental Programme for a Civilian Hungary*.[51] The Orban cabinet indicated that a primary task of the new government would be to strengthen civil control of the armed forces.[52] Crucially, by 1998 the contest for power between the president and the government had long since been settled. The first step in resolving this issue was the aforementioned ruling of the Constitutional Court in 1991. Further constitutional amendments in 1992–1993 and again in 1994 even more clearly defined the president's rôle as a titular – rather than operational – commander-in-chief and solidified the supremacy of the government and the minister of defence in the defence policy sphere.[53]

Notwithstanding the evident desire of FIDESZ to redress the weaknesses of civilian control which had grown so manifest under the previous government, and the resolution of the presidential–governmental conflict, a number of problems persisted throughout the late 1990s. To a certain extent, criticism of the system in Hungary centred on the perceived personal weaknesses of the minister of defence, Janos Szabo. As one non-governmental activist on defence policy argued, 'the new minister of defence is a civilian, however I can criticise him and the media criticises him because he is not professional at all'.[54] This perception of the minister of defence was also shared by officials within the ministry. One interviewee expressed his view that:

> Unfortunately, the ministers in this ministry have never been serious persons. Everybody called the former minister the 'spokesman' because he didn't make any decisions, he just communicated with the press. The current minister doesn't even do that.[55]

The unfavourable perception of the minister was probably deepened by the feeling that as a cabinet appointment the minister of defence was not considered particularly important. Szabo was not a FIDESZ member, rather he was a member of the smaller Independent Small-holders' Party which was in coalition with FIDESZ. Moreover, the minister was seriously hampered in the performance of his duties by the fact that he had virtually no permanent staff of his own:

> The minister has maybe five people who arrange his travel and telephones. He has maybe one advisor. Look at the phone book for how many people are

> under the minister. There is the head of the minister's secretariat, but this is not a real position – the others are typists. The advisory body of the minister has six places but only one person.[56]

In any event, while it was emphasised in interviews that formally the authority of the minister was unfettered, there were serious problems with the system in practice:

> I would say that we have all the institutions necessary for civilian control in the law. We have problems in the practice . . . The minister has the legal supervision over the defence forces, not only the general staff, but the whole military, but he does not use this competence. This is just the legal framework – what the minister can do. The other side of the issue is what he *dares* to do in practice. I think we have the legal framework for civilian control but this is just theoretical.[57]

Although civilian ministers of defence began to be re-appointed as early as November 1994 in Poland, the single most significant step in Poland's return to a civilian minister of defence was the election of Aleksander Kwasniewski as president in November 1995. With Walesa gone, the five-year campaign of manipulation of the top officials in the ministry of defence for the benefit of the presidency over the parliament began to come to an end. As opposed to Walesa, Kwasniewski was prepared to work with the Sejm so that the long-delayed *Law on the Duties of the Office of the Minister of National Defence*[58] which reinforced the authority of the civilian minister of defence, as well as a new *Constitution* in 1997[59] which cut back the prerogatives of the president were passed. Finally, in October 1997 Janusz Onyszkiewicz the architect of the 'Organisational Regulations' on which the *Law on the Duties of the Office of the Minister of National Defence* was based, was reappointed as minister of defence.

The passage of the *Law on the Duties of the Office of the Minister of National Defence* was a major turning point in Polish civil–military relations. The main thrust of the law was to end the dualism of civilian and military structures of authority within the ministry which had undermined the minister for so long. Under the provisions of the new law, the civilian minister of defence was the head of the whole defence establishment, with the general staff being integrated into the ministry. The chief of the general staff was made a deputy minister subordinate directly to the civilian minister – not to the president. Both the military intelligence services and military education were put under the control of the minister. The minister's directives and decisions acquired the status of direct military orders for all active service personnel, including the chief of the general staff. Basically, the new law signalled unequivocally that the civilian minister of defence was the ultimate arbiter of all things that went on in his department.

The 1997 Constitution limited the capacity of the president to interfere in the minister of defence's performance of his duties. It explicitly noted the principle of political neutrality of the armed forces and stated that they are 'subject to democratic and civilian control'.[60] The sole task of the armed forces was to 'protect the independence of the state and the indivisibility of its territory as well as to ensure the security and integrity of its borders'.[61] It also clearly stated that the president 'in times of peace, shall exercise command over the armed forces through the minister of national defence'.[62]

The main beneficiary of the legal developments in Polish civil–military relations was the minister of defence, Janusz Onyszkiewicz. In contrast with his Hungarian counterpart, the new Polish minister of defence gained not only the legal and institutional levers necessary to control the ministry, but as someone who had been deeply involved in defence and security issues since 1990, he also had intellectual expertise in defence.[63]

In summary, moving to a civilian minister of defence in Poland and Hungary was not simply a matter of declaration; rather it was a difficult process that took nearly ten years to achieve. Neither was it a straightforward process, as both countries experienced a period of re-militarisation. Crucially, we see that for civilianisation at the top level of the ministry of defence to succeed, it required the support of both president and parliament to enact the proper legislation and to avoid undermining the authority of the minister vis-à-vis his military advisers. Equally important, it was incumbent on new civilian ministers of defence to be pro active and actually *lead* their departments. In Poland, a particularly dynamic minister of defence working in a new legislative framework achieved positive results in imposing civilian control of the armed forces. In Hungary, on the other hand, a more passive minister, lacking sufficient staff and who may not have had the fullest support of his colleagues in cabinet, achieved much less impressive results. Ironically, this suggests that despite the far more serious and drawn-out transgressions of democratic civil–military relations in Poland, the resolution of the problem was more definitive there than it was in Hungary.

'Raisins in bread': integrating civilians in the defence bureaucracy

If obtaining a civilian minister of defence was a problem in Poland and Hungary, civilianising the bureaucracy of the ministry of defence was an even more complex challenge with even less positive results. The need to civilianise was widely acknowledged:

> Appointing a civilian minister of defence may facilitate civilian control of the military, but it does not guarantee effective civilian control. The new minister of defence also had to introduce a civilian presence lower down in the bureaucracy.[64]

There have been some signs of progress. For example, as of late 1999, civilian personnel represented about 46 per cent of the Hungarian ministry of defence. In Poland the percentage was lower at 33.5 per cent, but nonetheless there had been a tangible increase in the civilian presence in the ministry of defence.[65] On the other hand, the real influence of these new civilian officials in the ministry of defence remains a matter of considerable debate. When asked in 1999 what were the main problems of integrating civilians in the Hungarian ministry of defence, one long-time observer replied 'The short answer is that there is barely any integration.'[66] Similarly, in Poland it was estimated by one interviewee that 'less than five per cent of real decision making posts in the ministry of defence are held by civilians.'[67]

One barrier to the integration of the defence bureaucracy was the low skill level of civilians in the defence sphere. Efforts to inject civilians into staff positions in the ministry of defence merely for the sake of having certain functions performed by civilians often backfired. Frequently, it led to situations where under-trained and inexperienced civilian managers were dominated by their more skilful military counterparts. These situations in turn generated tensions between the military and civilians which impeded the development of mutual respect. Moreover, governments initiated 'only weak support' for the development of security studies in their national educational systems and, therefore, few experts were being educated for careers in the ministry of defence.[68]

The lack of support for the development of security studies may be attributable in large part to the inability of the state to properly fund education in general. However, there are indications that civilian governments also did not hold civilian defence experts in high esteem. 'I would say that the government tolerates civilian experts, or are just not very interested in the issue,' was the conclusion of an interlocutor in Budapest. While in Warsaw, 'The main problem in the last decade in this respect is the lack of understanding in the government of the need to have civilians in the ministry of defence.'[69] Neither did the West put much effort into redressing the imbalance of expertise between military and civilians in the Partnership for Peace states:

> To have civilian control of the military Central European countries need first of all 'cannons' – that is civilian experts in the field. Western countries, despite all the talk on civilian control and despite all kinds of training in other fields (from banking through ecology) has [sic] an exception and does not do much to train Central European civilian experts in international security.[70]

Partnership for Peace emphasised military participation in training programmes and military-to-military contacts, rather than partnership at the civilian bureaucratic level. The priority areas in Partnership for Peace were military–technical in nature: command, control and communications systems; standardisation; defence infrastructure; military education; exercises and training and so on. 'The few token civilians who participated in some of these programmes only give the illusion of change in both NATO and partner countries.'[71] In other words, the skill level of civilians was growing very slowly while the familiarity of military personnel with NATO command structures, standard procedures and operational style was increasing rapidly through a host of training opportunities. The lack of civilian expertise in defence in Central Europe stems from the facts that traditionally civilians were not trained in defence in the Soviet era, that security studies still is not a course of study available in many civilian universities, and a generalised feeling among civilians that military issues are best left to the military themselves. A Hungarian deputy state secretary of defence summed the problem up:

> The problem of integration is a historical one. Within the Warsaw Pact, the defence sector was closed. There was no teaching of defence and security issues at civilian universities; defence expertise was concentrated in the military colleges and the general staff; it was absolutely impossible for civilians to be involved in defence.[72]

A major factor in the *persistence* of the problem was the very low level of support on the part of national governments for building a really knowledgeable group of civilian specialists. Poland is somewhat of an exception in Central Europe in this respect since in 1995 a National Security Faculty was formed at the University of Warsaw as a tripartite venture of the university, the National Security Bureau and the ministry of defence.[73] Attracting well-trained civilians into careers in the ministry of defence is proving very difficult. In the post-communist era, a career in the military bureaucracy for a young, well-educated Pole was not very attractive. In 1998, for example, there was not a single graduate from the National School of Public Administration (the main source of graduates for careers in the public service) employed by the ministry of defence.[74] A Hungarian civilian defence official described his frustration working at the ministry of defence:

> I spent two years in the ministry of defence from 1995 to 1997. My main problem was that civilians are not accepted by their military colleagues as knowledgeable experts on security issues. Most of the civilians in the ministry of defence are retired military officers and simply being a retired military person does not make them a civilian in mind-set. It is hard for them to accept civilians . . . I was told in the ministry of defence that they did not expect reliable expertise from me because I am a civilian and that my knowledge of American defence planning and so on was not valuable. So my knowledge was not paid attention to. It is very hard in this part of the world to accept a civilian as someone who can make acceptable proposals about the military.[75]

An institutional culture which maintains a tradition that leaders must be officers and that civilians should not have command authority over military personnel, does not seem an attractive work environment for an ambitious young civil servant. On the other hand, there were indications in Warsaw that the barriers to civilianisation were more structural than attitudinal:

> The possible career path of young people in the ministry of defence compared to other ministries is rather poorer. The ministry of defence is still reluctant to absorb large numbers of young civilians – and the primary reason for that is not a negative attitude towards civilian control. But first of all it is the administrative problems it creates. The ministry of defence still has not developed

> a system that would enable a large number of civilians to continue their careers in the ministry. All these little regulations in terms of salary, sending people abroad, and everything else are aimed at officers. So the presence of civilians in this system causes bureaucratic problems. Therefore, in my opinion, it is first of all a problem of organisation and not a lack of will.[76]

There is another nuance to this problem: under the current personnel policy not only is it frustrating professionally to serve as a civilian in the ministry of defence, it can also be financially punitive. In Hungary, one interlocutor concluded:

> Why do we have so many military people within the system now? Its very simple: because of the salary. Many civilians join the ministry of defence and find that if they become an officer their salary will be one third higher.[77]

In Poland, the situation was similar:

> It is a question of market competition. I believe that national security specialists could be brought into the ministry of defence but it is a question of salaries and the ministry is not in a good position in this respect. The average salary here is half or a third what it is in civilian life. So it is a question of possibilities. I have a personal experience of cooperation with civilians in the international department and it was pretty good – but a lot of people are leaving the ministry of defence now because of the money. We cannot attract experienced people here, only young students. If they have experience then we cannot afford them – we call them 'raisins in bread'.[78]

The prospects for educating civilians in defence issues were lower in Hungary than in Poland. Aside from the defence economics department of the Economics University in Budapest, as of late 1999 there were no courses in security studies at any civilian university.[79] The main training centre for Hungarian civilians in defence issues is the National Defence University which began to admit civilian students to its department of security studies in September 1997. By late 1999, approximately 45 out of a total 142 students in the department were civilian.[80] The opening of the National Defence University to civilian students can be seen in both a positive and negative light. It indicates that the ministry of defence was trying to solve its shortage of civilian expertise with the limited educational resources at its disposal. On the other hand, it suggests that the government as a whole did not take the problem sufficiently seriously if it had made essentially no effort to support security studies in the civilian educational system.

In the short term, the security studies programme may alleviate some of the problems caused by lack of civilian expertise in the ministry of defence. In the long term it may contribute to the perpetuation of the problem. For one thing, several observers pointed out that political elites themselves are sceptical of civilian defence experts: 'political parties have retired generals who advise them on the military; politicians do not trust civilian advice; they do not believe in civilian expertise; when they have a question, politicians only want to hear from the military'.[81] Yet, one of the main reasons for having civilians in the ministry of defence is to have the benefit of a diversity of viewpoints on matters of defence and security. If the politicians themselves do not appreciate any need for a diversity of viewpoints; and if they are content to leave the responsibility for training civilian experts to the military – in the same school as military officers, using the same methods and with the same professors – then what is the point of having civilian cadres in the ministry of defence anyway?

Another potent barrier to the integration of civilians in the ministry of defence relates to the rather politicised appointment process. Some of Poland's problems in this respect have already been discussed in the context of appointing a civilian minister of defence. Naturally, the practice of making appointments to the ministry of defence based on political criteria rather than professional merit obtained at lower levels of the bureaucracy as well. Political appointees generated a lot of tension between the military and civilians in the ministry of defence. Within the bureaucracy there has been a very high turnover rate of civilian staff in both countries. Between 1990 and 1998 Poland had over 25 ministers and deputy ministers of defence, each representing different parties, and most unabashedly partisan. During Lajos Fur's tenure as minister of defence in Hungary, most of the senior leadership of the ministry of defence was civilian. Under Gyorgy Keleti, however, most of the senior, supposedly non-political, civilian posts were taken over by military officers. Then again, under Janos Szabo the ministry of defence leadership returned to being mostly civilian.

Aside from the period of re-militarisation, the really big problem of integration in Poland and Hungary has been the perception of the military that civilian appointments are politically rather than professionally motivated. In their view, not only did these new civilian bureaucrats lack any real expertise in defence, they were in the ministry of defence for too short a time to learn on the job, and because they were patronage appointees they were often not really interested in learning the job anyway:

> The biggest problem up to the latest election [1998] was that every new government tried to put its own people in the ministry of defence; the majority of them were not experts in any way – they were just family, cousins, friends, etc. Every new prime minister brings his own style of leading and his own people. Officials in the ministry of defence cannot connect with these people; it's hard because there is not enough time to build up a new system if the people change with every election.[82]

One of the main problems is that the civilian bureaucracy is not treated as a neutral, professional body which serves regardless of the political party in power; rather it is a politicised body which turns over with each election. Such systems are hardly unknown in the West where there is considerable variation in the depth to which political appointments may go: when the American secretary of defence changes so does a large portion of the personnel of the defence department, whereas in the

British system the bureaucracy tends not to change. In a country with a large talent pool of bureaucrats accustomed to working in the security sphere a high turnover rate is not an insurmountable problem. In Poland and Hungary, on the other hand, which have only a shallow talent pool of suitable civilian specialists, changing the bureaucracy with every new minister of defence is an extravagant luxury.

Several of the interviewees in Hungary shared the impression that the civilian bureaucracy was too political:

> For the military it was a real shock that immediately after the transition civilians started to do all kinds of jobs in the ministry of defence. It was not democratic at all but very political. Ninety-nine per cent of the civilians in the ministry of defence were political appointees – they were cousins or brothers, neighbours and supporters of some politicians, that is all . . . this created a negative atmosphere. It was not easy for military officers to be subordinated to a civilian, especially if the civilian was an untrained appointee who didn't know anything . . . To my mind this problem of political appointees is really difficult. Only the minister of defence and the administrative state secretary should be politicians. We still have that problem of young democracies, of replacing people all the time with political appointees, more than necessary, after each election for political reasons. It is still evolving, but the problem is not going away fast.[83]

Another problem was that the military and civilians appeared to lack a common vocabulary. As was discussed at the beginning of this chapter, the concept of civilian control was understood by civilians and the military in different ways:

> In the West, the concept of civilian control is quite simple but in Hungary it means something different. The meaning is much more on *control* of the military by civilians, not a shared responsibility for defence. It is a difficult relationship.[84]

On the one hand, military officers have little experience of working with civilians in a democratic context. On the other hand, due to the lack of civilian expertise and a poor understanding of the concept of civilian control on both sides, civilian and military officials cannot communicate effectively. What Sarvas called a 'symbolic blockage'[85] meant that military and civilians used different terms to describe similar problems, thus hampering the development of good civil–military relations. As a Hungarian military officer put it:

> [Civilians] think that the military has its own interests, special military interests – ranks, positions, salary, a big defence structure, the largest number of personnel and so on . . . And from the other side, we in the army can feel that civilians do not serve the interests of the military sphere; maybe they are serving the interests of the political parties, and political directions, different political directions . . .[86]

A final reason for the slow pace of integration was also the resistance of the existing bureaucracy to change. An obvious source of this resistance was the fact that with the change of regime officers in Central Europe felt the effects of the transition profoundly. Both socially and economically, military officers lost their formerly privileged positions. Ferenc Molnar, a Hungarian military sociologist and specialist on the effects of transition on the socio-economic conditions of Central European armies, pointed out a large number of reasons for the loss of morale in the military including: the poor personal financial situation of officers, the lack of societal support for the military, an unpromising career path and so on.[87] The result was that while many junior officers left the military for better jobs in the civilian sector, senior officers whose socialisation in the Warsaw Pact system made them most resistant to change remained. This created a serious bottle-neck:

> Optimally, we should have a pyramidal rank structure but what we have is an upside-down pyramid because about half of all officers are major or lieutenant-colonel in rank. It is at the lower level that we haven't enough . . . Only after eight years did we start to think about the human side of reforming the armed forces. In the first years we did not do too much in this respect . . . It is a problem because the civilians have no experience. They have no idea what should be reformed and how to see some real changes in the system. And of course the generals are opposing change because many times it seems they want to say 'its my place, its my chair, I don't want to change'.[88]

Reforming the general staff

However, the most significant source of resistance to the effective integration and empowerment of civilians in the ministry of defence was the general staff. In Hungary and in Poland the dilemmas were more or less the same: under the old system the general staff was the 'brain' of the army and many functions that should have been part of the ministry of defence such as planning and strategic analysis were concentrated there. Democratising civil–military relations, therefore, required that these functions be transferred to the integrated ministry of defence. Accomplishing this task, however, proved extremely difficult. Essentially the resolution of the problem had three complications:

1 civilians did not have the expertise to perform these tasks as well as the military;
2 for various reasons, both personal and professional, the military did not want to relinquish their roles to the ministry of defence; and
3 the weaknesses of defence legislation caused by the conflict between parliaments and presidents allowed them numerous ways of avoiding having to do so.

Most of these complications have been discussed above. Accordingly, this section will focus on a few details of the problem which are illustrative of the trends already sketched.

In Poland, the conflict between the general staff and the ministry of defence had at its centre General Tadeusz Wilecki, the chief of the general staff from August 1992 until March 1997. According to Michta, 'Polish institutional changes within the defence ministry in 1996–1997 largely focused on building a mechanism to constrain the chief of the general staff.'[89] Given that the civilian bureaucracy in Poland was highly politicised and subject to a very high rate of turnover, the general staff was reluctant through most of the 1990s to relinquish its prerogatives in the policy-planning sphere and its operational control of the troops to the officials of the ministry of defence. Until Walesa's defeat in the presidential elections of 1995, the general staff proved very successful in playing the president and the parliament off against each other, and thus managed to retain an almost complete independence from the ministry of defence.

The turning point was the 1996 *Law on the Duties of the Office of the Minister of National Defence*. This new law radically changed the organisational structure of both the ministry of defence and the general staff. First, it made the general staff a branch of the ministry of defence under the direct authority of the minister. Second, it merged with other administrative structures or wholly eliminated the 52 organisational units of the old ministerial/general staff structures down to a more streamlined structure of 34 administrations, offices and sections.[90] The really controversial outcome of the new legislation, however, was the creation of the Land Forces Command which became the command authority for the bulk of the armed forces in April 1997.[91] The Land Forces Command was not subordinate to the chief of the general staff; rather it was directly subordinate to the minister of defence. Whereas previously the minister of defence could command the troops only through the chief of the general staff, now he could issue directives through a ministerial structure which bypassed the chief of the general staff. Effectively, the general staff became the planning and advisory branch of the ministry of defence and lost the operational control of the troops which had contributed to its former independence. Thus, the former independence of the general staff from the ministry of defence was greatly diminished in line with the new strength of the civilian minister. On the other hand, the reform may have gone too far. The control of the minister of defence now extended to a very low operational level. This suggests that the military's former independence was simply replaced by civilian *micro-management*. The threat, according to Michta, is that, 'if the commands are not given the requisite freedom to implement orders and directives in a professional manner, civilian *control* of the military will have been taken almost literally to mean civilian *command*'.[92]

Though the root causes of the problem were similar in both countries, the conflict between the general staff and the ministry of defence was less openly dramatic, but also less definitively resolved in Hungary. Prior to the political compromises of 1989–1990 which led to the retreat of the communist party from power, the ministry of defence and the general staff were integrated under the command of the minister of defence who was both the highest-ranking military officer and a member of the government. The separation of the general staff from the ministry of defence, the declared intention of which was to isolate the armed forces from partisan political influences, could be seen as having been too successful: the general staff ended up becoming a buffer not just between the military and partisan politics, but also between the armed forces and the ministry of defence which made it very difficult for the government to implement its defence policy decisions.[93]

According to Zoltan Pecze, the institutional separation of 1989 gave the general staff the feeling that they were on an equal level with the ministry of defence. Senior military leaders preferred to view the ministry of defence as a provider of essential administrative needs, not as a superior.[94] As opposed to the Polish case, however, the position of the chief of the general staff as the subordinate of the minister was made very clear under the *National Defence Act*. Therefore, the tactic of the general staff to avoid submitting to reforms they did not like was typically not open confrontation with the minister but passive resistance to direction.

> It is true for the current chief of staff and for the previous ones that they don't know what civilian control is and they resist strongly when there are attempts to exercise civilian control. The previous chief of staff was dismissed because he resisted the current government's policies and individual orders. And then came another chief of staff who was told to be more loyal but my impression is that he also does not understand this whole idea and will cause problems – he already has caused problems . . . In Hungary, the commander bills himself as the strongest, most talented person in the company, regiment or whatever – and they hold on to this idea. A commander is a commander because he is the best ever in his area. When they come to the top they still think this way and regard the ministry of defence as a challenge to be overcome, as incompetent, stupid people who have no military knowledge and have no right (not in the legal sense) to say anything about military matters.

In 1996, some changes were made in various legal acts governing the armed forces, most notably to the *National Defence Act and the Service Acts* (Acts XLIII, *The Service Status of Profesional Soldiers*, and XLIV *The Service Status of Conscripts* of 1996) which addressed a variety of organisational, personnel and operational issues pertaining to the military but did not solve the underlying problems. In fact, one of the policies of the MSZMP government was to scrap plans for the merger of the military command and the defence ministry. Ultimately, all Hungarian governments paid lip service at least to resolving this problem. Even by the end of 1999, however, the chances of success were judged by several defence officials in Budapest to be fairly low:

> The first government made a resolution on integration in 1994, but that government left before it went through. The second government made some studies and promised to do this integration but never did. Now we have the third government trying which is, I am afraid, going to fail again.[95]

Indeed, in July 1999 the chief of general staff, General Ferenc Vegh, was forced to resign his post when a bitter dispute between him and minister of defence Janos

Szabo over the government's plan to increase the control of the ministry of defence over the armed forces became public. Vegh accused Szabo of managing a 400-strong 'shadow general staff' in the ministry of defence that advises decision-makers, while army commanders are pushed to the background.[96] The response of the ministry of defence was that 'the general staff must merge with the ministry and not vice versa. We shall quash anyone who opposes the government programme.' Szabo was also quoted as saying, 'there are matters within the ministry that can be settled only through orders'.[97] Undoubtedly, the position of the ministry of defence that it and not the general staff should control the armed forces was correct. Nonetheless, the rhetoric of the minister which amounted to saying 'shut up and obey!' was indicative of a worrying civil–military divide, internal tensions and operational disorders that cast doubt on the competence of the ministry's leadership.

Former Soviet Union

The Russian military has played a more prominent role in its political system than the Ukrainian military. Indeed, in the early 1990s there was real concern about the potential of a military coup in Russia. At a time when leading members of the government like Foreign Minister Andrei Kozyrev in September 1992 were asking, 'why is the military deciding highly important political questions? When tanks become an independent political force it is a catastrophe!', such fears did not seem wholly out of place.[98] By the mid-1990s, however, when the Russian military showed little inclination to try toppling the regime the efforts of scholars shifted to explaining the paradox of Russian military 'quiescence'.[99] A prevailing view emerged that the military was essentially passive in the face of malign neglect. There had been no attempt at a military take-over because, despite ample cause, the senior command was too corrupted to lead one, the officer corps was too divided internally to join one, and the army as a whole was too weak – relative to the array of other armed formations which might oppose it – to carry one out without touching off a civil war. In short, it was posited that the military posed no immediate threat to Yeltsin's regime and appeared to be resigned to a fate of marginalisation and disintegration.[100]

It is closer to the truth, however, to say that there was hardly any intention to put the Russian military under democratic civilian control in the Yeltsin era in the first place. The army was directly subordinate to an autocratic and erratic president who happened to be a civilian; that level of control was sufficient for the army and the president alike. From time to time, Yeltsin drew the army into his political fights – in putting down the opposition's revolt in Moscow in October 1993, then in attempting, first in 1994–1996 and then again in 1999, to restore Moscow's control over the breakaway Chechnya. In tradeoff for its support, he gave the military high command carte blanche to make defence policy more or less as it saw fit, provided its decisions did not conflict with any specific desires of the president or cost too much money. Wider society and politicians in the Duma, as one Russian politician observed, had virtually no role: 'They do not interfere in military affairs, having put all problems of survival and reform under the control of the military themselves.'[101]

Although there is much in common between Russia and Ukraine in terms of the dire social and economic plight of the armed forces, the Ukrainian military has not played nearly so active and obvious a role in the political life of the country. In general, calm has prevailed in Ukrainian civil–military relations. This is not to suggest that Ukrainian understanding of the concept of democratic civilian control was any deeper or subtler than the Russian. On the contrary, in a mid-1997 interview Ukrainian defence minister General Oleksandr Kuzmuk expressed a very primitive understanding of the concept: 'I am a member of the Cabinet of Ministers. I am also subordinate directly to the president, who is a civilian. I consider these to be sufficient controls.'[102] Yet, the dynamic in Ukraine was different from Russia. According to Sherr, the danger which the Ukrainian army posed to its society was not one of coup d'état, but of uncoordinated action between it and other security forces, and waste of scarce resources.[103] In a country lacking funds for spending on, inter alia, health care, pensions and education, a swollen and corrupt security establishment that was unaccountable for its spending and actions contributed to, and indeed came to symbolise, the general impoverishment and instability of the state.

In neither country did civilian integration in the defence establishment make much progress in the period under review. Let us look at the reasons why.

The minister of defence

Infrequently through the 1990s in both Russia and Ukraine concern about the weakness of democratic civilian control of the armed forces prompted calls for the appointment of a civilian minister of defence. Yeltsin's last military reform plan called *The Basic Principles (Conceptual Outline) of State Policy on Military Development up to 2005*, which was signed in 1998, reportedly dealt at length with establishing a civilian ministry of defence, anticipating that civilian control would make for better political and economic management of the armed forces.[104] The Council on Foreign and Defence Policy – a Russian, non-governmental research and lobby group – also called for a 'civilian defence ministry [that] could deal in greater detail with the social and political problems of the armed forces which seem to concern nobody now'.[105]

Igor Pustovoy, a defence critic and Rada deputy who was formerly head of procurement in the ministry of defence was a strong advocate of a civilian minister in Ukraine. He argued that one of the main principles of armed forces reform had to concern the question of its control by the public. In his view, this presupposed the occupation of the minister's office by a civilian minister supported by a civilian bureaucracy.[106] In fact, rhetoric about the desirability of a civilian minister of defence became reality in 1994 with the appointment to the post of Valeriy Shmarov, a prominent defence industrialist. However, this experiment with a civilian minister ended badly in 1996 with Shmarov's removal and replacement by a military man, General Oleksandr Kuzmuk.

It is difficult to show evidence of much progress toward the goal of installing an effective civilian leader at the top of the ministry of defence in either Russia or Ukraine. In fact, for much of the military and political elite in both countries the concept of civilian management of defence remains alien and superfluous.

The obvious place to begin building an integrated civilian–military decision-making structure for the Russian army would have been with appointing a civilian as the country's first post-Soviet minister of defence. Aside from being a clear indication of the intent of the new post-communist regime to put civil–military relations on a democratic footing, such a move would not have been impractical: there was at least one civilian, first deputy minister of defence Andrei Kokoshin, who could have filled the position. Nevertheless, with the appointment of General of the Army Pavel Grachev as minister on 7 May 1992, the prolonged debate over whether or not to have a civilian minister of defence was brought to a close. In interview with *Izvestia* shortly after his appointment, Grachev himself explained why a civilian minister of defence would have been a premature development for Russia:

> Let us look at it with a clear head. Is this the right time in Russia's life to have a civilian at the helm of the ministry of defence? I will say frankly that people in the military would not understand it. Not just the brass, but the ordinary officers too, the lieutenants and captains. That is the first thing. And second, right now, when the army is flooded by so many problems, for goodness' sake let someone who has breathed its air all his life deal with them.[107]

At the time, Grachev's view had some merit. The army was in the process of adjusting to massive psychological blows in the early 1990s, not least the fact that the new Russian army had become just one of 15 separate armed forces each belonging to a newly-sovereign Soviet successor state. Russia was also not unlike other post-communist states which, as Szemerkenyi pointed out, faced a serious dilemma due to the lack of civilian expertise in defence matters: 'They could appoint a minister of defence with democratic credentials, or one with knowledge of military issues' – but not both.[108] In a volatile political and socio-economic milieu Grachev was a good compromise between continuity of leadership in the military sphere and loyalty to the new regime. He was also not unpopular with the military[109] and was trusted by Yeltsin as a result of his support during the August Putsch of 1991. It was not at all an unusual development in a post-communist context. Many other transition states, like Poland and Hungary, either began transition with a military officer as minister or reverted to one shortly thereafter. Indeed, at least one analyst indicated that Grachev was seen initially as a transitional minister who when the ground became more fertile would be replaced by a civilian.[110]

The situation only worsened, however, and the ground grew less, not more, hospitable to a civilian minister. It was increasingly clear by the mid-1990s that Grachev's longevity as minister had less to do with providing continuity of military leadership than it did with the highly personalised pattern of civilian control which

Yeltsin had created. It seems that Yeltsin's understanding of civilian control was very simplistic:

> The president controls the army by appointing the minister of defence. Even though all Russia's defence ministers have been military they have served as the president's political appointees making sure that developments in the armed forces follow the directives of the president. Proceeding from his understanding of what the president wants, the minister appoints those generals to the top ministry of defence positions who are able to help him fulfil those tasks. This assures the loyalty of the ministry of defence leadership – and of the armed forces as a whole – to the head of state.[111]

Grachev's tenure was illustrative of the first and most important requirement of a minister of defence under Yeltsin: personal loyalty to the president. This relationship was symbolically underlined by Yeltsin on Defenders of the Fatherland day in 1996. At a ceremony in the Kremlin, Yeltsin awarded Grachev a gold medal with an image of himself on one side and the inscription 'from the president of the Russian Federation' on the other. Handing the medal to Grachev, he said 'this is not a state award, This is from me personally.'[112]

By July 1996 when, as part of a political bargain between Yeltsin and Aleksandr Lebed, General of the Army Igor Rodionov became minister of defence, few people lamented Grachev's passing. 'Pasha Mercedes', as he had become known, was widely reviled. Rodionov, by comparison, was thought to be an excellent choice by most observers. 'This is a man who merits respect,' said Lev Rokhlin who went on at length about the many fine qualities of the new minister.[113] In December 1996, Rodionov, having reached the mandatory retirement age of sixty, became Russia's first 'civilian' minister of defence. Yeltsin hailed this development as a 'sign of the democratisation of Russia'.[114]

However, despite his ideas and energy for military reform he was not a very effective minister. He was widely acknowledged to be a brilliant military officer (having been head of the general staff academy from 1989 to 1996), but he never seemed to figure out how to manage the cut-throat politics of the new Russia. By the autumn of 1996, his patron Aleksandr Lebed had been removed from all his official posts and Rodionov was without allies in powerful places. Quite quickly, the new minister of defence became embroiled in a conflict with Secretary of the Defence Council Yuri Baturin over defence reform and funding. What ensued was the bruising political battle that was discussed in Chapter 2 – a battle that Rodionov was ill equipped to fight and ended with his humiliating dismissal in May 1997. Rodionov's time as minister confirmed the first rule of civil–military relations under Yeltsin – Lebed forced him on the president and so his loyalty could never be fully assured. And suggested a second: the minister must not bother the president with demands on the federal budget, or embarrass the government by talking too loudly about the degradation of the armed forces.

The next minister of defence, Marshal Igor Sergeyev, seemed to have understood the rules better and was a better politician. The major distinguishing characteristic between him and Rodionov, wrote Oleg Odnokolenko, was that 'he did not link the success of military reform to the amount of funding provided to the Russian army. The president and the government probably surmised that such a link existed, and that it was a very direct one, but the minister did not press the point.'[115] In return, when Sergeyev reached sixty years of age, Yeltsin decreed that he was exempted from mandatory retirement until the age of sixty-five and, therefore, Sergeyev could stay on as minister in uniform (although the decree would have to be renewed yearly). By the time Sergeyev was appointed, a civilian minister of defence for Russia had simply become a non-issue. Duma deputy and member of the defence committee Sergei Yushenkov was one of the few politicians to consistently call for a civilian minister of defence.[116] Otherwise, few others pushed for it. This lack of interest stemmed in part from a recognition by Duma deputies that making proposals about the military in the face of the president's exclusive authority in the sphere of defence was futile: 'Duma members will not and cannot do anything, since as soon as they make any proposals they get a kick in the neck from the president [Yeltsin], who thinks he has exclusive authority over the military.'[117]

It came as no surprise at the end of March 2001 when President Putin announced that he would not renew the decree extending Sergeyev's exemption from retirement so that he could have continued to serve as minister of defence after turning 63 on April 20. In fact, most analysts felt the change was a long time coming since for several months prior a conflict between Sergeyev and Chief of the General Staff Anatoliy Kvashnin over proposed changes in the structure of the armed forces had paralysed the defence establishment.[118] But what relatively few predicted was that the secretary of the Security Council, newly-retired FSB Lieutenant General Sergei Ivanov, would be the man to take over. Ivanov was a noted Putin favourite and his star was obviously on the rise. But his old job heading the Security Council had a much higher profile than that of the minister of defence. Moreover, the appointment as minister of defence of a 'civilian' – or at least someone from outside the armed forces – appeared to contradict an earlier statement of the new president who, answering questions at the Russian PEN Center on 3 December 1999, had already made clear his views on civilians in the ministry of defence:

> It may be that a civilian should be at the head of the ministry of defence. In a normal state. But we have a weak state, and to make up for this state's weakness we have people from armed structures in places where civilians ought to work.[119]

In fact, Ivanov's appointment as minister was no demotion. But neither did it represent a sea change in the attitude of the Kremlin towards the civilianisation of the ministry of defence despite some of the rhetoric to that effect at the time; rather, it was another step in Putin's efforts to restore the 'vertical of power' in the Russian state. Ivanov was a trusted partner of the president who had already proved his mettle as secretary of the Security Council in seeing through to completion a new national security concept and military doctrine. Furthermore, and in addition to his demonstrated grit, as Putin's 'alter ego' in the ministry of defence, Ivanov represented a figure with whom even such fractious and openly ambitious generals as Kvashnin knew they could not trifle easily. On the other hand, as a starting point for the civilianisation of the ministry of defence, Ivanov's appointment amounted to very little since there was no further evidence of any intent to change the ministry of defence into a political rather than a military institution.

In fact, the real significance of the move lay elsewhere. First, it suggested that Putin really was taking seriously the need to push through a radical reform of the armed forces over the potential objections of the general staff.[120] Second, as Vladimir Shurygin wrote, it signalled that 'the role and place of the ministry of defence in the state system is being drastically changed. After almost a decade of languishing in second-rank roles, the ministry is becoming one of the main institutions of the state . . . From now on, the ministry of defence will once again be the main organ of strategic planning and state-building'.[121]

Even before the collapse of the USSR, Ukraine began taking steps towards the establishment of its own armed forces. The *Declaration of Sovereignty* passed by the Supreme Soviet of Ukraine in July 1990 asserted Ukraine's right to establish independent armed forces, its military neutrality, and its aspiration to be a non-nuclear state. In further legislation it was declared that Ukrainians would only perform their military service in Ukraine. A permanent commission of the Rada on defence was formed and tasked with preparing the legal basis for an independent Ukrainian defence establishment. And, a ministerial portfolio with responsibility for defence, security issues and emergencies – the main task of which was to liaise with the Soviet ministry of defence – was created.[122] Notwithstanding these developments, Ukraine did not begin to actively assert its control over the military forces deployed on its territory until after the failure of the August coup in 1991. By that time, since it had already created a rudimentary legal basis for an independent military and taking into account the weakened grip of the central Soviet authorities, Ukraine was able to move quickly in nationalising Soviet military assets. With the *Declaration of Independence* of 24 August 1991, Ukraine laid claim to all the military assets and personnel of the Soviet army deployed on its territory.

The problems encountered by Ukraine in turning the parts of the Soviet army on its territory into a national army instead of building a new army from scratch have already been discussed. Briefly, the factors underlying this decision were threefold. First, it was thought that the roughly 700,000 Soviet troops in Ukraine would be less likely to use force against the people if the new national authorities moved to assert control over them. A pacification campaign aimed at building the confidence of the troops and encouraging them to identify with Ukraine by guaranteeing their social rights, fulfilling their social needs and by treating them better than Soviet military units elsewhere in the Union was also launched in the lead-up to the December 1991 independence referendum. Second, building a national army equal in capability to the ready-made one already at hand seemed prohibitively expensive. Third, there was a perception among nationalists that one salient reason for the short existence of the independent Ukrainian National Republic in 1919 was the failure to create national armed forces.[123]

Building on the foundations of the *Declaration of Sovereignty*, the creation of an independent Ukrainian army was achieved inter alia through the *Declaration of Independence*, various pieces of other legislation, and the requirement of all servicemen to take an oath of loyalty to Ukraine. As part of the *Declaration of Independence*, the subordination of all Soviet troops to the Rada, as well as the creation of a ministry of defence were also resolved. In September 1991, the Law on Defence was passed which sketched the outline of a national security structure consisting of a ministry of defence, a defence council and a national security council (which were merged in 1995), the general staff of the armed forces, and the service chiefs.

As in Russia, the Ukrainian president is the most powerful figure in the security structure. He is the supreme commander-in-chief of the armed forces, in which capacity he is solely entitled to take all necessary measures to ensure the security of the state in the event of actual or threatened attack, including the declaration of war and martial law.[124] He is also the head of the National Security and Defence Council, which is the central co-ordinating body of the executive power in the sphere of defence.[125] Thus, either directly as supreme commander or indirectly as the head of the National Security and Defence Council, the president is able to keep all activities of the military under his control, co-ordinate all activities of state organs in the defence sphere, issue guidance on military matters, appoint and remove the minister of defence (the minister is confirmed by parliament) and the high commanders of the armed forces. Given the extensive powers of the president in the defence sphere, the powers of the minister of defence are quite circumscribed. The defence minister is responsible for the immediate, day-to-day control of the armed forces, the administration of defence policy and drafting the defence budget proposal. However, he has no control over the appointment of senior officers since under the constitution that is explicitly the responsibility of the president. Moreover, the president, without the agreement of the minister of defence may appoint the chief of general staff. There is also no constitutional requirement that the minister of defence be a civilian.

In general, the legal and constitutional system for civilian control in place by the early 1990s in Ukraine was sufficient to regulate the defence sector reasonably well and to preclude any egregious abuse of power by the armed forces. What was missing was a developed mechanism for the effective civilian management of the armed forces through a civilian minister of defence assisted by an expert civilian and military staff. There was no provision in the law for the introduction of civilian administrators able to monitor the real situation in the military. Some mechanisms that would have allowed a civilian minister to control personnel policy in the military were curtailed by presidential prerogatives. And, as with the other countries in this study the pool of civilians qualified for leadership positions in the ministry of defence was extremely shallow.

As was the case in Poland and Hungary, it is fair to say that questions of sound public administration of the armed forces were not foremost in the minds of

Ukraine's leaders when the first minister of defence, General Kostiantyn Morozov, was appointed in September 1991. In the volatile political and security environment at the time, as with the appointment of Grachev in Russia, the appointment of a military man to head the ministry was not necessarily a bad move. Although he himself was an ethnic Russian, Morozov oversaw the administering of the military oath of loyalty to the soldiers of the newly independent state. By February 1992, nearly 80 per cent of the military had taken the oath. Those personnel who chose not to were expected to resign from the military if they intended to reside in Ukraine, or to leave Ukraine if they wished to continue military service in another country.[126] As a result of this process, by the spring of 1992 Ukraine had secured effective control over the parts of the former Soviet military machine on its territory. That this transformation occurred peacefully and rapidly was a remarkable achievement that depended on a few key factors: The civilian leadership was strongly united behind the move, while Moscow was unable as a result of its own disorientation to put up much resistance. But much of the credit is due to Morozov's energetic and effective management of the process, especially in light of the fact that a majority of senior officers opposed the creation of the Ukrainian armed forces.[127]

Notwithstanding this success, Morozov remained in office only until October 1993 when he was compelled to resign after a vigorous disagreement with President Leonid Kravchuk over the Massandra meetings between Ukraine and Russia over the fate of the Black Sea Fleet. Morozov felt that Kravchuk had made too many concessions to the Russians. He wrote in an open letter to the president that if they were carried out he would disclaim all responsibility for Ukraine's defence in the south.[128] Morozov's successor, Vitaliy Radetskiy, was also a general. However, his impact on the ministry was less profound than Morozov's. Basically, during his tenure the reform of the military continued to stagnate. Radetskiy's main virtue – loyalty to President Kravchuk – eventually caused his downfall. Suspected of having encouraged military officers to support Kravchuk in the July 1994 presidential elections, he was dismissed by the new president, Leonid Kuchma.

In August 1994 Kuchma chose a long-time civilian colleague from the defence industrial sector, Valeriy Shmarov, to take over the ministry of defence. Expectations for Shmarov were high; he was relatively young (50 years old), a former deputy director of the Ukrainian National Space Agency, and a former deputy prime minister. In his own words: 'At present, the economy is not healthy and it has an impact on the army. So, it was the perception [of the state leadership] that the military should be headed by an individual with economic expertise who can balance the state's capabilities and the need to ensure protection of the country which prompted my appointment.'[129] Since military reform had stalled under his predecessor it was hoped that the new civilian minister would be better able to solve the economic problems of the military. All told, Shmarov had a reasonably promising start. By all accounts there was no passive resistance on the part of the military to having an effective civilian minister.[130] Yet, by February 1996, Shmarov was suing the Ukrainian newspaper *Vechirniy Kyiv* for defamation. The paper had accused him of inciting a revolution among the military with the intention of destroying the Ukrainian armed forces and the independence of Ukraine. Among other points, it was argued that the minister had formed a 'shadow general staff which has developed an anti-patriotic military policy', and that Shmarov 'tried to deceive Ukrainian President Leonid Kuchma, showing him documents that generals signed under pressure'. According to the paper the source of these allegations was a group of generals who opposed Shmarov's restructuring of policy and reforms.[131]

Ukraine's experiment with a civilian minister of defence came to an end in July 1996 with Shmarov's forced resignation amid scandal and recrimination. According to Grytsenko, the move was 'obvious, understandable, predictable and rather belated.[132] Why? Various reasons were speculated for his dismissal. By one account, the dismissal was a move by Kuchma to appease right-wingers in the Rada who disapproved of Shmarov's support for Ukraine's non-nuclear status. In return, they were to support the appointment of Prime Minister Pavlo Lazarenko. Another version held that it was done to appease left-wingers who disapproved of Shmarov's moves towards NATO, though the scenarios are not mutually exclusive.[133] What is clear, however, is that internally the ministry of defence under Shmarov was bitterly divided and deadlocked. Ultimately, Shmarov failed to meet the high expectations set for him; he implemented relatively few reforms of the ministry; and, as will be discussed below, he made little attempt to introduce other civilian staff in the ministry. These failings had less to do with the fact of his being a civilian than with his personality which generated conflicts between him and the senior leadership of the military.[134] Shmarov did not attempt to hide his lack of respect for his military subordinates. Reportedly, his leadership style consisted of 'gathering the generals in his office twice a week in order to haul them over the coals'.[135] In return, the generals refused to offer the minister the support required for his initiatives in the ministry to take effect.

Lieutenant General Oleksandr Kuzmuk was the next to be appointed Ukraine's minister of defence. This act was widely seen as a setback for the development of civilian control of the military. But it should be acknowledged that at least all Ukrainian defence ministers left their posts quietly and the military was never the object of such involved political machinations as was the Russian army. Moreover, though it was a setback for the first civilian minister of defence to have been a failure, Shmarov was proving to be a destabilising factor in civil–military relations. In that respect, Kuzmuk's appointment was timely in defusing increasing tensions between the military and political leadership.

The problem, however, went deeper than whether or not a civilian was at the head of the ministry of defence. Neither the Russian nor Ukrainian ministries of defence were structured in a way that would permit a civilian minister to exercise his authority effectively. Virtually no other civilians of any consequence were employed by the ministry in responsible positions and the division of powers and functions between the general staff and the minister were ill defined in legislation and in practice. In short, without substantive changes of the underlying structure, the presence of a Ukrainian civilian minister constituted little more than well-meaning rhetoric. In fact, according to one interlocutor Ukraine was not ready for a civilian minister:

> At present, the practice of high level appointments in the ministry of defence and other ministries is usually on the basis of political intrigues that are absolutely non-transparent for the public. The nominee's affiliation with particular political groupings and individuals is the most important factor. This raises the concern that a civilian minister of defence appointed by the president will stay beyond the control of any other agents of state power. In particular, the minister may be beyond the scope of control of the legislature, which will lead to an over concentration of power in the hands of the president.[136]

Numerous interviewees pointed to the basic problem that the highly concentrated presidential control over the military made the question of a civilian minister something of a moot point:

> The main problem we have in our system is with the society. Ukraine doesn't have a civil society. We don't have a civilian system. The president is the only civilian with any control over the armed forces. Therefore, it doesn't matter whether we have a civilian minister or not because the control is so personalized anyway. Take Shmarov, for example. His appointment didn't work. We had a civilian person at the head of the ministry of defence but we didn't have a civilian minister. He didn't have any civilian structures in the ministry of defence.[137]

Ukrainian parliamentarians were also critical of Shmarov's appointment for much the same reasons, considering that it was a mistake because the necessary conditions were not in place. What was needed was a strong military officer who knew the army and its problems in order to accomplish all that needed doing in terms of military reform. And, moreover, they felt that the security threat to Ukraine was not external, but internal – to and from the president.[138]

As opposed to Russia, Ukraine has not moved to appoint a civilian minister of defence; in 2001 in the wake of the tragic downing of a Russian civilian airliner over the Black Sea by a Ukrainian missile General Kuzmuk was replaced as minister by General Shkidchenko. The bigger problem , however, was that the structure of the ministry of defence in both Russia and Ukraine was still not conducive to civilian–military integration. The key missing condition for civilian control, in the words of a Ukrainian interviewee, was the 'creation of a civilian service for the ministry of defence and the armed forces that would strengthen control of the defence sector'.[139] Let us look at this issue next.

Integrating civilians in the defence bureaucracy

As in Poland and Hungary, finding a civilian minister of defence was only one side of the problem faced by Russia and Ukraine. Integrating civilian decision-makers in the defence bureaucracy was an even bigger problem. Until it was restructured in mid-2000, in the Russian ministry of defence there were two first deputy ministers of defence, one was the chief of the general staff, the other was an appointed civilian responsible for the ministry of defence's relations with the military–industrial complex. The first civilian to hold the rank of a first deputy minister of defence was Andrei Kokoshin – a former deputy director of the Institute of the USA and Canada – appointed in 1992. Kokoshin remains the only civilian to have had much influence over the Russian defence establishment from within the ministry of defence. Moreover, he was until recently the only civilian to have been seriously put forward as a candidate for minister of defence (in February 1992 by the 'Democratic Russia' and 'Soldiers for Russia' movements).

Unfortunately, Kokoshin was not a catalyst for the further civilianisation of the ministry of defence. In theory, the first deputy minister of defence was supposed to represent the military–industrial complex in the ministry of defence, lobby for the ministry of defence in the parliament, and supervise the arms trade. These tasks, however, overlapped with the duties of other officials in the ministry of defence, were defined vaguely, or were clearly impossible to achieve. In the case of the first mission, the persistent failure of the ministry of defence to pay invoices owing to military industries for past production gradually undermined Kokoshin's good relations with industrialists. At the same time, the army already had a chief of armaments with the same responsibility as the first deputy minister, confusing the situation even further. Neither of them had much money, but industry was more accustomed to dealing with the chief of armaments.[140] Taken together, these factors seriously compromised Kokoshin's ability to do his job effectively and reduced his influence in the ministry of defence.

His second job, to lobby for the ministry of defence in the Duma, was even more unfeasible. Kokoshin was, as far as the army was concerned, supposed to have good relations with the Duma (particularly in comparison to Grachev), but he was unable to get any money out of them for the ministry of defence. This inability to deliver the goods undercut his credibility. 'Sometimes I wanted to go into Kokoshin's office and ask him: "Andrei Afanas'evich, here you are all these years telling cheerful stories about new weapons, so why is the army crying that all they have in their hands is rusty old iron?"' commented a general staff officer.[141] Finally, Kokoshin had practically no way of supervising the arms trade. Too many more powerful people in Russia were interested in this lucrative business for it to be controlled by a first deputy minister of defence.

As in most large organisations, one good indicator of the influence of the deputy minister within the ministry of defence was the size of his staff. When Kokoshin's post was first created, in addition to regular military adjutants, he was to have a staff of twenty civilian aides, each equivalent to a lieutenant-general. In fact, the numbers in his office never reached this level and, according to one insider, gradually began to fall, to twelve, eight, and then to only four civilian staff members. Finally, the remaining civilian staff were demoted from 'aide to a deputy minister' to 'chief specialist' – equivalent to only a colonel or lieutenant-colonel. In the ministry of defence, there are hundreds of officers at the rank of chief specialist.

'Thus the actual influence of the civilian staff of the first deputy minister was cut down to a size which corresponded to the military's idea of what the desirable role of the civilian first deputy minister of defence should be.'[142] On the other hand, a serving military officer, also a chief specialist in the ministry of defence, who was in a position to work with Kokoshin's staff, put a different spin on the story:

> Kokoshin brought in a whole bunch of civilian idiots with him. After a year he had to fire them himself and replace them with military officers. They were inefficient and arrogant. They were like loose cannons, you couldn't manage them, you could only fire them. They just didn't care about anything. Corruption was a big issue. The sphere they were operating in – dual use technology, arms sales, German money for housing – they started a lot of 'shadow projects'. It just didn't work. I liked Kokoshin but dealing with his office was a pain in the neck.[143]

In 1996, by a decree of the president, the first deputy minister of defence was also named a state secretary of defence. The role of the state secretary, however, was, and is still, poorly defined. According to a former assistant first deputy prime minister, it equated to a formal role as 'the Tsar's eye in the ministry of defence, or a 'Commissar' if you will. But his real influence is very small.'[144] Theoretically, the state secretary had a degree of independence from the minister because he had the right to represent the ministry of defence in the Duma and the presidential administration. In practice though, the relevance of the state secretary as a representative of the ministry of defence depended on the personality of the minister. Grachev, for example, would never go into the Duma, which gave Kokoshin a wider and more stable representative role. Sergeyev, on the other hand, reputedly enjoyed the political work and spent quite a lot of time in the Duma which marginalised that function of the civilian first deputy minister. After the restructuring in mid-2000 the job of state secretary was disconnected from the duties of the civilian first deputy minister and transferred to a military officer – namely the former commander of the Moscow Military District, General Igor Puzanov.

Summing up, the first deputy minister of defence did not have a lot of bureaucratic weight in the ministry of defence. The ministry of defence bureaucracy regarded Kokoshin as an outsider and employed a number of means to marginalise him. His successor, Nikolai Mikhailov – a former top executive of NPO-Vimpel, a corporation specialising in anti-ballistic missile and space defences – was thought to be closer to the military which considered him one of their own: 'he wears shoulder-loops [flaps of fabric for holding an officers shoulder boards] under his jacket'.[145] Outside of questions of the military–industrial complex, however, Mikhailov probably had no more influence than did Kokoshin. Indeed, none of the military officers interviewed seemed to know what Mikhailov was supposed to do. As one senior naval officer put it, 'the only civilian official in the ministry of defence I have ever heard of is Mikhailov, but none of us know what his duties are or what he is doing'. Another naval officer claimed more simply that 'I am not aware of any role played by civilians in the military organisation.'[146]

A portentous change was Putin's creation of a new post in the ministry of defence – the deputy minister for finance – to which he appointed a female civilian, Lyubov' Kudelina. Throughout the 1990s the ministry of defence had been severely criticised for the poor quality of its accounting and finances. Two of Kudelina's predecessors were dismissed under a cloud of scandal. And a criminal case was launched against the former chief military financier Colonel General Georgiy Oleinik.[147] In the Yeltsin years, the finance ministry, as the enforcer of economic policies involving acute cutbacks in military spending, became in some respects the most important implement of civilian control. In her previous position as the top ministry of finance official in charge of defence spending Kudelina had won respect for her professionalism and tough-mindedness. Thus it was reasonable to expect a crackdown on the kind of creative accounting in the ministry of defence for which General Oleinik had been brought to book. On the other hand, while still with the ministry of finance, Kudelina also acquired a reputation for insisting on maximum secrecy of the military budget. Actually, members of the Duma defence committee said that Kudelina was the main obstacle to a more transparent budget.[148] In other words, the move suggested a crackdown on corruption but not more public scrutiny of defence spending.

As was noted above, Ukraine's only civilian minister of defence showed little interest in setting up an integrated military–civilian ministry. Why Shmarov tolerated his isolation as the only high-ranking civilian official in the ministry of defence is unclear. Nonetheless, the facts are clear. Only two senior civilian executives were appointed during his tenure: Anatoliy Dovhopolyi as deputy minister for procurement and armaments and Oleksandr Urban as head of the general staff foreign relations department. Neither Dovhopolyi nor Urban had so high a public profile as Kokoshin did in Russia, nor did they make much of a mark on the ministry of defence. Indeed, they were openly criticised by their peers in the ministry for their lack of knowledge of military issues.[149] Since Chief of the General Staff Anatoliy Lopatin was able to tell a meeting of military instructors in 1994 that 'the civilian defence minister is incompetent in his work',[150] and still kept his job until February 1996, this should not come as a surprise. All in all, the fact that in addition to the minister there were two civilians in high posts in the ministry of defence had little effect on the quality of civilian control. There was never a critical mass of civilian bureaucrats that would have allowed for mutual support in the Ukrainian ministry of defence. Given the absence of genuine civilian expertise in military issues, the government expected military professionals to maintain 'civilian' control of the armed forces:

> Ironically, the Cabinet of Ministers allows serving officers to maintain control over the military, partly because they are considered the only real experts in this field, underlining the need for establishing firm democratic civilian control over the armed forces.[151]

Under Kuzmuk's leadership of the ministry of defence there were no civilian executives in the ministry of defence at all.[152]

Throughout the 1990s according to the Russian research group 'Panorama', the only civilians of any consequence in the ministry of defence were Kokoshin and Mikhailov.[153] According to the deputy chief of the department of contract workers and civilian employees, although as of late 1998 the ministry of defence employed a little more than half a million civilians, they were 'not meant to have command authority over military personnel'.[154] Aside from clerical and janitorial duties, these civilians performed a range of support roles in the armed forces such as scientific personnel in research facilities and defence laboratories, provided specialised technical service and repair on certain equipment, or were teaching staff at military universities and institutes. But, 'they do not occupy any key positions and the entire decision-making process is in the hands of the military'.[155] As another officer explained it:

> If someone is in the chain of command they must have a rank. It is a wartime system. When you are at war you get a rank. Maybe our system is still in the Cold War, but you can't change the system, even from the inside. Guys like Kvashnin have so much power, and they don't want civilians. There is a stereotypical position in the military about civilians: Why do we need them? They don't know anything.[156]

The situation was rather similar in Ukraine. The civilian defence establishment of the ministry of defence counted 157,000 personnel in 1997, decreasing to approximately 90,000 people as of 2000 in line with the overall reduction in the size of the ministry.[157] The positions they filled, however, were mainly in the personnel, medical, financial, economic, educational and administrative departments, but these areas remained firmly in the control of mostly retired military officers.[158] As far as decision-making positions were concerned,

> There is no role for civilians in the ministry of defence because there are no civilians in the ministry of defence. And there are no ideas for putting civilians in the structure; only a few discussions. The army is very closed and bureaucratic. To get someone from the society inside the military system with the power to control how it works is not acceptable to the military. Moreover, this issue is not pushed by politicians. The centrists, social democrats, etc., have put forward the notion of having military reform, of having a professional armed forces and so on. But this is only at the level of declaration.[159]

In the West, although it is increasingly difficult to draw a line between civilian and military occupations, there is a key difference between civilian and military personnel. Civilian personnel are intermediaries between the military and government, and between the military and society. Their effectiveness, and hence their career prospects, are determined by how well they play this mediating role. If they perform well, they can rise within the bureaucracy to the highest levels. This cannot be the case in the Russian or Ukrainian ministries of defence where to occupy a high position one must have a military rank. 'If civilians are always subordinate to military officers, and if a civilian wants to make a career in the ministry of defence, he literally has to turn himself inside out to represent the interests of the military.'[160] Obviously, under such circumstances civilians cannot play an independent role and mediate between the interests of the military and the government, or society as a whole. Therefore, according to an interlocutor in Kiev, civilians have . . .

> no role. No influence. There are no influential civilians in the ministry of defence. There are some civilians in low-key positions but there are zero at the top. There are few remarks about the development of civilian control in the laws that say civilians should occupy certain positions. According to the law on defence the armed forces have a minister of defence – he could be a civilian, but he could not be. There is no legal requirement either way, neither is it set out anywhere what positions in the ministry should be held by civilians or military.[161]

The fact that there was no legislation beyond general labour law governing the rights and responsibilities of civilian personnel in the Russian or Ukrainian defence establishments made the problem particularly intractable. In the absence of appropriate laws specifying who should be given what authority, it is difficult to imagine significant civilian appointments in the ministry of defence of either country. On the other hand, there is no ban on civilian appointments to important ministry of defence positions, such as the chief of a main administration, but in practice matters of staffing are decided by the ministry of defence leadership on the basis of their own internal rules.

In Ukraine as well there are reports that the poor socio-economic situation in the military was a generator of conflict in the ministry between civilian and military employees. According to one interlocutor, civilians were advocating civilian control of the military only because in the process of reforming the military civilians in the defence establishment would obtain permanent work, higher salaries and the same pension that military personnel already received.[162] Jaworsky has also claimed that the armed forces were further demoralised by downsizing because the civilian side of the defence establishment had suffered less from the budget and personnel cutbacks of recent years.[163]

The influence of academia on the defence policy debate and in terms of preparing civilian defence experts was judged to be minimal in both Russia and Ukraine. Perhaps reflecting the USSR's centralisation of foreign and security policy expertise, more civilian defence experts could be found in Moscow than in Kiev. One Russian interviewee reported that inspite of this:

> The influence of academics is clearly insufficient. First, the existing potential of the academic community in military affairs is not utilised fully. Second, the military have their caste-bound tradition of not entrusting civilians with military matters. And third, the academic community has very limited resources (especially for fundamental research) because of the government's neglect, and it is preoccupied with its own survival.[164]

Or, in the succinct words of another interlocutor, 'The academic community has no impact on policy. There are just a few people there who understand anything about military matters and they are like so many cockroaches in a jar, who cannot get out and are eating each other.'[165]

In Kiev, the defence community is small but reasonably vibrant and in some cases, such as the Ukrainian Centre for Economic and Political Studies, very publicly active. Nonetheless, the problems were very similar to those in Russia.

> Not one civilian in the ministry of defence has a decision-making role. There are 300,000 soldiers and 100,000 civilians but they do not influence policy. We need to train civilian experts for the ministry of defence but we don't.[166]

In other words, there were few civilians in the Russian and Ukrainian defence establishments at the end of the 1990s, little indication that more were likely to be introduced, and very few facilities existed for the education of civilian specialists in defence.

Dealing with the general staff

As was noted at the beginning of this chapter, a powerful general staff was a characteristic feature of the Soviet defence establishment. This powerful body dominated defence policy planning and monopolised the defence expertise of the state. In practice, the chief of the general staff could be as influential or more than the minister of defence. Both Ukraine and Russia struggled with the advantages and disadvantages of inheriting a general staff. Understanding the inner workings of the ministry of defence requires understanding the relationship between the minister of defence and his nominal subordinate, the chief of general staff.

In a democratic system it is fundamental that a minister of defence have unfettered access to all the information necessary to make sound policy choices. In the West, this is achieved through an integrated ministry of defence which clearly delineates which functions of the ministry are political (a civilian responsibility), administrative (a shared civilian and military responsibility) and operational command (a military responsibility). In Russia and Ukraine these distinctions are far from clear. For one thing, the distinction between the structures and personnel of the general staff and the ministry of defence is not intuitive for military officers socialised in the Soviet system where the defence establishment was a homogeneous military organisation.[167] Nowadays, there are no *glaring* structural or legal contradictions between the powers of the minister of defence and the chief of general staff in either Russia or Ukraine. In both countries the chief of general staff is defined in the law as a deputy minister of defence and, therefore, subordination to the minister is implied. The problems lie in the avenues of political control and influence over the military and, as in Poland and Hungary, especially in the inter-relationships of the chief of general staff, the minister of defence and the president.

In some ways, the term ministry of defence is misleading because it implies the existence of a bureaucratic structure that acts as a buffer between the armed forces and the state authorities whereas in actual fact no such buffer exists. Indeed the distinction between political, administrative and operational command functions loses its meaning in a ministry where there are virtually no civilian decision-makers. In the opinion of one Russian interlocutor, 'there is no such thing as a civilian ministry of defence, it is just a cover for the army. In fact, there is no ministry of defence. The minister of defence has a staff of twelve people . . . its all an enormous bloc made up of military directorates. The defence minister and his staff are more like supervisors.'[168]

In Russia in particular it is difficult to deconstruct the exact nature of the relationship between the chief of general staff and the minister of defence because there are numerous contradictory indicators. In the law, there was no question that the chief of general staff is the subordinate of the minister and is tasked with the operational control of the armed forces. The question is how real was the minister's supremacy over the chief of general staff? The answer for both Ukraine and Russia was: as real as the president decided it should be. One might then ask, why does the president not simply subordinate the chief of general staff directly to himself as supreme commander of the armed forces and cut the minister out of the chain of command entirely? In Russia, such a plan was rumoured to have been in the works in late 1994 and early 1995.[169] It was proposed that the general staff would be separated from the ministry of defence and attached to the presidential administration. The general staff would then act as the overall command for all the armed services – not just the army – leaving the minister of defence with responsibility only for the logistics and administration of the army and for relations with the legislature.

In the end, nothing came of the idea and the general staff remained an integral part of the ministry of defence. One may speculate on reasons why the plan was not adopted. By one account, the move was strongly advocated by Lebed who thought it would eliminate the inefficient command over the multitude of military formations that were making the war in Chechnya so complicated to fight.[170] Perhaps, its association with Lebed tainted the idea in the mind of the president. It might also have been the case that the president was unwilling to allow the concentration of command over all the military formations in the state under a single authority, which would not have fitted well with Yeltsin's divide and rule leadership style. Another potential reason was that if the minister and the chief of general staff were mutually dependent on each other and also totally beholden to the president, a kind of extra-legal check and balance on both of their powers emerges. Neither could too openly criticise the other without fear that they would both lose their jobs. Moreover, neither would be able to use the forces of the ministry of defence as a power-base against the president.

Given the evident concern of the Ukrainian president about internal threats it is not unlikely those considerations would pertain in Kiev also. Nonetheless, there are subtle differences in the Ukrainian approach to this question. Until August 1997, when the division of responsibility between the ministry and the general staff was finally set out by presidential decree, the ministry of defence was a poorly concealed battleground between the minister and the chief of general staff. As minister of defence, Shmarov tended to intrude into professional military matters while General Anatoliy Lopata, his chief of general staff, tended to pursue his own political agenda. Lopata was the first casualty in the feud between the two when Kuchma dismissed him in February 1996. Allegedly, the cause was Lopata's 'making public of what amounted to state secrets' during a public dispute with the minister over the size of the armed forces, but rumours of internal plots to remove him had already been circulating for over a year.[171] (Five months later Shmarov was himself dismissed.) By some accounts, the vague division of functions worked in favour of the minister who tried to delay clarification of the respective competencies of the minister and the chief of general staff. Bearing in mind the immaturity of his own administrative apparatus, Shmarov might have felt that if any strict delineation of functions were carried out on the basis of competence he might be compelled to concede so much authority to the general staff as to make his position merely symbolic.[172]

According to the presidential decree *On the Division of Responsibilities of the Minister of Defence of Ukraine and the General Staff of the Armed Forces of Ukraine*,[173] the functions of the ministry of defence and the general staff were delineated roughly as follows:

1 The ministry of defence, inter alia, is responsible for military–political leadership and administrative support of the armed forces day-to-day activities, the implementation of state policy in defence matters, participates in the formulation of the defence budget, and reports to the Cabinet of Ministers on the implementation of the budget.
2 The general staff is the body through which the *president* executes command and control of the armed forces. It is responsible for defence planning and the operational command and control of the armed forces.[174]

On the face of it, the decree made it somewhat clearer that the ministry of defence was responsible for mainly administrative matters and the general staff for operational matters. What it did not make clear was the subordination of the chief of general staff, since the decree entitled the president to appoint the chief of general staff without the minister's consent and, moreover, implied that the president was the direct superior of the chief of the general staff. Nonetheless, since the appointment of General Kuzmuk as minister of defence such distinctions have grown less important as a balance of sorts was achieved between the minister and the Chief of General Staff General Shkidchenko. However, as Grytsenko pointed out, what was achieved was not a *civil*–military balance, but a *military*–military balance.[175] This suggests that Ukraine has some of the forms of a democratic system of civil–military relations without much of the substance. However, it was only when a civilian minister was in place that the weakness of the substance was strongly revealed.

Comparative conclusions

Civilianising the bureaucracy of the defence establishment in all the states under review proved to be a gravely difficult task. In Central Europe as of late 1999 the process of integration had really only just begun. Even then, the skill gap between military and civilian officials was still quite apparent in the region and may, indeed, have been growing as military officers acquired more and more expertise through contact with NATO, while their civilian counterparts had much less access to training opportunities at home or abroad. Russia and Ukraine made hardly any progress in integrating civilians in their ministries of defence in the period under review. The differences between Russia and Ukraine in this respect pertained more to their starting conditions. Russia inherited a bigger, more sophisticated but also more entrenched and cumbersome defence bureaucracy than Ukraine. Politics in both countries, however, shared most of the same democratic deficits, while the understanding of the concept of democratic civil–military relations was rudimentary and elite appreciation of the need for civilians in the defence establishment was low (though rhetorically more seems to have been made of the issue in Ukraine).

By no means, however, were these problems exclusive to the former Soviet Union states. Generally, the slow progress in creating integrated military–civilian ministries of defence can be blamed on both sides of the civil–military equation. On the civilian side, it was only in the late 1990s that governments began to articulate reasonably clear defence policy programmes. It should be no surprise then, that civilian control was weak. When presented with a clear and unambiguous programme, such as the integration of civilian decision-makers in the ministry of defence, the military really only has two choices: obey or not obey. Overwhelmingly, professional military officers in Eastern Europe preferred to obey legitimate orders, especially if there was a legal and institutional framework to monitor their activities and punish any transgressions appropriately. Absent any specific plan, however, as was the case for most of the 1990s, the military had a multitude of choices: do nothing, do what they thought the civilians wanted, or do what they thought was best. Naturally, if there was no compelling reason not to, they tended to choose the last option. In other words, civilians were not exerting their right to control the defence establishment preferring, for the most part, to leave figuring out the problems of the army to the army itself.

A major problem for civilians was that they had few opportunities to acquire the necessary expertise and knowledge to take on a more active role in the ministry of defence as the equals of their military colleagues. With the exception of Poland, all the governments in the study invested little or no effort into training that rare breed: the civilian defence expert. Western training programmes, meanwhile, were also not much help as they tended to focus on military–technical needs. In Central Europe the politicised appointment process of civilians in the ministry of defence also aggravated the problem and generated considerable ill-will toward civilians in the minds of many military officers; though more generally it can be said that scepticism about – or open hostility towards – civilian defence expertise was endemic amongst much of the military *and* the political elite in the region. The instability of the political scene was a major factor in the poor showing of civilian integration. On the one hand, the battle for control between presidents and parliaments compromised the ability of both to exert control over the military. On the other hand, particularly in Central Europe, the short active period of the election cycle also limited the amount of time civilians had available to learn on the job. In short, the military came to view civilians as transitory, politically partisan, not very well-informed and not very interested in the job – quite often it was a true characterisation.

Finally, civilians had a sometimes narrow understanding of the concept of civilian control which facilitated the emergence of a rather hostile atmosphere of antipathy between civilians and the military in the defence bureaucracy. This, in turn, hampered efforts at real cooperation between the two. It is a bit like the ‘chicken and egg’ paradox: did the military’s passive resistance to civilian direction fuel the civilians’ distrust of their motives, or did the civilians’ distrust of the military provoke the military to resist out of a sense of resentment? For soldiers, the integration of civilians and the tensions that created presented them with a real dilemma: did their loyalty to the nation and to their profession mean that they should try to prevent the degradation of the army as a result of the ill-conceived reforms of an incompetent civilian elite? Was it their duty to save the civilians from themselves? Moreover, at a bureaucratic level, the integration of civilians posed problems for ministries of defence where the legislation and internal regulations on defence personnel were never designed with civilian officials in mind.

The military also carried other heavy burdens in all the countries in the study. On the one hand, society saw the army as a serious financial drain on the state. On the other hand, civilian governments were rarely willing to take up the *responsibility* for civilian control of the army because that would impose on them a difficult and politically dangerous obligation to explain to the populace why expenditure on the military was necessary even in a time of great fiscal tightness. Yet, this is precisely what was needed. The military needed competent civilians on its side if it was going to obtain the long-term financing it needed to modernise. Civilians needed a reasonably efficient army, not least in the Central European states to serve as a tangible symbol of their deepening integration into Western structures, notably NATO. A well-organised, integrated military–civilian ministry of defence is the best way to create such a symbiosis. By late 1999, both Poland and Hungary were still some distance from this goal but making progress.

Russia and Ukraine, however, appeared even further away. Neither country had much success with a civilian minister of defence: Russia did not even try it until 2000 (assuming one sees Ivanov as a civilian); while Ukraine’s single experiment with a civilian minister backfired. Below the level of the minister, neither country made much progress in installing civilian executives in the defence bureaucracy. In Russia, a very capable, well-known civilian defence expert was gradually marginalised in the ministry and his authority reduced such that his real influence was, in the end, small. His replacement had lower aspirations and took care not to ruffle the feathers of his military peers, but he too was forced out of the ministry of defence. A senior civilian bureaucrat from the ministry of finance was transferred to the defence ministry but for a variety of reasons it is difficult to characterise this as the beginnings of a wave of such appointments. In Ukraine, even less progress was made: Two unremarkable civilian executives held fairly marginal positions for a few years; they left and were replaced by military officers. Among the rank and file of both ministries the relatively large size of the civilian side of the defence establishment belied the negligible impact of civilian employees on decision-making. In fact, a substantial portion of civilian employees were simply retired military personnel supplementing a pension.

Finally, the general staff in both countries appeared to act as a brake on integration by guarding its dominance of policy-planning and its monopoly of defence expertise. In both cases, the president played an instrumental role in perpetuating the conflict between general staff and ministry of defence for partisan political reasons.

One may conclude about civilian integration in the ministries of defence of Russia and Ukraine quite simply: there was almost none. Nor do the trends point to positive improvement in the near future. Ukraine will pay lip-service to the notion of building an integrated ministry of defence for as long as its political leadership favours ever closer links with NATO. But on the substantive issues progress seems unlikely without radical changes in the country's economic fortunes and political climate. The situation is fundamentally the same in Russia. Although it too was experimenting with a nominally civilian minister by 2000, his suitability for the post was based on personal loyalty to the president not democratic credentials and his success will be determined by his skilful employment of the subjective control mechanism of actively monitoring military loyalty, rewarding those who exhibit it and punishing those who do not. These trends were well established in the 1990s.

4 Agencies of civilian oversight

Democratic states employ a number of mechanisms in order to control, manage and give guidance to their defence establishments. One of those mechanisms was examined in the previous chapter: having a civilian minister of defence and qualified civilians working within the ministry of defence helping to formulate security policy options for decision-makers and seeing to the implementation of policy. Another is having civilian officials outside the ministry of defence performing similar duties as part of legally constituted bodies of civilian oversight. That is to say, that in having a democratic system of civil–military relations, the presence of civilians in the ministry of defence is only one side of the coin. The other side is having effective institutions of civilian oversight in the parliament, the presidency and the government. With respect to the present chapter, four institutions are of specific interest:

1. parliamentary defence committees, particularly the effectiveness of their budgetary oversight;
2. personnel directorates or commissions on higher military ranks within the administration of the president which advise the head of state on the exercise of his prerogative to award higher military ranks;
3. Security Councils which serve as the main inter-agency body for policy coordination between the security services, other key ministries, and top government officials;
4. Military Inspectorates which check up on the activities of the armed forces.

Not all the states in the study created all these institutions in the 1990s. Hungary, for example, had still not established a standing security council by the time of its accession to NATO. Similarly, military inspectorates varied from country to country in composition, in leadership and to whom they reported. And the real importance of the commissions on higher military ranks depended greatly on the relative strength of the presidency vis-à-vis the parliament in the political systems adopted by Poland and Hungary, Russia and Ukraine. Moreover in all of the states various ad hoc commissions on such issues as defence reform and military finance also played a significant role in the exercise of civilian oversight from time to time. But this is merely to acknowledge the obvious: the institutional architecture of civilian control varies to some degree from one country to another, even in the long established democracies. On a more general level though, it is fair to say that the existence of democratic civil–military relations depends on the existence in one form or another of the institutions noted above – and, with a few caveats, they were created in all the states under review. Yet creating said institutions and imbuing them with legal force was very much the easy part of the job. Szemerkenyi wrote of the Central European states in 1996:

> Legal control may be in the hands of civilians, but effective control depends on the advisors and close associates of the top-ranking leadership in the ministries of defence: largely military personnel. In these circumstances, civilian oversight of the military is becoming virtual oversight.[1]

That is to say breathing life into the system, enabling it to give real substance to the notion of civilian control was very much the more difficult task. Accordingly, the current chapter will focus more on the process of *strengthening* the agencies of civilian oversight than on the act of their legal establishment. In practice, this means seeking answers to two key questions. First, what is the *composition* of the agencies in question? Are they staffed by military personnel or by civilians? In short, can they really be called 'civilian' agencies? In all the states under review, but particularly in Russia, serving or retired military officers tended to dominate in such agencies making this question exceedingly pertinent. Second, what is the *effectiveness* of the agencies (most importantly the effectiveness of parliamentary oversight of the defence budget)? Does their membership possess the knowledge and expertise to conduct its affairs well? Do they have credible, independent expert staffs to support their work? Is the budget sufficiently detailed to allow real review? If so, do the agencies have the expertise to understand it? Indeed, even if civilians in these agencies have the legal wherewithal to exert control do they actually have the *desire* to do so?

Civilian oversight of defence in the Soviet era

The process of Soviet defence decision-making has already been discussed in the introduction to previous chapters. There is little to add, therefore, except to reiterate the basic facts. In the Soviet system civilians did not exercise democratic control over their armed forces because the structures of the various communist parties were not formed according to any notions of democratic accountability or legitimacy, nor did they give credence to the concept of an open civil society. The leading organs of the communist party – the Politiburo and the Central Committee – were not democratically elected; they were made up essentially by a system of cooption from the top. In such a context parliaments were mere window-dressing – a rubber-stamping façade for a political system that utterly lacked transparency and political responsibility. Constitutional checks and balances were altogether missing. The armed forces, like every other societal institution, were dominated and closely monitored by a single political authority which placed no value on the norm of public accountability. To the extent that the state scrutinised the pattern of resource allocation to military purposes this activity took place in secret within such bodies as the Commission of the Presidium of the USSR Council of Ministers for Military–Industrial Questions and the Defence Industry Department of the Communist Party's Central Committee Secretariat.[2] In short, in terms of public scrutiny of defence policy and the military budget all the post-communist parliaments were starting from zero.

The office of the military inspectorate, however, merits some examination because it is somewhat foreign to Western armies which either never fully adopted or have since moved away from a classical general staff system. The Russian military inspectorate has its roots in the traditions of the Imperial armed forces, having been created by Peter the Great at the beginning of the eighteenth century, but was preserved in Soviet practice. The ostensible function of the military inspectorate was to check up on the training, maintenance and readiness of military forces. At times the inspectorate served as an alternate avenue for the political leadership of monitoring the activities of the military from outside the chain of command. At other times the office was subsumed by that of the minister of defence. Yet the inspectorate also played another important function in the Soviet system: allowing trusted older generals to move out of the chain of command into relatively powerless but respected and comfortable sinecures, thereby permitting younger generals to move into senior leadership positions.

Central Europe

Before looking at the Hungarian and Polish agencies of civilian oversight it is necessary first to point out a final difference between the two countries that has had considerable impact on their development: the nature of their legislative– executive relations. Although both Poland and Hungary adopted mixed presidential-parliamentary constitutional models, the relative strength of their presidents vis-à-vis their parliaments differed considerably. In the Polish system the president is directly elected by the people while the Hungarian president is elected by the parliament. The much greater constitutional prerogatives of the Polish president in the sphere of defence and security reflected this qualitative difference in electoral mandate. The Polish president had a limited authority over the formation of the Cabinet of Ministers, in particular from 1994 until the passage of the 1997 *Constitution* when he had complete discretion over the selection of the defence, foreign affairs and interior ministers. He also had the deciding voice in the content of strategic defence policy.

The upshot of this difference in executive–legislative relations was the relatively stable political scene in Hungary throughout the 1990s compared with the highly volatile Polish situation. The crux of the problem in Poland was the battle between President Walesa and successive Polish governments dominated by former communists. The core of Walesa's political agenda appeared to be preventing the return of the reformed communist party to power by all means available. This over-arching concern relegated civil–military reform to a subsidiary goal at best.

It also led Walesa to try and maximise his powers, including control of the armed forces, vis-à-vis other political actors no matter what damage was done to democratisation of civil–military relations. Indeed, by early 1995, in an effort to keep the military out of the hands of parliament, Walesa told the Sejm that 'military people should run the military'.[3] In short, Walesa made every effort to concentrate control of the armed forces in the presidency which he saw as the only way of ensuring that former communists did not gain control over the country's military and foreign policy. Failing that, the president's preference was that the military remain independent of both president and parliament. Naturally, this situation allowed the military considerable leverage in Polish politics and a high degree of independence from civilian control – a situation which did not begin to change until the election of Aleksander Kwasniewski as president in 1995.

Hungary had a somewhat analogous problem in the early 1990s which boiled down to a dispute between President Arpad Goncz, Prime Minister Joszef Antall, and Minister of Defence Lajos Fur about who had ultimate authority over the armed forces. The conflict came to a head in October 1990 when taxi drivers protesting a hike in the price of fuel launched a blockade of the country's roads. The prime minister and defence minister wanted to use the military to break up the roadblocks, but the president as commander-in-chief ordered the military to stay in their barracks. This constitutional conflict was submitted to the Constitutional Court which ruled on 23 September 1991 that the president was entitled only to give guiding principles to the military, not direct orders. In peacetime, direct orders can only be given to the military by the government through the minister of defence.[4]

Parliamentary oversight of defence

It is an axiom of democratic civil–military relations that citizens play a role in the formulation of public policy and ensuring that it is implemented faithfully. A strong civil society does not limit itself to maintaining a strong and representative parliament for this task – independent media, for example, also provide a forum for public debate on the crucial issues of the day – but parliament is the *main* avenue through which it exercises oversight of its defence establishment. In respect to the issue at hand, parliamentary defence committees bear the weightiest responsibility. They need to be intellectually and practically capable of judging developments in the defence sector independently of the government and the executive. They must also perform detailed oversight of the military budget – their strongest power. At the same time, parliamentarians must understand that it is not their place to *command* the military. The logic of active military operations – emergencies by definition – will not allow time for parliamentary debate; operational direction of the armed forces is rightly the responsibility of the government working in concert with its military leadership. In other words, parliament must walk a fine line, balancing the demand for general oversight of policy while resisting the temptation to micro-manage the armed forces. It must also perform detailed oversight of the budget which means it must know where funds are being allocated, for what reasons, and be able to judge that monetary inputs are justified by security outputs. Though their different constitutional models produced different stresses on civil–military relations, both the Hungarian and Polish legislatures experienced considerable difficulties in achieving the required balance. For the most part the legal architecture of parliamentary oversight was in place at an early stage; breathing life into the system was a more difficult matter.

Leslie Holmes wrote of hybrid constitutional models like Poland's that, 'Since the government is more or less equally answerable to both the president and the parliament, it can be caught in the crossfire between the two if there is a major conflict, which in turn can result in policy-making stalemate.'[5] As was seen in previous chapters, the reform of the Polish military and the restructuring of civil–military relations was very much a victim of such a stalemate under the presidency of Lech Walesa. The *Little Constitution* adopted on 17 October 1992 failed to set out a clear division of powers between the president and the parliament. It granted the president extensive powers in the field of foreign and security policy.[6] At the same time it charged the government with the responsibility for the realisation of foreign and security policy.[7] As a consequence, the factual meaning of presidential oversight vis-à-vis that of the parliament was quite murky.

From the beginning of transition the president had played a major role in the selection of some members of cabinet, but in 1994 Prime Minister Pawlak acceded fully to presidential demands that he have sole discretion over the selection of the heads of the security ministries (defence, internal and foreign affairs), thus producing an odd situation whereby three ministries were partly excluded from the authority of the prime minister.[8] Among the many problems caused by this state of affairs was that the prerogatives entrusted to the president with regard to the oversight of the armed forces were accompanied by only crude tools for the exercise of that oversight – such as the veto or the right of legislative initiative. The intention of the constitutional measures strengthening the president was to insulate the armed forces from the roiling and unstable Polish political scene with its rapid changeover of governments. The effect, however, was to aggravate the turmoil creating a political milieu in which the salient importance of effective parliamentary oversight of defence was diminished in the minds of the military's leadership, in society generally, and in the minds of parliamentarians in particular.

The Polish parliament exercises oversight on security matters mainly through the work of the Sejm Committee on National Defence. However, the functional capacity of the committee to carry out its work during the period under review was deeply handicapped by a number of practical factors. The rapid turnover of governments, especially between 1989 and 1993 when the simple proportional electoral system meant that the legislature was made up of a myriad of weak political parties, was a main problem. Another more intractable problem was the insufficient quantity and quality of expert staff available to assist and advise the committee. A year after Poland's accession to NATO, the defence committee still had no dedicated advisory body. There was a Sejm research department with a staff of approximately seventy people tasked with preparing answers to specific questions for individual parliamentarians and ministerial committees on various issues. But the foreign affairs section of the research department consisted of only four persons, only one of whom was designated to handle defence matters.[9] The defence committee itself had a secretariat of four persons, three of whom fulfilled administrative and clerical functions while only the fourth (a retired general) acted as an adviser.[10] The morale, motivation and competence of members of parliament to perform oversight roles in the defence committee was also an issue. As one Polish analyst put it:

> It happens that some members of parliament just end up as members of the defence committee but have no particular interest in or knowledge of the area. There is not a long tradition here of involvement of civilians in defence issues so it is a very simple problem: lack of information made worse by lack of experience. Sometimes, parliamentarians try to get that experience and knowledge. But in my opinion definitely there is still space for improvement of their work.[11]

According to another interviewee, the life experience of Polish politicians tended to tell them that the military was a 'hermetic institution that should be left to itself'.[12] A few parliamentarians recognised the need for a more pro-active interest in defence matters but improvement has been slow.

Even by 2000 the number of politicians with experience in the defence sphere was very limited. Invariably, those who did have some knowledge ended up as members of the defence committee. As a result, around one third to half of the committee had some defence background – for example, former ministers and other high officials of the ministry of defence such as Janusz Onyskiewicz and Bronislaw Komorowski – or at least showed a desire to deepen their knowledge. Unfortunately, the trend was for the parliament to rely on this small group for discussion of defence matters while largely ignoring military issues in the wider assembly. So, in general there was still a restricted public debate on security.[13]

In the mid-1990s, at the National Defence Academy in Warsaw a higher defence course was made open to defence committee members, civilian personnel of the ministry of defence and other civilian agencies where necessary. The course was designed for developing defence awareness in civilian officials with no military background. Extremely flexible in delivery time – the course ranged from as little as five to as much as seventy hours in length – the subject matter of the course was still quite limited. In the opinion of some of the instructors it seemed to be enough to give the participants an overview of the defence system but only at a very general level. Moreover, the focus tended to be on the local official rather than the parliamentarian. 'Our motto is that the most important thing is to create cooperation between the military and the local administrations because it is there that most of the problems are located: stationing of troops, transporting of arms and dangerous goods, local employment, and so on,' said one course organiser.[14] Another criticism aimed at the quality of the higher defence course was that it suffered from the same problems as the whole of the military education system which is not flexible enough to adapt to new procedures while at the same time it preserves many aspects of 'old thinking'.[15]

As discussed in the last chapter, the passage of the 1996 *Law on the Duties of the Minister of National Defence* and the 1997 *Constitution* significantly increased the authority of the minister of defence while diminishing the authority of the president. Nevertheless, what did not occur as a result of this strengthening of the minister of defence was a commensurate strengthening of parliamentary oversight. The minister added to his portfolio considerable powers but without being subject to greater parliamentary scrutiny. The continued weakness of the parliament provoked Michta to question whether the army, while firmly under civilian control, was at risk of becoming merely a 'bureaucratic extension of the government . . .'[16]

The experience in Hungary shows both contrast and continuity with that of Poland. On the one hand, (as was noted above), for the most part the constitutional dilemma between the executive and the legislative powers with respect to the oversight of the armed forces was settled in favour of the parliament by the constitutional court in September 1991. Indeed, the parliament has very well-founded and extensive authority over the armed forces to the point of micro-management. Szenes wrote that this situation caused tremendous problems for the army, particularly with regard to the deployment of foreign and national armed forces abroad and at home. By law, only the parliament is authorised to resolve such issues. So, for instance, the ministry of defence must seek parliamentary approval for such mundane matters as foreign military units coming to Hungary to participate in military exercises, or Hungarian troops going abroad for the same purposes. Similar proceedings are required even in a state of emergency or under the threat of war. 'These regulations', wrote Szenes, 'are not suitable in the new political, security and military environment and do not meet the flexible military cooperation requirements of NATO.'[17] Or as Zoltan Martinusz put it, 'the authority and influence of the parliament is often wasted, side-tracked by issues of lesser importance in the greatest detail while it allows issues of key importance to pass with only the most perfunctory attention.'[18]

As in Poland, the real competence of the committee to perform effective oversight of the military was quite low. In the words of a deputy state secretary for defence 'Civilians on the parliamentary security and defence committee have very low skill levels in the area of defence issues. They are simply not well versed in this area.'[19] The majority of interviewees in Budapest in a position to observe the activities of the committee admitted a very low opinion of its work. As one put it:

> I do not have a high opinion of the defence committee. They are unable to exercise effective control. From what I see they usually debate some proposition of the ministry of defence or the general staff but they do not have the knowledge and capacity to judge matters the ministry deals with effectively. It does not mean that they do nothing but I think that practically they have only a marginal role; sometimes it could be more than marginal, but in general because the membership of the committee has no staff – actually it has only one lawyer and nobody else, just some typists – they are not prepared for

> exercising effective control. They also have no theoretical knowledge so they do not know what they should be controlling.[20]

As this interviewee indicated, the lack of expertise of the membership as well as the inadequacy of its support and advisory staff was a main problem with the Hungarian defence committee. So too was the fact parliamentarians on the defence committee were, in the polite words of Tamas Wachsler, 'not elected from the first line of representatives from the political parties'.[21] Efforts to improve the standard of competence proved rather unsuccessful. Officials in the ministry of defence and elsewhere in the defence community expressed considerable frustration that, although a short, modular training program on security issues akin to the Polish higher defence course was designed before the 1998 elections for parliamentarians and their staff to be delivered at the National Defence University on weekends or evenings, 'MPs did not have time or did not want to attend and it did not work out.'[22]

To the extent that individual members of the Hungarian defence committee had access to expert advice it was not through the committee itself (which had no advisory staff) but through the structures of their political parties. The problem with this was that advisers to political parties were chosen in large part because they identified with the political programme of the party and tailored their advice and proposals on that basis. So from this point of view the exercise of their expertise was quite restricted. A further problem was that such advisers tended to be long-retired former military officers most of whom lacked familiarity with modern military thinking and spoke no foreign languages.[23] Moreover, the membership of the defence committee tended to be dominated by retired military officers. One reason for this was that former military officers saw the defence committee as an area where they could contribute usefully to the work of parliament. Another was that, like their Polish counterparts, Hungarian politicians tended to relegate former officers to the defence committee both because they were perceived to have the requisite expertise and because the defence committee was not considered an especially interesting post by most other politicians.[24] Unfortunately, retired military personnel serving in parliament generally did not act as generators of alternative ideas and plans to those provided by the military; rather than providing knowledgeable critique, more often than not, they behaved as spokesmen or lobbyists for the military's plans in parliament.[25]

The main function of parliament in the system of civil–military relations is to exercise detailed oversight of the military budget. On this issue the opinion of many interviewees in Warsaw and Budapest was split on how effective that oversight was. In Warsaw, for example, an official of the budgetary department of the ministry of defence maintained that, notwithstanding many problems in the past, by the late 1990s the committee paid close attention to the military budget:

> The defence committee analyses the draft budget [usually submitted in September] very carefully and they are tough guys. The ministry of defence organises about one hundred pages of detailed information for the committee

> debates on the budget. They discuss the assumptions and details in all the subsections of the draft budget. The army chiefs, service commanders, and ministry officials have to speak to the committee. After the discussions are finished the committee sends their findings to the committee of public spending which presents the whole government spending plan to the parliament. Then the president has to approve it. After that the budget holders can use their funds. The last part of the process is in December.[26]

The short approval period for the Polish budget from analysis of the first draft in September to presidential approval in December would suggest that parliamentary oversight was superficial. Yet the notion that the parliament practised fairly stringent control over the budget was echoed in other interviews. According to an official in the National Security Bureau: 'The committee asks many questions of the ministry of defence [about the budget] and the ministry of defence must answer to parliament. I would say that the committee is fairly effective in this respect.'[27] While the director of the ministry of defence's legal department spoke positively as well:

> I think the defence committee is quite effective. They have a big influence on the matters which concern them. They discuss the projects of the government. They discuss the budget. They monitor how we in the ministry implement the budget. I don't know how they could have more control; really they have enough power to do all their jobs.[28]

No doubt one reason why scrutiny of the budget seems to be taken more seriously by Polish parliamentarians than the exercise of more general oversight is due to the clear primacy of the Sejm vis-à-vis the president on fiscal matters. As opposed to more general defence policy questions the president can only sign the budget or send it to a constitutional tribunal for adjudication – but he may not veto it in whole or in part. As a result, the president is not in a position to force the government on matters of defence expenditure. In Hungary, on the other hand, judgments on the state of the military budget and the quality of parliamentary oversight were highly critical. With respect to the actual planning of the military budget it was widely agreed that the process was under military control. Said one interlocutor,

> The system is still very rigid and important changes in the budgetary process have not taken place. The planning is almost the same as it was in socialist times. We feel the practical difficulties of this. On the one hand we are supposed to make all sorts of plans but the plans cannot be realised because when we go to ask for money it becomes clear that we do not have any. My guess is that the planners simply do not have the economic data to make proper decisions on defence spending. The starting point in the budget is what they received last year. Army units ask for money but there is no serious analysis of what they need, or why.[29]

In other words, the Hungarian defence committee had great difficulty auditing defence spending. There was no defined mechanism for controlling spending objectively in order that funded programmes were in harmony with political guidelines. The budget was not transparent, nor was it very detailed: 'It is not precise enough to make judgements. There are only some big sums for big purposes, no real details,' said one interviewee. Even as late as 1997 the budget of the ministry of defence was reported to have been not more than six pages in length.[30] The structure of the budget, moreover, did not allow effective evaluation of inputs in relation to outputs because it was itemised by spending on institution (eg., central administration, background institutions, logistics and so on) rather than by programme. In fact, the budget in 1997 included under a single item – 'Hungarian Home Defence Forces' – two thirds of the entire defence expenditure! Reportedly, due to the extensive defence reforms the general staff was unable to offer any further detail.[31] In short, the Hungarian defence committee was unable to effectively evaluate whether they were getting good value for their money in defence spending.

One should not, however, overstate the Polish parliament's greater effectiveness than the Hungarian parliament in the sphere of defence oversight. Within the limitations of the data provided them, parliaments have been reasonably effective at controlling the *implementation* of the budget, particularly major acquisitions of equipment. Since 1995 there has been a State Audit Office in Hungary controlling the economics of the defence forces, monitoring spending in the defence budget and reporting directly to the parliament. While in Poland the National Audit Office performs the same role. Therefore, in general, parliament was able to assess whether the budget was fulfilled according to the law. But this is the easier side of civilian budgetary oversight. Parliament is also supposed to ensure that military funding complies with national security goals and with other budgetary priorities. As such, parliament must be able to debate the purposes for which funds are allocated and be assured that the spending estimates of the proposed budget are reasonable and justified. This is the more difficult side of budgetary oversight.

In both Poland and Hungary, however, such levels of sophistication still remained beyond the means of parliament on the eve of their accession to NATO. In practice, in both countries military personnel worked out defence spending priorities, developed the defence budget, estimated the level of expenditure required, and saw to the implementation of the budget. Parliament could follow up retroactively what the military did with its funding, sometimes revealing fiscal abuse – 'control through scandal', one interlocutor called it[32] – but it lacked the expertise to seriously challenge military thinking at any level or to develop alternate policies to those recommended to them by the ministry of defence. Indeed, in the opinion of some analysts, legislators quite often did not know what issues were important and worthy of attention or what questions to ask to get such information.[33] A Hungarian analyst commenting on the effectiveness of his nation's defence committee outlined a relationship of mutual incomprehension between military and civilian officials:

> I regularly attend the sessions of the defence committee and I experience that opinions clash there during the debates in the following way: a political standpoint is described; to this the soldiers present say – and they may be right – that it is already a military area, a professional issue and policy should not penetrate. If soldiers state their views about certain issues politicians say this is not the soldier's task, it belongs to the field of policy.[34]

Presidents in the system of civilian control

As noted above the main difference between the Polish and Hungarian systems of civil–military relations was in the nature of their executive–legislative relations. In democratic states the head of state plays an important role in the system of civil–military relations – normally as the commander-in-chief of the armed forces. However, the practical powers which accompany the title commander-in-chief differ from one state to another depending on constitutional practice. In Poland, the president enjoys broad powers over the armed forces, especially issues relating to the appointment of senior personnel. In Hungary, the president plays a more symbolic role with effective control of appointments lying with the government. As with parliamentary oversight there is a balance to be achieved in executive–governmental relations concerning the armed forces. Taking different paths, Poland and Hungary encountered somewhat different problems. In Poland, the concentration of power at an early stage in the hands of the presidency undermined the influence of the government and helped to stalemate needed reforms. The story there is one of reducing presidential prerogatives and slowly bringing into line the government's responsibility for the defence establishment with the power to direct its development. In Hungary, by contrast, the president had few prerogatives after September 1991. The problem, as discussed above, was that the government devolved too much of its control functions to a weak parliament unable to exercise them in a timely and efficient manner.

In Poland military contestation of civilian policy was fostered by the wider disagreement among civilian political elites over whether parliament or president would dominate the political system. To the extent that the military was able to articulate its preference on the matter it tended to see its corporate interests as being better served under a presidential model. Accordingly, particularly during the tenure of General Wilecki as chief of the general staff (as discussed in the previous chapter), the army leadership showed a partisan support for President Walesa. In this sense, the change of leadership from Walesa to Kwasniewski in presidential elections in 1995 was a highly significant event presaging broader changes in legislation that reduced the power of the presidency vis-à-vis that of the government and reined in the independence of the general staff. On the other hand, even after these changes the Polish president retained major powers over the armed forces. Under the *Constitution* of 1997 and other normative acts the president:

1 executes general leadership of the field of state security;
2 is the highest 'supervisor' of the armed forces;

3 decides on the armed forces development program, plans for the defence of the state and coordinates the nation's defence strategy;
4 awards officers' commissions and general officers' ranks, appoints the chief of the general staff and the commanders of the army, navy and air force; and
5 is head of the National Security Council.

The problems of working out the practical meaning of the president's 'general leadership' of the defence sphere has already been discussed, as has the president's influence over the defence reform programme and military doctrine in Chapter 2. Let us look then at the impact of the president's constitutional prerogatives concerning the appointment of senior ranks in the armed forces.

In Poland after the 1997 Constitution, the president retained the capacity to award higher military ranks in all the uniformed services (military, border guard, police, fire services, etc.) to persons *proposed* by the prime minister and the minister of defence. The president could not appoint senior commanders without the authorisation of the minister of defence. On the other hand, the president was not *required* to promote the officers proposed by the minister and might refuse to promote an officer at his own discretion. Moreover, in the case of the chief of the general staff and the commanders of the military services (army, navy, air force) the president did not require any proposal at all from the prime minister or minister of defence. Who would be the chief of the general staff and the service chiefs was entirely the choice of the president.

According to one of his advisers in the National Security Bureau, in the Polish system of civil–military relations the president is meant to be the representative of the armed forces in government and in society. 'When the soldiers need some help then it is the president's responsibility to see that they get it. He is their commander, supervisor and protector.'[35] Essentially, the president is not meant to be a passive, ceremonial figurehead. On the contrary, he is supposed to play an active role in the direction of the armed forces. 'Our president is not like the queen', explained an interviewee. 'He has a role in defence but not over the whole defence system . . . Of course our constitution, like all constitutions, is general and it will have to be established by practice how things will work in the future but the president should be influential.'[36] This situation of cohabitation put the capacity of the executive and legislative powers to compromise and cooperate with each other at a premium. Under Walesa, compromise and cooperation was all but impossible and the president had too much influence over the defence system to the detriment of the reform of the armed forces. Under Kwasniewski confrontation was greatly muted: 'The president would *like* to have more power with respect to the military but the government says that it has all the responsibilities as concerns defence and that the person who has the responsibility should have the power also.'[37]

A year after Poland's accession to NATO the debate over the respective competencies of the president vis-à-vis the government in the sphere of defence was still on-going. A draft *Law on the Competencies of State Organs in the National Security System of Poland* was being debated in the defence committee that was expected to finally clarify such issues as the division of responsibility for defence between the president and the government (Council of Ministers) and the practical meaning of the president's 'supervision over the armed forces' as opposed to the government's 'responsibility' for the defence establishment of the state.[38] Although the law had not yet been passed, the trend by mid-2000 was more and more toward matching responsibility for the defence system with the power to command it, thus implicitly strengthening the government over the president.

The National Security Bureau is a subordinate body of the Office of the President designed to assist the president in the performance of his duties in the defence sphere. It is headed by a state secretary who also serves as secretary of the National Security Council (discussed further below). Within the bureau there are a number of divisions:

1 the cabinet of the head of the National Security Bureau;
2 an advisory group;
3 an undersecretary of state;
4 the National Security Council Department;
5 the Department for the President's Supervision of the Armed Forces; and,
6 a number of ad hoc groups focused on specific problems of defence.[39]

For the moment let us concentrate on the main divisions: the department for the president's supervision of the armed forces and, later, the national security council department. The former department is responsible for advising the president on a wide range of general and specific matters including the following: general overview of the armed forces, its organisational structures and chain of command; preparing analytical papers relating to bringing the armed forces into line with NATO standards, civil democratic control of the military, and changes in the legislative basis of defence; inspecting and assessing the education, training, maintenance, operational readiness, etc., of the armed forces; advising on the promotion of senior officers, and appointment of the top commanders of the armed forces; and, awarding of medals and other honourable decorations.[40] Thus, the department for the president's supervision of the armed forces appears to combine the functions of a military inspectorate with advisory and protocol functions.

By contrast with Poland, in Hungary after September 1991 the prominence of the president in the system of civil–military relations was not a major issue. According to the Constitutional Court in 1991: 'The function of the president of the Republic as the commander-in-chief is a constitutional function and is not a . . . position or rank. Accordingly, the commander-in-chief is not a superior in the chain of command of any of the armed forces.'[41] Unlike the Polish president the Hungarian president *is* meant to be a ceremonial figurehead. The president has the authority to appoint senior military personnel, but such appointments have to be countersigned by the prime minister and the minister of defence who thereby take political accountability for them. Formally, appointments are the prerogative of the president but the expectation and practice is that the president merely confirms the selections of the minister of defence for promotion to high military rank. The president also appoints the chief of general staff, but only on the proposal of the minister of defence who initiates and manages the appointment process.[42]

In line with the comparatively restricted role of the president in the Hungarian system, by 1995 the Military Office of the President amounted to no more than a few officials whose functions were almost exclusively protocol.[43] The president did not have a military inspectorate reporting to him, not even in the somewhat watered down form possessed by the Polish president. In fact, Hungary did not create a state military inspectorate as such. Instead, the inspection function is one of the responsibilities of the chief of general staff. It would be a mistake, however, to imply that the Hungarian system was better than the Polish one merely because it was less susceptible to the policy stalemates that afflicted Poland as a result of the conflict between its executive and legislative authorities. Hungary had a different problem. The ministry of defence was not a plum political posting in the Hungarian cabinet and, therefore, was usually given over to the junior party in a coalition government. Taking into account this fact, in addition to the deficiencies of parliamentary oversight noted previously and the weak role played by the president, the ministry of defence tended to be beyond consistent oversight from *any* quarter and was therefore vulnerable to being treated as the personal fief of the minister and his political party.

National security councils

National security councils have been important and controversial institutions in all the states under review. Important, because where they exist they have tended to become the locus of decision-making in the sphere of defence. Controversial, because they were often vaguely defined in constitutional and legislative terms and because of a perceived linkage to the powerful defence councils of the old system which were thought to have had too strong an ideological content.[44]

In fact, security councils are often seen as a 'Russian' innovation which perhaps adds to their controversy.[45] This is not without reason since security councils in the robust 'Russian' form are unusual in the West. Their elite membership and closed nature putting them beyond easy public scrutiny, and the way they tend to acquire de facto decision-making powers can make them seem contrary to the principle of transparency. Moreover, most mature democracies do not require strong agencies for policy-coordination because they have civil services that usually are able to coordinate policy between ministries informally or in ad hoc inter-ministerial groupings without compromising effectiveness. In the post-communist context, however, public administration rarely possessed the maturity to coordinate policy on this basis. Arguably, this puts a premium on agencies such as security councils. Yet Poland and Hungary took different approaches to the issue, with the former creating a strong National Security Council while the latter eschewed this potent form of policy coordination in favour of a diverse collection of less powerful institutions. Nonetheless, by the end of the decade neither country was really satisfied with the structures they had chosen.

From the very beginning of Poland's democratic transformation in 1989 there was a general conviction among politicians that the president should play a main role in the resolution of defence matters. As such the president was equipped with special powers with regard to the armed forces. In particular, it was decided that the president would play a main role in the determination of the state's strategic security goals and how they would be realised. These powers were enshrined in the 1992 *Little Constitution* and then reiterated in a less robust form in the 1997 *Constitution*. According to a well-respected insider, however, the point was not to increase the powers of the president per se; rather, it was to heighten the powers of the chairman of the National Security Council – a post held by the president.[46]

That is to say, the National Security Council was meant from the beginning to play an important role in the defence sphere. Politicians accepted the council as the main architect of security policy and both the 1992 *Principles of Polish Security Policy* and the *Security Policy and the Defence Strategy of the Republic of Poland* were enacted by the president in his capacity as chairman of the council. The attractiveness of the council in the Polish system of presidential–parliamentary cohabitation lay in its broad composition which included the following: president, prime minister, chairmen of the Sejm and the Senate, defence minister, interior minister, finance minister, foreign affairs minister, chairman of the central bank, and the head of the National Security Bureau. In addition there was a Permanent Political Advisory Group to the council made up of representatives of the parliamentary opposition that, while not part of the council itself, allowed some opposition input to policy debates.

The staff of the National Security Council were provided by the National Security Bureau of the Office of the President, specifically its national security council department which, according to a staffer, played the role of 'executive body of the National Security Council . . . an advisory body and part of the secretariat of the president. [It] plays a monitoring and advisory role.'[47] Judging from its listed functions, however, the national security council department did play an important agenda setting role. Among its more important functions were:

1 organisation of National Security Council meetings;
2 preparation of briefing materials for the president and the head of the National Security Bureau, including preparation of meeting agendas, decision and discussion papers;
3 monitoring the preparedness of internal and external security units and submitting reports to the council;
4 advising the president and the head of the National Security Bureau on all aspects of the Polish foreign and security policy; and
5 participating in inter-agency working groups on defence and foreign policy issues.[48]

The vast majority of staffers in the national security council department at the time interviews were conducted were retired or serving military officers seconded from the ministry of defence. It did not seem, however, that military personnel felt beholden to the ministry of defence. That is they did not believe that their career prospects were in any way limited by the degree to which they identified with or lobbied for the armed forces and its institutional priorities in the workings of the council. Indeed staffers typically had no intention of returning to regular military service.[49]

At a higher level of abstraction, the story of the Polish National Security Council fits the pattern of civil–military developments in that country more generally. In the early years of transition the voice of the president was supreme in defence matters. The minister of defence was a member of the Council of Ministers and subject to the authority of the prime minister, but at the same time he was also supervised by the president who had power over his appointment. In other words, the minister of defence was subordinate to the president. This relationship, in turn, was reflected in the National Security Council where the minister held the post of vice-chairman under the president. Towards the latter part of the 1990s, however, pressure was growing to reduce the power of the National Security Council – and by implication the power of the president. Parliamentarians pointed out that the council was barely mentioned in the 1997 *Constitution* which stated only that: 'The advisory organ to the President of the Republic regarding internal and external security of the state shall be the National Security Council.'[50] As such, it did not merit such extensive powers.

A year after Poland's accession to NATO it seemed possible that the council would be shut down.[51] What would replace it was unclear. In 1994 under Prime Minister Pawlak a Committee for Defence Affairs was established within the Cabinet of Ministers with responsibility for the coordination and management of ministries involved in defence. It consisted of a small sub-cabinet of ministers, the most important being the minister of defence, the minister of foreign affairs and the minister of finance. The legal basis of the committee was an act of the cabinet of ministers and its head was appointed by the prime minister. But it had no permanent staff; support and advice were provided to the committee by the general advisers of the prime minister and by advisers of particular ministers. Moreover, since its establishment, the coordination role of the committee has gradually diminished and it has become mainly an advisory body.[52]

Like Poland, under the old system Hungary had a defence council that managed the inter-agency coordination of governmental policies on security matters that were not easily resolved under a single ministerial portfolio due to the size and complexity of the issue or because of institutional conflicts. Unlike Poland, after the change of regime the Hungarians chose not to preserve the defence council. Instead, there was a constitutional provision for the creation of a National Defence Council or 'war cabinet' during times of emergency, while for the purposes of inter-ministerial policy coordination there have been a number of ad hoc agencies housed within the prime minister's office as well as in the cabinet.

Article 19 of the Hungarian constitution identifies parliament as the supreme instrument of the state in the defence sphere: ultimately, only parliament is empowered to decide the main issues such as the declaration of a state of war and subsequently to terminate hostilities. The article also authorises the parliament to establish the National Defence Council in times of national emergency. Once established, the council is presided over by the president and includes the speaker of the parliament, the leaders of the parties represented in parliament, the prime minister and other members of the government, as well as the chief of staff of the armed forces. The council exercises numerous emergency powers including authorising the employment of the Hungarian defence forces internally or externally. In some superficial ways the National Defence Council resembles a security council, notably in its broad and high-level membership and wide decision-making powers. But it is not a standing body; rather, it is only formed in time of extreme emergency, has no permanent staff of its own, no real policy-coordination role except in wartime, and its decisions are valid only for the duration of the emergency that precipitated its formation.

In fact, Hungary has never had cause to form the National Defence Council. Shortly before the Kosovo crisis in 1999 the government formed instead another institution – the National Security Cabinet – as the main decision-preparing and decision-making body for the duration of the crisis. The National Security Cabinet is one of several subordinate bodies of the Council of Ministers which includes a Government Cabinet and an Economic Cabinet. The membership of the National Security Cabinet fluctuates but typically includes the foreign, defence, interior, finance, justice and national security ministers. According to some analysts it also includes the chief of defence staff and is led by the prime minister.[53] Other sources, however, indicate that it is headed by the interior or defence minister and the chief of defence staff is not mentioned.[54]

Both Hungarian and foreign observers have long recognised the serious problems caused by the lack of a high-level policy-making committee that could link the defence ministry with the foreign and other ministries and the top civilian leadership. As discussed in Chapter 3, without such a committee Hungary had great difficulty working out an overarching security and defence policy bridging the gap between foreign affairs and defence. The National Security Cabinet was a step in the right direction but insufficient on its own. The various cabinets of the Council of Ministers are only meant to facilitate *in-cabinet* discussions of policy issues on many priority areas of government including national security. They have no decision-making powers of their own; they formulate positions on various security matters and make recommendations for decisions of the government. Moreover, as a subordinate body of the Council of Ministers, the cabinet also has no expert staff of its own relying instead on the resources of the individual ministers.

There was a final institution created in Hungary in 1998 for the coordination of defence policy – specifically the updating of the 1993 *National Security Principles* and the *Basic Principles of National Defence* – the secretariat for security and defence policy in the office of the prime minister. The secretariat for security and defence policy was one of three headed by the National Security Adviser, Bela Gyuricza, until his death in spring 1999.[55] Its aim was to coordinate national security policy and ensure that future changes in the defence sphere be conducted on the basis of thorough analysis as opposed to the ad hoc and spontaneous way it had happened in the past. After Gyuricza's death, however, the influence of the secretariat was greatly diminished; its policy-coordinating role became negligible and its secretary came to operate more as an adviser to the prime minister on security matters.

Former Soviet Union

The Russian and Ukrainian political systems bear more in common than do those of Poland and Hungary. Both countries adopted strong presidential constitutional models. In both, presidents have a direct electoral mandate, have strong legislative powers (i.e., they may issue decrees which carry the force of law provided they do not contradict existing legislation), have the decisive voice on cabinet selection and survival, and control security policy formulation. Civilian control of the defence establishment in both countries is overwhelmingly a matter of presidential concern and precludes intervention from other political actors. The predominance of presidential authority over the armed forces in both countries has produced a situation wherein the vertical chain of civilian control from president to the armed forces is strong while oversight from other societal agents – notably the parliament – is greatly underdeveloped. Moreover, owing to the rather limited number of expert civilians in the vertical chain it is difficult to call even the strong presidential oversight of the military truly 'civilian'. In the previous chapter we saw that there were, and still are, almost no civilian executives in the Russian or Ukrainian ministries of defence of any consequence. In this chapter we will see that the military is represented in, or heads, all the main bodies of 'civilian' oversight – defence committees, security councils, military inspectorates and, indeed, presidential administrations thus calling into question the reality of 'civilian' control of the armed forces.

The political systems of both Ukraine and Russia have been characterised by strong, long-serving presidents able to rule by decree, volatile and weak legislatures dominated by the left which were unable to put much of a brake on presidential prerogative, and rapid turnover especially of prime ministers, but also of ministers of defence and chiefs of general staff (particularly in Ukraine). The legislative basis of the defence establishment in both countries has been discussed at a general level in previous chapters. At this point it is worthwhile revisiting that discussion with a more specific focus on the legal architecture of civilian oversight and, in particular, on the relation of the executive and legislative powers in the sphere of defence.

In Russia, the defence establishment is regulated in three main documents: the 1992 *Law on Defence*, the 1993 *Constitution of the Russian Federation* and the 1996 *Law on Defence* According to the 1992 law on defence, the president and the parliament were accorded roughly approximate powers. The president was named commander-in-chief of the armed forces, but responsibility for such issues as the direction of state military policy and doctrine, deciding the size and structure of the military, overseeing promotions, discharges and awards of high military posts within the military, ordering partial or complete mobilisation of the armed forces and declaration of a state of war, were shared. The president was in control of the 'nuclear button', but parliament had a say in defining the conditions under which nuclear arms could be employed.[56]

The 1993 *Constitution of the Russian Federation* – enacted after the October crisis of that year – substantially changed that balance. It became the sole prerogative of the president to: appoint and remove the army's high command;[57] to introduce martial law and states of emergency throughout the Russian Federation or in individual localities with notification of the Federation Council (the upper house of parliament);[58] and to approve the military doctrine of the state.[59] The Federation Council retained a level of influence over military developments under the new constitution – mainly the capacity to confirm the introduction of martial law or a state of emergency by the president, as well as the right to decide on the possibility of employing the armed forces outside the territory of the Federation.[60] However, as the president controlled the military doctrine and military policy which defined what would constitute a state of emergency, in practice he had little need to ask the Federation Council to confirm any decisions, including both Chechen wars. The Duma was left with virtually no powers except passing and providing oversight of the federal budget and adopting laws on various matters concerning defence and on issues of war and peace.[61]

The updated 1996 *Law on Defence* merely confirmed the centralisation of control over the military in the hands of the president already implied by the *Constitution*. The powers of the president listed in the law were extensive, accounting for twenty paragraphs.[62] The Federation Council merited four paragraphs, retaining the right to 'confirm' declarations of the president on martial law and states of emergency, passing the federal budget, overseeing the passage of laws by the Duma on matters of defence and war and peace, and deciding on the use of military force abroad.[63] The State Duma's powers were occupied in only two paragraphs (3 lines) covering the passing of the federal budget and the passage of laws on defence.[64]

A new law entitled *On Control of the Military Organisation of the Russian Federation* was drafted by a group of experts working for the Duma defence committee in the latter half of the 1990s. While proceeding from the premise that the president would continue to provide the main focus of civilian control of the military, the draft envisaged strengthening the role of the legislature in terms of supervising the budget process as well as through the establishment of a parliamentary 'Commission on Civilian Control'. By the end of the 2002, however, the draft still remained a working document and had not been formally introduced or discussed in the legislature.[65]

In the period under review Russia has had both a Defence Council and a Security Council playing policy-preparing, policy-coordinating and advisory roles in the system of defence management.[66] The interrelation of these institutions, whose responsibilities and authority overlapped considerably, is complex and will be discussed further below. At this point it bears mentioning, however, that both councils were executive bodies headed by the president and were in no way accountable to parliament. The legal establishment – by presidential decree – of the State Military Inspectorate occurred in autumn of 1996.[67] Initially the inspectorate was designated an independent sub-department of the presidential administration. In 1998, however, the military inspectorate was transferred to the authority of the secretary of the Security Council.

The *Constitution of Ukraine* sets out the range of responsibilities and authority of the various players in its system of civilian control. The system is very similar to Russia's, particularly in respect to the concentration of powers in the presidency. The President of Ukraine: is the commander-in-chief of the armed forces in which capacity he appoints and dismisses the high command of the armed forces and other military formations and 'administers' in the spheres of national security and defence;[68] heads the National Security and Defence Council of Ukraine;[69] and confers high military ranks.[70] Some of the president's powers are shared with the Verkhovna Rada, notably the declaration of a state of war or emergency in Ukraine or in individual localities necessitating the employment of armed force.[71] The General Military Inspectorate, which is not mentioned in the constitution, is a subordinate body of the presidential administration with no links to parliament. It was established in 1995 by a decree of the president.[72]

Constitutionally, the authority of the Verkhovna Rada of Ukraine in the defence sphere would appear somewhat stronger than that of the Russian parliament. In addition to its control of the budget, the remit of the Rada includes: determining the principles of domestic and foreign policy;[73] confirming the general structure and numerical strength, and defining the functions of the armed forces, the security service and other military formations;[74] approving decisions on providing military assistance to other states, on sending units of the armed forces abroad, or on admitting units of armed forces of other states on to the territory of Ukraine.[75] At the same time, the constitution contains significant ambiguities. It states that the Rada approves 'national programmes of economic, scientific and technical, social, national and cultural development, and the protection of the environment',[76] explicitly leaving out programmes of *military* development. Ukraine's National Security and Defence Council is also described in the constitution, according to which it is the coordinating body of the president on national security and defence issues. That is to say, the council is an executive body under the chairmanship of the president who controls the composition of its personnel and enacts by presidential decree decisions taken in council.[77] The Ukrainian parliament only began drafting a law on civilian control of the military sphere in 2000.[78]

Parliamentary oversight of defence

As discussed in the last chapter on Poland and Hungary, parliaments play a crucial role in the system of civilian control of the military. They are the main vehicle for societal scrutiny of the activities of the armed forces and they oversee the military budget. To an even greater extent than Poland and Hungary, the Russian and Ukrainian parliaments were unable to perform their oversight function in the 1990s. In general, one might say that the problems which plagued parliamentary committees in the former Soviet Union states were in the same categories as those encountered in Central Europe but at a greater level of intensity: the Russian and Ukrainian presidents arrogated to themselves even more power than the Polish president, while at the same time the inexperience, lack of expert assistance and de-motivation of parliamentarians also undermined their effectiveness.

In some respects, the reasons for the Russian and Ukrainian failure to exercise effective oversight of their respective defence establishments were practical, resembling the problems encountered by Poland and Hungary – neither committee possessed permanent advisory bodies to assist them in their duties. Instead, they have relied on the expertise of individual members, analytical reports of the ministry of defence, their parliamentary staffs or whatever research organs might be available from their political parties.

In general, analytical support to the Ukrainian defence committee was considered to be 'unsatisfactory'.[79] As of 2000, the committee had twelve clerical staff and twenty-one members, about a quarter of whom had a military background. The committee itself had no analytical staff of its own, relying instead on the analytical sections of the ministry of defence and occasionally outside agencies like the National Institute of Strategic Studies.[80] The same applied to the Russian defence committee which also had no permanent analytical staff, relying as well on analytical reports of the ministry of defence or on ad hoc advisory groups of outside experts such as the one that worked on the draft law on civilian control.[81] In the words of the deputy chairman of the defence committee, Alexei Arbatov, not only in the defence committee but also in the budget, tax, finance and banking committees the number of '. . . people with an understanding of defence questions are an insignificant minority . . .'.[82]

As in Poland and Hungary, due to the scarcity of defence expertise the trend in the Russian and Ukrainian parliaments was to rely on a small group of members with military backgrounds for discussion of defence matters while the wider membership largely ignored such issues. In the Russian Duma, with the exception of a few civilians like Alexei Arbatov and Andrei Kokoshin, this group centred on the '"Duma Generals" – retired military men elected as deputies who are the only members possessing any expertise in defence . . .'.[83] Indeed, most of the defence committee's chairmen have been military officers, including Colonel (ret.) Sergei Yushenkov, Lieutenant-General (ret.) Lev Rokhlin, Colonel-General (ret.) Edward Vorobyev, Major-General (reserves) Roman Popkovich, and General of the Army Andrei Nikolayev. The situation in Ukraine bore some similarity with a number of prominent 'soldier-politicians' serving in the Rada, including former minister of defence General Vitaliy Radetskiy, former Chief of the General Staff Anatoliy Lopata, and General Vilen Martirosyan among others.[84] However, such individuals did not always end up as members of the defence committee, prompting one close observer to lament:

> In Ukraine, the parliament has some ability to oversee the military but not much and not very strong. Part of the problem is the type of people we have on the committee here. In Russia they have people like Nikolayev, Kokoshin, Arbatov and so on but here we don't have any such military experts. The past head, Kriuchkov, had some ability but no one does now. Although the committee passed a lot of laws, basically it is quite weak.[85]

Leaving aside the question of the competence and wherewithal of the defence committee to perform a substantive oversight role, another problem was the *reluctance* of many parliamentarians to get involved in scrutinising military issues. In Russia, a point was made by one interlocutor that because becoming fully knowledgeable about defence policy would make the member of parliament a bearer of state secrets – and hence subject to stricter limitations on foreign travel – many were simply unwilling to take on a more concrete role in defence oversight:

> If you get the clearance [to view secret material], you become a bearer of state secrets, which would give some petty clerk the power to bar you from foreign travel, and who would want to give up one's vacation on Bali?[86]

There was general agreement among interviewees in Moscow and Kiev that the defence committee system worked very simply. In Russia, 'The defence committee acts like a military lobby by trying to get the government to allocate more funds to the military, and in exchange tries to gain some influence in the military.'[87] From time to time, the Duma was in a position to exercise some authority over the military through specific acts of legislation. When this occurred, such as when the *Law on Alternative Service* was being debated, according to a former member of the Security Council, 'the military lobbied hard to bend the legislation in their own interest, and sometimes used their allies to kill those bills they did not like'.[88] Moreover, 'the low professional level of most legislators makes it impossible for them to make serious, well-thought-out policy decisions, which results in the ministry of defence virtually dictating to members of parliament decisions on how the armed forces and defence industry should develop'.[89]

In Ukraine, 'The parliament rubber stamps what the military develops and brings to the Cabinet of Ministers or the administration of the president various projects or problems for their decision.'[90] In other words, the existence of a defence committee that would work systematically on civilian oversight was

> a long way off, because if you look at the personnel of the committee – particularly its chairmen – you see that they are not trained or experienced with the military in any way. This causes from the very beginning a kind of inequality. It is not a body that can provide any sort of critical judgement. It really just represents the military in parliament.[91]

The opinion of serving military officers on the work of the parliament is telling. According to a senior Russian naval officer, 'The parliament plays no role in controlling the armed forces. The parliament can always make the military's life more miserable, though.'[92] Similarly, a senior Ukrainian army officer concluded that 'parliament can screw things up and make them more complicated'.[93] In effect, parliaments in Russia and Ukraine actually seemed in some ways to undermine the loyalty of the military to the new order. Due to the financial constraints on the military budget they were forced to withdraw military benefits like free metro passes and income tax exemptions. In Ukraine the officer quoted above continued:

> parliament really earns the military's anger in a lot of ways because they have voted to reduce the priveleges formerly allowed to officers like rest homes, subsidised housing, subsidised bills, travel and allowances etc. Such cutbacks have reduced my salary by about twenty-five per cent – this really generates a lot of resentment in the army.[94]

In Russia, the periodic efforts of the Duma to restore some of the benefits of military service usually stayed in the realm of populist rhetoric and were not translated into public policy. 'In the end,' concluded a Moscow researcher, 'the military need the politicians primarily for the money, little as there is of it, and are accumulating resentment against them for their systematic neglect of the army's needs. Relations between these politicians and the military are those of a mutually unpleasant neutrality.'[95]

The effectiveness of defence committees in both countries, however, was undermined at an even more fundamental level: the overwhelming concentration of authority over the armed forces in the presidency made parliamentary oversight a moot point. Defence committees could, in theory, discuss any aspect of defence policy which interested them, but their practical capacity to do anything about it was essentially limited by the legal restrictions on their authority. In Russia, even on an issue as publicly unpopular as the first war in Chechnya, the Duma was unable to exert much pressure on policy. Russia's laws on defence give the Duma little to no accountability over the formulation of military policy at any level. Neither the ministry of defence, nor any other 'power ministries', are *required* to report to parliament on their activities; the minister of defence is subordinate to the president and reports to him, not the legislature. The committee has a purely declarative role. Its members, can point to problems in the army, and criticise the government's defence and security policy, but they have little authority; any decisions they might take carry at best moral weight if they do not accord with the policies of the president. Even the freedom of the parliament to pass new legislation on defence is circumscribed because it must not contradict the military doctrine which carries legal force and thus acts as something akin to a military constitution. Parliament may pass legislation on defence issues, but only in accordance with the dictates of military doctrine which, of course, is determined by the president.

The powers of the Verkhovna Rada with respect to the military are also quite limited. 'In fact, it does not operate a single lever of influence on the power structures.'[96] According to the constitution, the Rada does not have power over the approval of long-term development programmes in the military sphere, does not give consent to key appointments in the ministry of defence, does not play any role in the personnel policy of the armed forces, and does not have oversight of the combat readiness of the military.[97] According to a committee staffer, relations between the ministry of defence and the committee are workable:

> When we need their input it is provided. They provide detailed analyses and support the activities of the committee. With respect to the minister, relations are also OK. The committee cannot demand that he testify or give reports, but

> neither has it ever tried to. When required the ministry of defence will send a deputy minister.[98]

On the other hand, according to another interviewee, 'the real effectiveness of the parliament, its influence, for example when there were parliamentary hearings on military reform, is a matter of real debate. The level of sophistication of debate is very low. The main point for the ministry of defence to talk to the parliament at all was to lobby for more money.'[99] Legally and in practice 'only the presidential structures have control over the military and force structures. Parliament has no real control. Even the nomination of the minister is the prerogative of the president . . . The ministry of defence is responsible primarily to the president, to a certain extent to the cabinet of ministers, and to the ministry of finance.'[100]

In democratic theory, to achieve civilian control parliaments must have substantive and detailed, not just perfunctory, parliamentary oversight over security policy and spending; 'a parliament which is limited, or which limits itself through lack of interest, to a rubber-stamp role in the oversight of defence is a clear indication of poor civilian control'.[101] Neither the Ukrainian nor Russian parliament exercised substantive and detailed oversight of security policy and defence spending in the period under review. While there is a constitutional provision for parliamentary oversight of the budget in both countries, in reality this mechanism does not work. Opinion on why this was the case was virtually the same in Moscow and Kiev. According to a Russian analyst,

> when the budget is in such poor condition as nowadays, the issue of control loses its meaning. Secondly, while the constitution does provide for the parliament's role, there is no developed system for legislators to effectively carry out the task of budgetary control – a system which would compel the military to inform the lawmakers about their plans for military development, and to persuade them to support their proposals and fund them.[102]

Ukrainian analysts voiced almost the same concern that the level of spending on defence was so inadequate as to make budgetary scrutiny by parliament 'irrelevant'.[103]

Indeed, the detail of the military budget was insufficient to allow thorough analysis by parliamentarians. In Russia from 1994 to 1997 the budget consisted of only seven articles on appropriations for the ministry of defence, military pensions and military programmes of the ministry for nuclear energy. According to 1998 amendments of the *Law on Budgetary Classification*, the defence budget must contain at least 130 open positions. The military budget was also supposed to show the distribution of appropriations to the military by function, by the types of armed forces being supported with what types of weapons, as well as by its main missions and so on; but it did not. From 1998 to 2000, the budget of the ministry of defence contained only three main articles: maintenance of the armed forces (alone counting for up to 90 per cent of the total), mobilisation readiness, and programmes of the nuclear ministry. This level of secrecy effectively denied the parliament any real opportunity to exercise oversight of the military budget and opened the way for the ministry of defence to manipulate appropriations.

Analysts in Ukraine offered similarly sober assessments of the capacity of the Verkhovna Rada to perform detailed oversight. In a lengthy paper on parliamentary control of the military in Ukraine, Vadim Grechaninov dwelled for only two paragraphs on the question of budgetary scrutiny saying:

> The main work of the committee is control of the military budget. But . . . ; the capacity of such control from the committee is, on the whole, extremely insignificant.[104]

Another interviewee noted that the Rada reviewed only the 'military budget at large and in general, not at all in detail – there is practically no transparency in defence spending'.[105] In fact, the Ukrainian system of budgeting fits well with the broader tendency to reform by declaration noted in previous chapters. According to a Western defence attache with five years experience in his post in Kiev:

> They have here what I call a system of budgeting by decree: 'The army will work!' Who cares how it happens. That's their problem. This means that the budget is virtually meaningless. It doesn't reflect how much money the army will get or how it will be spent. Let me give you an example of my assistant who was a conscript in the army and told this story. He and a couple of soldiers were told by an officer that a particular wall had to be painted. They weren't given brushes or paint or any direction how to do it. That was their problem. They were ordered to do it and they had to figure out how. That, in microcosm, is how the whole system works.[106]

In Russia throughout the 1990s there was a lot of concern about the role of 'soldier-politicians' in the legislature. Such as, for example, during the 1995 parliamentary elections when Grachev ordered 123 military officers to run for office in order to 'represent the interests of the military' in the Duma.[107] Although the legal right of serving Russian officers to serve in the Duma is strange to Western observers, it did not represent a particularly potent threat to Russian democracy. The 'soldier-politicians' represented a very small percentage of Duma deputies and since they were divided among nearly every political party did not represent a coherent military bloc in the legislature. Moreover, with one exception (the chairman of the Duma defence committee) they did not hold any of the senior positions in the house. The real threat of military men in politics was more subtle. They undermined the ability of the Duma to exercise its only real means for control of the military: review of the defence budget.

To the extent that budgetary oversight was carried out in the Duma it was performed not by civilians but by the military itself through its retired members in the Duma. The system worked very simply: a few mainly military members of the Duma defence committee would study a classified defence budget containing data not open to normal members of the legislature, work on it with the ministry of defence, and submit generalised conclusions to the other members of the legislature with regard to the adoption of the budget as a whole. After approval, the same mainly military members of the committee would monitor spending on the basis of classified data they received from the ministry of defence, which normal members would never see.[108]

The situation was made even more complex by the fact that the process of defence appropriation was very tricky. There were actually three defence budgets, each controlled by a different body: the federal budget voted for by the Duma which would become law; the real budget allocated to the ministry of defence by the ministry of finance, and the actual spending of the ministry of defence. Legally, failure to implement the budget was a crime, but no one was ever charged because the government simply did not have the money to fulfil all its obligations. The ministry of finance disbursed whatever funds really existed and then the military spent what it got as it saw fit. In the end, 'the system works with the kind of quality which can be expected in a situation where the government does not have the means to implement the budget. At the current level of defence spending, there is not much control to do.'[109]

Presidents in the system of civilian control

Without doubt, control over the security forces in Russia and Ukraine stems unambiguously from the president and his administration. Indeed, to the extent that civilian control of the armed forces exists at all, it is because the president is a civilian and the power of all other agencies derives, directly or indirectly, from his office. 'Generally speaking,' said one Russian interviewee, 'the ministry of defence is not under the authority of the government: it is directly controlled by the president.'[110] While in the words of a Ukrainian interlocutor:

> The president has built up an impenetrable chain of command over the power structures. It goes directly from the president through the National Security and Defence Council staff and on to the power ministries. In this vertical line of executive command and control there is no room even for input from the cabinet of ministers.[111]

Within the Russian and Ukrainian presidential administrations there existed a range of comparable institutions for exercising control of the military: a national security adviser, a commission on higher military ranks, and a general military inspectorate. In Russia, the military branch of the personnel directorate of the presidential administration also played a small role in the military appointment process, and the military branch of the main control directorate had responsibilities focused mainly on fiscal accountability and the military–industrial complex.[112]

The position of national security adviser has been a powerful one in both countries. In Ukraine, Volodymyr Horbulin had a strong influence as adviser to the president and as secretary of the National Security and Defence Council from

1994 until December 1999 when he was replaced as secretary of the council by Yevheny Marchuk, a retired general and former presidential candidate. Indeed, some interviewees suggested that Horbulin's influence over defence policy was not diminished by losing the secretariat of the council. He retained his post as adviser to the president, and much of the staff who reported to him as secretary of the council were simply moved to the presidential administration.[113] That said, according to Parfionov, the national security adviser played no real role in the system of civilian control.[114] In Russia, on the other hand, the post of national security adviser had some influence from 1993 to 1998 when it was held by Yuri Baturin. But after Baturin's dismissal from all his posts in 1998 the post was subsumed by the head of the presidential administration (General of the Army Nikolai Bordyuzha who held the post from December 1998 to March 1999).

Less is known about the activities of the commissions on higher military ranks which, while important, tended to go about their work outside of the public eye. In Russia until March 1997 the commission on higher military ranks was also headed by Yuri Baturin, at which point the functions of the commission were transferred to the authority of the newly-appointed vice premier, Anatoliy Chubais, who had been ordered by the president to take responsibility for the direction of military reform. Then, in 1999, the functions were transferred again to the Security Council under the direction of its secretary. Yeltsin's byzantine machinations to keep the commission on higher military ranks out of the hands of his political enemies testifies to its importance as a mechanism for control of the armed forces.

In Ukraine the reality of the president's power over military appointments was made evident through the National Security and Defence Council.[115] Military inspectorates provided another important lever of presidential control over the armed forces. The Ukrainian General Military Inspectorate amounted to around forty (mostly military) personnel as of 2000 under the command of a colonel general. The primary function of the inspectorate was to inspect and oversee the activities of all the armed services and report on their readiness to the president. However, opinion on the effectiveness of the inspectorate is divided. Sherr wrote:

> The inspectorate, resting on subordinate inspectorates and on information-analysis departments in each armed service, is a potent institution, and it provides the president with an effective means of supervising military structures as well as making their activity more transparent.[116]

Yet, in the estimation of an interviewee in Kiev, the role of the general military inspectorate was merely to be,

> used as the army's golden parachute. It's a way to let old retired generals keep their cars and privileges and to stay involved in things. It's a total replica of the old communist system whereby older comrades kept a hand in the system as inspectors. They kept their privileges and so on, but they were removed as rivals for the new cadres.[117]

One Western defence attache's assessment of the inspectorate points a way to understanding this contradiction. 'The inspectorate is slightly a mystery to us,' he said. 'They seem to be feared by the rest of the ministry. I assume they have some impact, but not very much I think.'[118] The key words here are *feared* and *not very much impact*. The inspectorate can hardly have much impact in an army facing as dire a crisis as Ukraine's. After all, it would not take very much effort to reveal grievous standards of readiness, training, maintenance and morale in virtually any unit of the armed forces. On the other hand, the findings of the inspectorate could be used as a pretext for disciplining a particular commander who was in disfavour with the president for some other reason.

Such was likely the case with the navy commander-in-chief Vice-Admiral Volodymyr Bezkorovainy. In October 1996, the inspectorate found the performance of Bezkorovainy unsatisfactory and asked him to resign. According to the head of the inspectorate, General Valeriy Hubenko, Bezkorovainy's failings included allowing the Russian-controlled fleet to conduct exercises in Ukrainian waters 'whenever and wherever it pleased' and he criticised the commander's performance in ensuring the navy's battle worthiness.[119] Nevertheless, the timing of the resignation, on the eve of a reported breakthrough in Russian-Ukrainian talks on the status of the fleet, fuelled speculation that the real cause was Bezkorovainy's too public disagreement with concessions made in the negotiations. In other words, the inspectorate was feared as an instrument for presidential censure of individual commanders for reasons having little or nothing to do with the operational readiness of the forces under their command – which were uniformly bad throughout the armed forces.

The Russian State Military Inspectorate was approximately double the size of the Ukrainian inspectorate with some 100 personnel of which 80 were seconded from the security services.[120] It too was empowered to inspect all of the security services, not only those of the ministry of defence. The establishment of the inspectorate in 1996 was connected with efforts to reinvigorate the process of defence reform; it was hoped that the inspectorate would not only perform political control of the armed forces, but also control its reform. In fact, the idea of a State Military Inspectorate outside of the ministry of defence was mooted by Igor Rodionov in 1995 prior to his appointment as minister of defence. In his view, an inspectorate was warranted because,

> The defence ministry . . . taking advantage of the lack of real oversight is deceiving the political leadership and the country's public as regards the combat readiness and progress and quality of the reform of the armed forces.[121]

In fact, the inspectorate did not live up to these hopes. The political leadership was not deceived, as Rodionov wrote, by the military as to the real state of the moribund military reform or the critical weakness of the armed forces. By 1995 anyone who could read a newspaper knew how dire the situation was in the military; they simply did not consider it of sufficient importance relative to the other crises facing them to take action. When the inspectorate uncovered double bookkeeping in the interior ministry and reported it to the president, Yeltsin upbraided the minister, Sergei Stepashin, while at the same time decorating him with a state order. In other words, like Ukraine, when and what the president might do with information provided him by the inspectorate was entirely a matter of his own discretion.[122]

Presidential control of the military in both Ukraine and Russia is clearly strong and effective. What is less clear is the extent to which presidential control can be equated with *civilian* control. Generally speaking, it can be said of the various controlling agencies of the presidential administration that they could be led by either a civilian or a military man depending on the will of the president. And, indeed, certain civilians such as Baturin in Russia and Horbulin in Ukraine have exercised great influence. Yet, at the same time, in Russia the numerous members of the security services serving in the presidential administration – such as General Alexander Korzhakov (head of the presidential security service from 1991 to 1996), General of the Army Mikhail Barsukov (commandant of the Kremlin from 1992 to 1995; director of the FSB in 1995-1996), and General of the Army Nikolai Bordyuzha (head of the presidential administration from December 1998 to March 1999) – leant it a strongly military flavour. Similarly, according to experts of the Ukrainian Centre for Economic and Political Studies, the predominance of active or retired servicemen in the structures of the Ukrainian presidential administration pointed to the 'military nature' of presidential control in their country as well.[123]

Security councils

Through the 1990s security councils in both Ukraine and Russia have attracted considerable interest as they slowly evolved de facto powers seemingly beyond their constitutional remits. The Russian Security Council, created on 7 July 1992 by a decree of the president entitled *On Procedures for Implementing Decisions of the Russian Federation Security Council*, was originally supposed to be a consultative body on matters of national security, but gradually it became the main inter-agency coordinating body for the security services and seemed to acquire de facto decision-making powers, although legally it had no mandate for decision-making. The Ukrainian National Security and Defence Council – under the uninterrupted direction of Volodymyr Horbulin from 1994 to December 1999 – experienced a similar evolution.[124] Constitutionally, it too was an advisory body assisting the president in the exercise of his control functions; in practice, the council became one of the most influential and effective state structures.[125]

The influence of the Security Council fluctuated throughout the course of the 1990s. In its early days it was far from obvious that the Security Council would perform any serious functions. Indeed, by August 1993 Vitaly Marsov, writing in *Nezavisimaya Gazeta* claimed that Marshal Yevgeni Shaposhnikov was resigning his post as secretary of the council after only three months because he had realised that,

> first of all, what was required of him was political loyalty to the president and a minimum of activity, and that the Security Council is nothing more than a

> part of the president's staff that is intended only to organise conferences between Boris Yeltsin and the heads of particular departments . . .[126]

By the mid-1990s, however, the Security Council was becoming a major player in the defence sphere attracting the attention of domestic and foreign analysts of military–political matters in Russia. Much of that attention centred on the potential of one figure – Aleksandr Lebed, a challenger for the presidency in the 1996 elections who served as secretary of the council from June to October 1996 – to use his position as secretary of the council to take on the mantle of 'security Tsar'. However, only a month after Lebed's appointment Yeltsin created the highly comparable Defence Council. The similarity in mission, structure and composition of the councils prompted many to wonder why Russia needed two such institutions.[127] Two theories were proposed to explain this situation. The first was that there was a functional division of labour between the councils. As Vladimir Klimenko – the chief of staff of the Defence Council – outlined it, the council would concentrate solely on 'questions of military structure and military reform, separating these tasks from the whole issue of national security into a separate problem'.[128] The tasks of the Defence Council and the Security Council were to be interconnected, with the Security Council defining the security interests and requirements of the Russian Federation, while the Defence Council worked out how the armed forces would meet those requirements.

The second theory was that the Defence Council was created to ensure that Lebed did not acquire too much power. Yeltsin could award Lebed a high position while, at the same time, the powers of his office were transferred to a more reliable functionary. The trouble with this theory, which has become accepted lore, is that while some powers were transferred from the Security to the Defence Council, the powers of the Security Council secretary were also strengthened in some important respects: most importantly he was given the power to control the personal staffs of the heads of all the ministries and agencies having to do with security matters.[129]

In short, the evolution of the Security Council defies easy interpretation. Lebed was never able to manipulate the powers of his office to really acquire the status of 'security Tsar' because he was too busy trying to negotiate a settlement to the war in Chechnya. At the same time, the extent of his potential powers did arouse insecurity among other state officials who helped engineer his downfall.[130] In this respect, the establishment of the Defence Council was likely connected *in part* with a desire to neutralise Lebed's growing power. Certainly, the abolition of the Defence Council in 1998, only two years after its creation, with Lebed safely gone, would tend to confirm this thesis.

When Andrei Kokoshin took over as secretary of the Security Council on 3 March 1998 there was talk about Russia having taken a step toward achieving real civilian control of the armed forces. By this time, Kokoshin was already the head of the State Military Inspectorate which became a branch of the Security Council. In combining the two agencies it was thought that a kind of 'super, civilian minister of defence' who could control all the security services would be created. Moreover, as a public politician, Kokoshin, while remaining subordinate first of all to the president, would also be open to influence from the Duma and the public. It is difficult to say whether this is what Yeltsin intended when he appointed Kokoshin, but it seems unlikely; after only six months as secretary, Kokoshin was fired by Yeltsin for no stated reason and replaced by Nikolai Bordyuzha.

As a body of civilian control, however, the Security Council was not likely to be very effective, under Kokoshin or anyone else, for the simple reason that it was not really a civilian body – a substantial portion of its membership and most of its staff were from the security services. For example, of the roughly 70 ranking officials who have been members of the council since its inception in 1992, at least 25 were officers from the security services. Out of a total of ten secretaries, there have been four generals and one colonel (Putin). And of those five, two have been in active service (Nikolai Bordyuzha from the Border Guards and Sergei Ivanov from the FSB). The military inspectorate branch of the Security Council was almost completely staffed by the security services themselves. In 1998, a general, Nikolai Barsukov was its head while eleven of its thirteen inspectors were also generals.[131] Finally, the majority of the Security Council's 207 staff (as of 1997) were military officers posted there from the security services whose long-term career prospects depended on how well they protected the interests of their home ministry.[132]

A Russian defence analyst who in 1990 worked with Kokoshin writing proposals for the creation of the Security Council commented in late 1998 on the effectiveness of the council as a body of civilian control:

> it is not working nowadays. Actually, it is unclear why the president created it at all. It seems its establishment was connected with the idea of creating the post of civilian minister of defence. But today the president won't let anyone but himself control the power ministries.[133]

Basically, the Security Council under Yeltsin was an agency tailor-made for departmental lobbying between the power ministries, not for the exercise of civilian oversight.

The evolution of Ukraine's National Security and Defence Council was less dramatic than the Russian Security Council. More consistency in leadership – Volodymy Horbulin, as noted above, was secretary from 1994 to December 1999 – as well as the more general level of calm that prevailed in Ukrainian civil–military relations contributed to this smoother development. Its powers are somewhat broader than those of the Russian Security Council. According to the *Law on the National Security and Defence Council of Ukraine* of 5 March 1998, the council is responsible for the coordination and realisation of the control of the executive in the sphere of security and defence. In its meetings the council discusses and prepares recommendations for presidential decision on a wide range of defence matters including concepts of national security, military doctrine, reform programmes, military finances, military readiness, and so on.[134] In short, the council is responsible for coordinating policies and assisting the president in exercising the myriad functions in the defence sphere entrusted to him by the constitution. Indeed, the National Security and Defence Council is an integral part of the presidential administration – unlike the Russian Security Council which, in theory if not in practice, is kept at arm's length from the presidential administration.

The membership of the council includes the president, the secretary of the council, the prime minister, the head of the security service, the minister of interior, the minister of defence, the minister of foreign affairs, and others. As of late 1999, due to the continuing domination by men in uniform of the top posts in the 'power-ministries' the 15-strong membership of the council had a certain military flavour with seven of its members being in uniform.[135] The staff of the council, however, 'is much more civilian', according to a former staffer (a military officer). 'Especially the economic and foreign relations directorate have more civilians. They have retired military too. But the council employs mostly civilians.'[136] The civilian staff are employed by the council directly, while the military personnel are paid by the council though they wear military uniform. Importantly, the staff are independent. According to the same staffer:

> The staff of the National Security and Defence Council are independent. There was no pressure on me to defend the ministry of defence as an adviser. I was totally independent. The military people, even in the military inspectorate, are independent.[137]

Moreover, the quality of work coming out of the council, as discussed in Chapter 2, particularly the 1997 *National Security Concept*, was of a high standard.

On the other hand, by the end of 1999 it was clear that all was not well with the workings of the National Security and Defence Council. It is telling that the most influential experts on the council staff, such as Anatoliy Grytsenko who worked on the *National Security Concept*, felt it necessary to leave. After publishing his analytical report 'Military Reform in Ukraine: Start or Another False Start?',[138] the Ukrainian Centre for Economic and Political Studies found itself in a cold war with the armed forces. The military were offended by the energy and argumentation of their civilian 'opponents' and their proposals.[139] The confrontation between the generals and the state leadership on the one side and the outside defence experts on the other was hard to hide. In any such confrontation two outcomes are possible: either the truth will be borne out in time, or each side will go its own way ignoring productive cooperation. At the end of the 1990s the latter outcome seemed the more likely.

Other analysts pointed to a sea change in the strength and influence of the council at the end of the decade. Until 1999, it had the National Institute of Strategic Studies under it doing the scientific and analytical work on military reform and other issues. But then the institute was transferred to the presidential administration.

> This means that today the National Security and Defence Council has practically no analytical capacity. It has some people on its staff but they are mostly bureaucrats. They cannot analyse what is going on in the army, the security structures and so on. Practically, the presidential administration controls all the military reform and the security sector in general.[140]

Comparative conclusions

Poland and Hungary, Russia and Ukraine all encountered difficulties in creating truly effective agencies of civilian oversight. In general, the legal establishment of control agencies was accomplished at an early stage. Yet, in practice, civilian oversight has been quite weak. Parliaments, in particular, proved lacklustre. Parliaments may have had the legal right to perform general and budgetary oversight of the defence sector, but for practical and political reasons failed to do so. On the other hand, such as in Hungary, they tended to use their authority over the armed forces in order to micro-manage its affairs – to meddle in details of trifling importance while dealing in a perfunctory way with matters of great consequence. Defence committees, which bore the weightiest responsibility with respect to the discharge of parliamentary oversight, ended up performing an altogether different role – instead of being the avenue through which *civilian* society exercised its voice in defence matters, they tended to act as the *military*'s lobby in the legislature. Parliaments to some extent, especially in Central Europe, exercised control over the implementation of the military budget, and were able to determine how much money was spent in total and (more or less) on what, but at the same time proved utterly unable to judge that monetary inputs were justified by security outputs.

To some extent the reasons for this ineffectiveness were ubiquitous in all the countries in the study. Parliaments lacked sufficient analytical support for their work; they were extremely inexperienced in defence issues; in general, the level of detail in budget submissions was insufficient to allow really sophisticated analysis; and, moreover, many parliamentarians lacked a strong interest in the material. In other words, the accountability of the armed forces to civilian authorities, their openness to public scrutiny, and the ability of political authorities to sanction their behaviour were weak and ineffective in all the states under review, but more so in Russia and Ukraine than in Poland and Hungary. But let us look at the issues raised systematically.

It has been said that one of the main factors influencing whether democracy functioned smoothly or was riddled with conflict in the post-communist states was a state's constitutional form: 'Constitutions with the best outlook for promoting stability provide a clear delineation of authority over cabinet ministers and the primacy of the legislature over the president in the passage of laws.'[141] The same may be said of civil–military relations; indeed, conflict over who should control the military – parliament or president – rather than the desirability of civilian control per se, was the main issue in Poland and Hungary, Russia and Ukraine with the partial exception of Hungary.

In this respect the countries under review represent the full spectrum of possible models from strong parliamentary in Hungary, mixed presidential–parliamentary in Poland, to strong presidential in Russia and Ukraine. In Hungary after the ruling of the Constitutional Court in September 1991 the prominence of the president in the system of civil–military relations was no longer a major issue. In Poland, by contrast, the battle between President Walesa and successive Polish governments was a major issue in civil–military relations giving the military considerable independence from civilian control up until 1996-1997, after which the balance seemed to be tipping in favour of the government. In Russia and Ukraine, however, the overwhelming concentration of authority over the armed forces in the presidency made parliamentary oversight a moot point – irrelevant even. The vertical chain of control from president to armed forces was very strong in both countries. On the other hand, due to the presence of so many military officials in this chain it is hard to see this control as truly 'civilian'. Moreover, the closed nature of this strong form of presidential control of the armed forces was effectively impenetrable by any other societal actors seeking to perform scrutiny of the armed forces.

In an effective system of democratic civil–military relations, civilian authorities – particularly in parliament – need to perform general oversight of defence matters while resisting the temptation to micro-manage the armed forces. With respect to the countries under review, there was again a spectrum of models. Let us look at the extremes.

At one end, in Russia and Ukraine, the system worked very simply: the president appointed a defence minister who was accountable directly to him without interference from parliament. General Yuri Popov (ret.), a prominent independent military expert, testified at an international conference on civil–military relations held in Moscow in 1998 to the 'excessive, almost absolute, concentration of formal political authority over military affairs in the hands of one person – the president of the Russian Federation, whose real activity as commander-in-chief is very weak', and a 'tight curtain of secrecy, as a result of which society has no way of knowing how military–political decisions are made and implemented, while the decisions themselves acquire an anonymous and irresponsible character'.[142] At the other end of the spectrum there was Hungary, where the parliament had very well-founded and extensive authority over the armed forces to the point of micro-management. This situation caused tremendous problems for the army, particularly with regard to the deployment of foreign and national armed forces abroad and at home.

Feaver wrote that, 'Civilian competence, in the general sense, extends even beyond their competence in a particular sense.'[143] By this, he meant to draw attention to the fact that civilians often have great difficulty controlling specialised, technically-sophisticated organisations like the armed forces because they lack deep knowledge of the issues involved. This was a major problem in all of Eastern Europe because civilian authorities tended to lack sources of independent, non-military advice on defence matters. Only Poland took a relatively pro-active approach to increasing the defence expertise of parliamentarians and their civilian staffs, but progress there was glacially slow. The trend in all the parliaments, though perhaps mostly in the Russian Duma, was to rely on a small group of deputies with military backgrounds for discussion of defence matters while the wider membership largely ignored such issues. In this context it is reasonable to ask, who is controlling whom? As Donnelly noted, 'if all advisers to defence policy-makers are military, and policy-makers are ignorant of military realities, then the army, not the government, is controlling defence policy.'[144]

Budgetary oversight is not mere accounting, it is a process of ensuring that military funding complies with national security goals and with other budgetary priorities. In this respect, progress among the countries in the study was mixed. In Poland, opinion was that control of the budget was fairly stringent. In Hungary, on the other hand, judgments on the state of the military budget and the quality of parliamentary oversight suggested it was quite superficial. In Russia and Ukraine, the disaster in state finances generally tended to make parliamentary control of the budget dubious from the beginning. That said, the level of transparency of the defence budget was clearly inadequate in all the countries under review – with the partial exception of Poland. On the other hand, through audit bodies civilian authorities in Poland and Hungary were able to control military spending at least in some limited degree: they knew what they had authorised to be disbursed to the ministry of defence and could control how it was spent in broad categories – sometimes revealing fiscal abuse. But they lacked the expertise to judge whether they were getting good value for money for their defence dollars.

The weaknesses of budgetary oversight in Russia and Ukraine were of a different magnitude. In most countries, the budget is a real funding plan for the nation for the next twelve months. In Russia and Ukraine, on the other hand, the budget throughout the 1990s was more of a statement of *intent* which few people expected the authorities would actually fulfil. In other words, defence budgets were, for the most part, completely fictitious: they did not represent what the military would actually get nor did they explain how funds would actually be spent. The last time the appropriations in the Russian defence budget were fulfilled in real spending was 1993. The situation was fundamentally the same in Ukraine. In short, the abysmal state of the federal budget in general meant that there was not all that much oversight to be done in the defence sector. To a great extent, the ministry of finance became the main enforcer of fiscal discipline in the armed forces in both countries. But this control was similarly opaque to public scrutiny. Indeed, as Sherr noted, 'transparency is simply the ability to measure and see. When People's Deputies fail to challenge the ministry of defence's claim that the defence budget meets 38 per cent of minimal requirements, is this because they endorse the claim or because they have no basis for judgement?'[145] The latter would seem to be indicated.

Stepan wrote that the leadership of the national security councils which serve as fora for high-level discussion of security and defence matters must be civilian: 'The very point is that such a council be democratically controlled by civilians, and that the military participate as advisers to the civilian leadership.'[146] In both Russia and Ukraine national security councils evolved into the most powerful centres of defence decision-making. Conceivably, given that they possessed strengths where other oversight bodies, notably parliament, possessed weaknesses – high level membership, de facto decision-making powers, substantial expert staffs and so on – they could have played a main role in the exercise of civilian oversight. In fact, as was discussed when Andrei Kokoshin took over as secretary of the Security Council there was talk of a kind of 'super, civilian minister of defence' who could control all the security services having been created. In practice, however, the exercise of civilian oversight by national security councils was never a priority. Judging from its membership, the Russian council was hardly a civilian body in the first place. In essence, national security councils served as venues for inter-agency bargaining between the 'power ministries' over resources and missions and for the exercise of the president's authority over the armed forces – not as bodies of civilian control.

Conclusion

The problem of civil–military reform in Eastern Europe was not a matter of preventing direct military intervention in politics; rather it was a problem of how democratically-elected civilians could exercise efficient management, direction and oversight of their armed forces in a way that did not undermine development in other sectors of the polity and economy. Two broad patterns were evident in how civil–military reform progressed in the countries in the study. In Poland and Hungary, there has been a slow, difficult and still incomplete process of adopting new norms of democratic civil–military relations. In March 1999 these countries received recognition of their advances by their admission to NATO. In Ukraine and Russia, by contrast, the transition of the state to *some form* of democratic governance in general, and the transition to *some form* of democratic civil–military relations in particular, has been halting, marked by significant crises and setbacks which still must be resolved.

That said, it is important to recognise that the gap between Russia and Ukraine, on the one hand, and Poland and Hungary on the other, is not so large as to invalidate comparison: as Donnelly noted, '. . . there is not a single Central and East European country which has a civil military relationship which it can consider satisfactory . . .'.[1] In other words, while Poland and Hungary accomplished much in terms of reforming civil–military relations, they also had much left to accomplish at the end of the period under review. Similarly, while Russia and Ukraine made less progress, this is not to say they made *no* progress. In Ukraine, the 1997 *National Security Concept* and the 1999 *State Programme on Armed Forces Reform and Development Until 2005* betrayed a significantly more mature and pro-active approach to solving the problems of the armed forces than had been the case before. In short, contrary to conventional wisdom, there has been some improvement in Ukrainian civil–military relations, albeit tentative and dependent on more general developments in the polity and economy which may still undermine the progress made.

Russia entered the new century with an unreformed military and with civil–military relations in disarray. Just as in many other areas, developments in civil–military relations in the 1990s were shaped more by the logic of disintegration of the old state than by the logic of new state-building. A vicious circle formed. It was hard to expect productive and consistent efforts toward development of stable democratic civil–military relations from a state in a shambles. At the same time, because the military has always occupied a special place in society, it was impossible to create an efficient state without building sound civil–military relations. Russia's shift to a more authoritarian type of government in 1999, and the signs that the new president was more resolved about addressing the problems afflicting the armed forces than was his predecessor, represented an attempt to find an exit from this vicious circle. However, the authoritarian relapse represents only one of many factors of Russian politics. The shape of the new Russian state and of the system of civil–military relations will be determined in the course of intensive struggles, involving major political forces and many citizens; international events will have a great impact, too.

It is also important to recognise that all the states in this study faced fundamentally the same problems in terms of civil–military reform. First, they had to reform their obsolete armed forces, bringing them into line with the new economic and strategic realities of the post-Cold War world. Second, they had to create new bureaucratic structures for their defence establishments in which civilians played the key policy-making roles. Third, they had to strengthen political institutions tasked with oversight of the armed forces. In each of these areas the onus of reform was chiefly on the civilian side of the civil–military equation. That is to say, it was not so much a problem of changing the attitudes and behaviour of the military towards civilian and political society as it was a problem of changing the attitudes of civilian and political society towards the military. Put differently, it was incumbent on civilians to actually empower themselves to perform civilian control of the military. Civilian authorities had to take responsibility for military policy decisions. They had to actively participate in the formulation of defence policy and monitor its implementation. And they had to learn to provide substantial and detailed oversight of the military through various legally-constituted bodies of civilian control. Let us look at the key issues raised.

Reforming the armed forces in Eastern Europe was a major undertaking, which was by no means complete by the end of the 1990s. Though it is fair to say that the former Soviet Union states accomplished *less* reform than those in Central Europe, the main accomplishment of Poland and Hungary was more in avoiding the extreme examples of degradation in the armed forces that plagued Russia and Ukraine than in actualising a profound change in their armies to a new level of effectiveness. In other words, they avoided a negative result more than they achieved a positive one. By the time of their accession to NATO there is little doubt that Poland and Hungary were democratic states and their problems of civil–military relations were of a democratic nature.[2] Although problems remained in both countries – for example, in the continuing division of the Hungarian general staff and ministry of defence – the centre of gravity of defence policy-making had shifted to the civilian political realm. The *quality* of defence policy could be questioned but not, for the most part, the legitimacy of the way in which it was formulated.

The same cannot be said of Russia and Ukraine. In both countries the quality of their defence policy products was not the *main* question; rather, it was the quality of the democratic functioning of the state in general. In some cases, notably the 1997 Ukrainian policy statements *National Security Concept* and the *State Programme on Armed Forces Reform and Development Until 2005*, the sophistication of policy was high. What was lacking was evidence of strong civilian direction of the formulation of these policies outside of the narrow and non-transparent confines of the presidential administrations.

Civilianising the bureaucracy of the defence establishment in all the countries being studied proved to be a gravely difficult task. In Poland and Hungary as of late 1999 the process of integration had only just begun. The skill gap between military and civilian officials was quite apparent and may, indeed, have been growing as military officers acquired more and more expertise through contact with NATO, while their civilian counterparts had much less access to training opportunities at home and abroad. There were few civilians in the Russian and Ukrainian defence establishments at the end of the 1990s, little indication that more were likely to be introduced, and very few facilities existed for the education of civilian specialists in defence. Among the rank and file of both ministries the relatively large size of the civilian side of the defence establishment belied the negligible impact of civilian employees on decision-making. In fact, a substantial portion of civilian employees were simply retired military personnel supplementing a pension.

The Central European states had somewhat more success than the former Soviet Union states, but their problems were by no means solved. Moving to a civilian minister of defence in Poland and Hungary was not simply a matter of declaration; it was a difficult process that took nearly ten years to complete. Neither was it a straightforward process, as both countries experienced a period of re-militarisation. Crucially, we saw that for civilianisation at the top level of the ministry of defence to succeed, it required the support of both president and parliament to enact the proper legislation and to avoid undermining the authority of the minister vis-à-vis his military advisers. Equally important, it was incumbent on new civilian ministers of defence to be pro-active and actually *lead* their departments.

In general, in all four states, with the partial exception of Hungary, military contestation of civilian policy was fostered by the wider disagreement among civilian political elites over whether parliament or president would dominate in the political system. This was a very serious issue in the former Soviet Union states – where presidential dominance of the political system effectively excluded other societal agents from the system of civilian control – though it was also an issue in Poland until approximately 1996-1997.

Parliamentary control of the armed forces was especially lacklustre. In general, parliaments lacked sufficient analytical support for their work; they were extremely inexperienced in defence issues; the level of detail in budget submissions was insufficient to allow really sophisticated analysis; and moreover, many parliamentarians lacked a strong interest in the material. In other words, the accountability of the armed forces to civilian authorities, their openness to public scrutiny, and the ability of political authorities to sanction their behaviour was weak and ineffective in all four states, but more so in Russia and Ukraine than in Poland and Hungary.

The study suggests two distinctive trends or modalities of civil–military reform. In Central Europe, there was a strong tendency amongst reformers to try and simply adopt the forms of democratic civil–military relations without seeking to understand the logic behind them: reforms were designed without understanding, and they were implemented because NATO required them, not because they were seen as intrinsically necessary. The result was a process of imperfect copying of liberal-democratic norms of civil–military relations which resulted in systems of civil–military relations that were liberal-democratic in form but idiosyncratic and sui generis in practice. In the former Soviet Union there was a different trend of increasing centralisation of authority over the armed forces in the hands of the executive. Particularly in Russia, the need to build democratic civil–military relations was derided as Western patronising and meddling by many in military circles; while in a time of profound budgetary crisis the armed forces were left to fend for themselves absent any effective civilian scrutiny or interference except that exercised infrequently by the head of state in his capacity as commander-in-chief. The result was the systematic denial of any role in civilian oversight of the armed forces of all political and societal actors excepting the president and his administration.

This dichotomy dovetails with the 'insider' and 'outsider' status of the countries under review.[3] On the one hand, Poland and Hungary (as 'insiders') saw entering NATO as integral to a broader return to the 'European fold' and their comparatively successful transformations were supported by the expansion of NATO and the prospect of inclusion in the European Union. On the other hand, Russia and Ukraine (as 'outsiders') seemed to be growing more and more distant from the 'New Europe' by the end of the 1990s. The profound impact of NATO on civil–military reform in the countries in the study had positive and negative consequences. On the positive side, NATO offered examples of good practice as well as advice and assistance at a crucial time. Whether or not their political and military elites internalised the reasons for reform, working toward NATO membership acted as a powerful motivator for Poland and Hungary to undertake certain normative changes in their systems of civil–military relations. To some extent, the impact of NATO on reform planning in Ukraine was also growing toward the end of the 1990s. In Russia, however, the impact of NATO was quite negative – indeed, the Russian politico–military approach to the Alliance obstructed a major restructuring of the armed forces away from a Cold War, preparation-for-war-with-NATO paradigm.[4] As an 'outsider' looking in, Russia viewed NATO with distrust. The still unresolved puzzle for Western policy-makers, and for reformers in Russia, has been how to overcome this distrust.

In the Central European states after the collapse of the Warsaw Pact neither the political nor military elites had much experience with strategic issues. As a result of the backlash of these new elites against anything smacking of the old ways, their strategies came to be largely inspired by Western ideas. This is in contrast to the former Soviet Union states which had much more experience in strategic thinking and had less desire to adopt Western ideas in preference to their own, homegrown military traditions. In short, political and military elites in Warsaw and Budapest were much more inclined to adopt new norms of behaviour from NATO than those in Moscow.

It must also be recognised, however, that for most of the 1990s NATO membership was understood by Poland and Hungary as an end in itself rather than as a means to an end. Their military and political elites expected – and most likely would have welcomed – NATO solving their problems for them. It took most of the 1990s for them to get over this expectation and begin to design their own solutions. Ukraine too showed this desire at times for NATO to simply tell them what they should be doing. Moreover, the Partnership for Peace programme was, in some respects, detrimental to the development of democratic civil–military relations in Central Europe. It focused on military to military contacts between member and aspirant states and on providing training opportunities for military officers, thus highlighting and helping to deepen the skill gap between military and civilian officials in the defence establishment which has been such a problem.

Despite repeated statements that one of the government's priorities was military reform, the Russian military at the end of the 1990s was essentially a poor, shrunken, and angry version of the Soviet Army. It was not at all clear that Russia's military leadership had learned much from ten years of transition: they were still resistant to looking at their defence needs and potentials from a first-principles perspective, let alone adopting Western behavioural norms they saw as patronising and ill-suited to Russian conditions; they preferred, it seemed, to continue trying to preserve – or restore – the Soviet military system in a reduced form. Fundamentally, civil–military relations reform could not be effected if elites did not want it to be. In Russia especially, it appears that neither military nor civilian elites were particularly committed to building a liberal-democratic civil–military relations regime. In the hostile political atmosphere which characterised the 1990s it proved preferable for presidents – as the main stake-holders in civilian control – to have a partisan military – provided it was partisan in their favour. For military elites similarly, it was preferable to build personal relationships with the president as that was seen as a more effective means of protecting the military budget.

In the end, the crises in the armed forces reflected the crises of society at large. At a time of massive economic distress making substantial reforms in the armed forces was very difficult. Similarly, where the political system was characterised by deep conflict between civilian political actors achieving a broad consensus on the desirability and direction of civil–military reform was nearly impossible. On the economic side, improvements came earlier in Central Europe than in the former Soviet Union states. On the political side, Poland did not see a major change until the passage of the 1997 Constitution which drastically curtailed the prerogatives of the president in the sphere of civilian control of the military. In Ukraine and Russia the need to reform was both more acute than in Poland and Hungary and delayed for longer. Only at the end of the 1990s were there signs of real steps to halt and reverse the ten-year decline of the armed forces, but even those signs were equivocal. It seems significant, however, that these signs of progress appeared only when there emerged signs of improvement in the economy. This would accord with the experience of Central Europe where economic improvements by the mid-1990s began to permit some modest steps to redressing the material decline of the armed forces. Nonetheless, the major sources of doubt about future developments in civil–military relations in Russia and Ukraine stem mainly from the still uncertain political environment and the dubious commitment of their political elites to the rules of a democratic game.

On a more methodological point, it is worthwhile pointing out the salience of interviews as a research technique in the area of civil–military relations. There is much written material available to the researcher in this area; legislation on defence is published and often translated into English, structures of the ministry of defence are quite often laid out in official publications, doctrines and concepts are usually also available. The problem in all the states in the study is the gap between the rhetoric about the way things are supposed to work – the formal system – and the way things actually work – the informal system. Interviews with people in the system or local experts with considerable experience in the area is effectively the only way for the researcher to figure out the underlying dynamic of the national system of civil–military relations.[5]

A new direction for civil–military relations research and theory

Traditionally, the study of civil–military relations has been a study of dichotomies: civilian vs. military; general oversight vs. micro-management of the armed forces; policy-makers vs. policy-implementers; Huntington's 'professionalism' model vs. Janowitz' sociological one; and so on. These dichotomies are all, to a large extent, false and misleading both in the post-communist context of the Poland and Hungary, Russia and Ukraine and, perhaps, in a more general context as well.

What sort of questions of civil–military relations are being asked in the democratic states nowadays? In many, the status of homosexuals in the military has excited an occasionally acrimonious debate between civilian and military authorities, as has the integration of women in combat units. The question of how civil–military relations may be optimised in peacekeeping operations is also a main problem which raises the issue of *who* is in control. In Canada and the UK, for example, the departments of foreign affairs are becoming the prime-users of the military and they are starting to affect what kinds of capabilities the forces build. This occurs below the level of parliamentary oversight and is increasingly formalised as policy advisers from foreign ministries are attached at lower and lower levels (brigade, national contingent, and even battalion). There are, moreover, serious questions, especially in the United States, as to whether senior military figures have usurped too much authority over military–political decisions. Nonetheless, for the most part the main concern in civil–military relations is over how far the armed forces need to reflect the society they serve, not over how the armed forces need to be controlled.

Indeed, the issue of civilian *control* of the military is looking increasingly anachronistic in the democratic states. The need for effective civilian control in the West nowadays is understood mostly in terms of preventing (largely fiscal) irresponsibility and avoiding the evils of bureaucracy, not for preventing military takeovers. Yet if, as Douglas Bland has argued, the modern problems of democratic civil–military relations are those confronting societies in which the political power of the military has effectively been curbed,[6] then what makes the control and management of the defence establishment any different from other sectors of state activity where the prevention of fiscal irresponsibility, avoiding the evils of bureaucracy, and obtaining good value for money are also germane? Increasingly little, it seems.

This, combined with the shift in focus from questions of control to questions of management and effectiveness suggests that civil–military relations theorists should be looking less to the fields of political science and sociology and more to the field (or sub-field) of public administration for theoretical insights. As a start, it is useful to look at the two main approaches to the study of any public policy: the political and the managerial. The former is concerned with questions of accountability and the control of policy. The latter approach emphasises more the rules for the effective organisation of action. The two approaches meet in that they are both concerned with the structure of formal authority, but otherwise they cover different ground. Extant theory has tended to focus on the control of policy while ignoring the mechanics of administration. The present study suggests there are good grounds for shifting the analytical focus of civil–military relations research to a managerial approach and a concentration on the civilian side of the civil–military spectrum.

In this respect, applying the sort of scheme outlined below used by scholars of public administration for evaluating the effectiveness of public bodies begets useful insights. Any effective public organisation possesses: effective outside political control; flexible organisation; good leadership and management; internal delegation of responsibilities; meritocratic personnel management; internal cooperation; continuous review and research into objectives, methods and results; a professional morale antipathetic to bureaucratic methods; effective publicity; and widespread public understanding through interest, criticism and control.[7] Under such a scheme applied to civil–military relations, outside political control remains a primary criterion but, rather than being the sine qua non of civil–military relations, it is only one of a number of areas of concern.

Essentially, this has been the main thrust of this book. In the states discussed here, each of the above noted points was a problem. More often than not, Central and East European armies based on the Soviet model were inflexible and resistant to organisational change. Similarly, the delegation of tasks from higher levels to lower ones did not work well because of an institutional culture of avoiding responsibility for decisions. The practice of avoiding culpability for failure by continuously seeking further clarification for each decision was endemic. Internal cooperation was stymied by formal and informal divisions between general staffs and ministries of defence. Systems of meritocratic promotion were a fair way off due to an enduring norm of senior officers acquiring protegés and advancing their interests. Strategic planning and review was very much a new and unfamiliar activity for armies accustomed to receiving directives in minute detail from the general staff in Moscow. And public understanding and respect for the military was at a low ebb in many of the post-communist states, signalling, inter alia, a dismal record of public relations.

The aim of a new model of civil–military relations should not be to overturn Clausewitz' dictum 'War is nothing but a continuation of political intercourse, with a mixture of other means.'[8] In other words, a rejection of the extant theoretical edifice of civil–military relations is not required. In the current context the military takeover seems no longer a main concern, but that does not mean the threat is entirely gone. The experience of Poland and Hungary, Russia and Ukraine would indicate, however, a necessity to modify the traditional paradigm of civil–military conflict to a paradigm of *civil–military integration*. Whereas extant theory directs our attention to how the armed forces and politicians can be kept at arm's length from each other, the issues in Central and Eastern Europe have been about how soldiers and civilians can work together to achieve the highest 'value for money' in planning the security and defence of their countries. Essentially, this is a problem of effective public administration, not of civilian control per se.

Notes

Introduction

1 For the sake of convenience, in this work the term Eastern European states is used when referring to all the states in the work; Central European states when referring to Poland and Hungary; and, former Soviet Union states when referring to Russia and Ukraine.

2 Where necessary for explanatory purposes or in order to demonstrate particular trends, events prior to July 1991 and after March 1999 will be discussed. In general, however, every effort will be made to focus on the time period noted.

3 Christopher Donnelly, 'Defence Transformation in the New Democracies: A Framework for Tackling the Problem', *NATO Review*, Vol. 45, No. 1 (January 1997), pp. 3–7.

4 These terms are taken from John Löwenhardt, Margot Light and Stephen White's research project entitled *The Outsiders: Russia, Ukraine, Belarus, Moldova and the New Europe* (project grant L213252007) which is part of the ESRC's 'One Europe or Several' Programme.

5 NATO and the European Union were not the only significant external actors for the Russian Federation. India, China, other former Soviet republics, and old Soviet partners in the Middle East such as Iran and Iraq also impacted on their policy outlook. For reasons of brevity and clarity, however, the book looks only at the Russia–NATO axis.

6 For an elaboration of the role of the armed forces in the collapse of the communist regimes in the non-Soviet Warsaw Pact countries, see Zoltan Barany, 'East European Armed Forces in Transitions and Beyond', *East European Quarterly*, Vol. 26, No. 1 (Spring 1992), pp. 1–30.

7 These included mainly the air forces under Marshal Shaposhnikov and the airborne forces under General Grachev. See: John W. Leppingwell, 'Soviet Civil-Military Relations and the August Coup' *World Politics* (July 1992), pp. 539–572.

8 Guillermo O'Donnell, Philippe Schmitter and Lawrence Whitehead, *Transitions from Authoritarian Rule: Prospects for Democracy*, Baltimore, MD: Johns Hopkins University Press, 1986, passim.

9 Donnelly, 'Defence Transformation . . .'

10 Timothy Garton Ash referred to it as 'Refolution'; a term which was meant to refer to a process of political, economic and social changes that combines elements of structural reform and revolution. In essence, this means that the new regime did not totally destroy the old system; rather, it is based on the old system – both in terms of structure and personnel. See: Timothy Garton Ash, 'Refolution: The Springtime of Two Nations', *New York Review of Books*, 15 June 1989, pp. 3–10.

11 Jon Elster, Claus Offe and Ulrich K. Preuss, *Institutional Design in Post-Communist Societies: Building the Ship at Sea*, Cambridge, UK: Cambridge University Press, 1998, pp. 7–8.

12 Zoltan Barany, *Soldiers and Politics in Eastern Europe, 1945–1990: The Case of Hungary*, New York, NY: St. Martin's Press, 1993, p. 147.
13 Dale Herspring, '"Refolution" in Eastern Europe: The Polish, Czech, Slovak and Hungarian Militaries' *European Security*, Vol. 3, No. 4 (Winter 1994), pp. 664–690 (esp. note 6); and, Andrew A. Michta, *The Soldier-Citizen: The Politics of the Polish Army After Communism*, New York, NY: St. Martin's Press, 1997, p. 82.
14 Throughout the work, for the sake of convenience, the term 'general staff' is used although national practice may be to refer to the institution by another term, such as 'defence staff'. Unless otherwise indicated, the term refers to the general staff of the armed forces as a whole, not to service staffs such as the army, in particular. Similarly, 'chief of general staff' is used generally though national practice might be to have a different title, such as 'chief of defence staff'.
15 James Sherr, 'Civil-democratic Control of Ukraine's Armed Forces: To What End? By What Means?', in David Betz and John Löwenhardt (eds.), *Army and State in Post-Communist Europe*, London and Portland, OR: Frank Cass, 2001, p. 65.
16 Christopher Donnelly, 'Civil-Military Relations in the New Democracies', in Betz and Löwenhardt (eds), *Army and State . . .*, p. 9.

1 Approaches to civil–military relations

1 Daniel Nelson, 'Civil Armies, Civil Societies and NATO's Enlargement', *Armed Forces and Society*, Vol. 25, No. 1 (Fall 1998), p. 137.
2 Samuel Finer, *The Man on Horseback: The Role of the Military in Politics*, 2nd Edition, Harmondsworth, Middlesex: Penguin Books, 1976, p. 4. 3rd Edition, Boulder, CO: Westview Press, 1988.
3 Sun Tzu (Thomas Cleary trans.), *The Art of War*, Boston, MA: Shambhala Publications, 1998, p. 78.
4 Ibid., p. 114. Imperial Chinese civil–military relations broadly approximated the liberal model of civilian control: 'rule by the pen [the civilian bureaucracy] rather than the sword formed the ideal, if not always the reality of Confucian political reality'. See Claude E. Welch, 'Civil-Military Relations: Perspectives From the Third World', *Armed Forces and Society*, Vol. 11, No. 2 (Winter 1985), p. 186.
5 Niccolo Machiavelli (W.K. Marriott trans.), *The Prince*, London: E.P. Dutton and Co., 1920, p. 97.
6 Carl von Clausewitz, *On War*, Middlesex: Penguin Books, 1968, p. 402.
7 Ibid. Clausewitz also wrote: 'If in the next place, we keep once more to the pure conception of War, then we must say that the political object lies out of its province . . .' (ibid., pp. 122–123).
8 Ibid., p. 405
9 Samuel Huntington, *The Soldier and the State: The Theory and Politics of Civil-Military Relations*, Cambridge, MA: Harvard University Press, 1957, p. 56.
10 Ibid., p. 84.
11 Ibid., p. 83.
12 Ibid.
13 Ibid., pp. 83–85. Some analysts of Soviet civil–military relations would have strongly disagreed with Huntington on this point. Timothy Colton argued quite the opposite: 'On balance, the Main Political Administration [of the Soviet army] has probably made a positive contribution to military efficiency.' See, Colton, 'A Participatory Model', in Dale R. Herspring and Ivan Volgyes, eds, *Civil-Military Relations in Communist Systems*, Boulder, CO: Westview Press, 1978, p. 59.
14 Morris Janowitz, *The Professional Soldier: A Social and Political Portrait*, Glencoe, IL: The Free Press of Glencoe, 1960, p. 418.
15 Specifically, he points to three 'major devices' of control: civilian budgetary control, civilian discretion on the allocation of military roles and responsibilities, and the

provision of independent (non-military) advice to the executive on security aspects of international relations. Ibid., pp. 363–366.

16 Ibid., p. 440.

17 Rebecca L. Schiff, 'Civil-Military Relations Reconsidered: A Theory of Concordance', *Armed Forces and Society*, Vol. 22, No. 1 (Fall 1995), pp. 7–24. Schiff argued that: 'under certain cultural conditions, civilian institutions or the very idea of 'civil' may be inappropriate. Therefore, the specific type of civil-military relationship adopted is less important than the ability of the three partners [military, political elite and society] involved to agree on four indicators: the social composition of the officer corps, the political decision-making process, recruitment method and military style.' (pp. 7–8)

18 William E. Odom, 'The Party-Military Connection: A Critique', in Dale R. Herspring and Ivan Volgyes (eds), *Civil-Military Relations in Communist Systems*, Boulder, CO: Westview Press, 1978, pp. 35.

19 Finer, *The Man on Horseback*, pp. 22–23. He quotes as an example General MacArthur who said in 1952: 'I find in existence a new and heretofore unknown and dangerous concept that the members of our armed forces owe primary allegiance or loyalty to those who temporarily exercise the authority of the Executive Branch of Government rather than to the country and its constitution which they are sworn to defend.' (p. 23.)

20 Ibid., pp. 23–24.

21 Ibid., pp. 23–24.

22 Alfred Stepan, *Rethinking Military Politics: Brazil and the Southern Cone*, Princeton, NJ: Princeton University Publishers, 1988, p. 3.

23 Ibid., p. 3.

24 Ibid., p. 4.

25 Ibid., pp. 128–129.

26 Ibid., pp. 129–130.

27 Ibid., p. 133.

28 Ibid.

29 Ibid., pp. 137–138.

30 Ibid., p. 139.

31 Ibid., p. 141

32 A.J. Bacevich, 'Tradition Abandoned: America's Military in a New Era', *National Interest 48*, (Summer 1997), p. 17.

33 *OSCE Code of Conduct on Politico-Military Aspects of Security*, Chapter VII, Paras. 20–23.

34 *Study on NATO Enlargement*, (Brussels: NATO Integrated Data Service, September 1995), Chapter 5, Parts A-D, Sections 68–78.

35 Ibid., Chapter 5, Part B, Section 72.

36 Donnelly, 'Defence Transformation . . .'

37 Marco Carnovale, 'NATO Partners and Allies: Civil-Military Relations and Democratic Control of the Armed Forces,' *NATO Review* (March 1997), pp. 32–35.

38 Donnelly, 'Defence Transformation . . .'

39 Carnovale, p. 33.

40 Ibid., p. 33.

41 Donnelly, 'Defence Transformation . . .'

42 Peter D. Feaver, 'The Civil-Military Problematique: Huntington, Janowitz and the Question of Civilian Control', *Armed Forces and Society*, Vol. 23, No. 2 (Winter 1996), pp. 149–178.

43 Douglas Bland, 'A Unified Theory of Civil-Military Relations', *Armed Forces and Society*, Vol. 26, No. 1 (Fall 1999), pp. 7–26; Bland, 'Managing the 'Expert Problem' in Civil-Military Relations', *European Security*, Vol. 8, No. 3 (Autumn 1999), pp. 25–43; and, Bland, 'Discovering Westminster: The Transformation of Civil-Military Relations in Central Europe', in D. Haglund, S. McFarland, and J. Sokolski, eds, *NATO's Eastern Dilemmas*, Boulder, CO: Westview Press, 1994.

44 Nelson, 'Civil Armies, Civil Societies . . .'
45 Feaver, p. 152.
46 Ibid., p. 152.
47 Ibid., p. 152.
48 Ibid., p. 154.
49 Bland, 'A Unified Theory . . .', p. 13.
50 Ibid., p. 13.
51 Ibid., p. 13.
52 Ibid., p. 9.
53 Ibid., p. 10.
54 Bland, 'Managing the 'Expert Problem . . .' p. 25. In fact, the 'expert problem' in civil-military relations was a notion of Huntington (*The Soldier and the State*, p. 20) which Bland developed further.
55 Ibid., p. 38.
56 Nelson., 'Civil Armies . . .', p. 143.
57 Ibid., p. 143.
58 Ibid., pp. 9–10.
59 Donnelly, 'Defence Transformation . . .'
60 Richard H. Kohn, 'How Democracies Control the Military', *The Journal of Democracy*, Vol. 8, No. 4 (October 1997), p. 141.
61 Ibid., p. 143.
62 Janowitz, pp. 363–366.
63 Chris Donnelly, 'Defence transformation . . .'
64 Bland, 'Managing the "Expert Problem" . . .', p. 40.
65 Bland, 'A Unified Theory . . .', p. 20.
66 Donnelly, 'Defence Transformation . . .'
67 Interview with a chief specialist in the Directorate of International Military Cooperation, Ministry of Defence, Ottawa, Canada, March 1998, and Moscow, January 1999.
68 A plausible explanation for this might be the very different experiences of Russians, as opposed to Central Europeans, in the Warsaw Pact. The non-Soviet former Warsaw Pact countries were accustomed to receiving political directives from abroad which were expected to be implemented without question. Russians were not similarly accustomed. On the contrary, they were conditioned to the reverse: issuing directives
69 Kohn, 'How Democracies Control . . .' p. 144.
70 Donnelly, 'Defence Transformation . . .'

2 Security policy-making and defence reform

1 Christopher Donnelly, 'Defence Transformation in the New Democracies', *NATO Review*, Vol. 45, No. 1 (January 1997).
2 Steven Meyer, 'Decision-making in Defence: The Soviet Case', in Carl G. Jacobsen (ed.), *Strategic Power USA/USSR*, London: Macmillan Press, 1990, p. 254.
3 Ibid., p. 251.
4 Gerald Snel, *From the Atlantic to the Urals: The Reorientation of Soviet Military Strategy, 1981–1990*, Amsterdam, Netherlands: VU University Press, 1996, p. 119.
5 Ibid., pp. 118–119.
6 Ibid., p. 120.
7 See Carl G. Jacobsen (ed.), *The Soviet Defence Enigma: Estimating Costs and Burden*, London: Oxford University Press, 1987.
8 Sebestyen Gorka, 'Hungarian Military Reform And Peacekeeping Efforts', *NATO Review*, Vol. 43, No. 6 (November 1995).
9 James Sherr, 'Civil-democratic Control of Ukraine's Armed Forces: To What End?

By What Means?', in David Betz and John Löwenhardt (eds), *Army and State in Post-Communist Europe*, London and Portland, OR: Frank Cass, 2001, p. 69.

10 Ben Lombardi, 'An Overview of Civil-Military Relations in Central and Eastern Europe', *Journal of Slavic Military Studies*, Vol. 12, No. 1 (March 1999), p. 18.

11 Ivan Volgyes, 'Military Politics of the Warsaw Pact Armies', in Morris Janowitz (ed.), *Civil-Military Relations: Regional Perspectives*, London: Sage Publications, 1981, pp. 211–212.

12 Ivan Volgyes, 'Hungary: Problematical Performer', in Volgyes (ed.), *The Political Reliability of the Warsaw Pact Armies: The Southern Tier*, Durham, NC: Duke University Press, 1982, pp. 60–86.

13 Zoltan D. Barany, *Soldiers and Politics in Eastern Europe, 1945–1990: The Case of Hungary*, New York, NY: St. Martin's Press, 1993, pp. 129–130 and 152–153.

14 Keith Crane, Steven Popper and Barbara Kliszewski, *Civil-Military Relations in a Multiparty Democracy*, Santa Monica, CA: RAND Corporation, R-3941-RC, 1990, p. 47.

15 A. Ross Johnson, Robert W. Dean and Alexander Alexiev, *East European Military Establishments: The Warsaw Pact Northern Tier*, New York, NY: Crane, Russak, 1980, pp. 23–32.

16 Stefan Sarvas, 'Professional Soldiers and Politics: A Case of Central and Eastern Europe', *Armed Forces and Society*, Vol. 26, No. 1 (Fall 1999), p. 103.

17 Interview with LTC Andras Ujj, Deputy Director, Institute for Strategic and Defence Studies, National Defence University, Budapest, 1 December 1999.

18 This brief history of the early Polish reform debate owes much to an interview with BGEN Stanislaw Koziej, Director, Defence System Department, Ministry of Defence, Warsaw, 20 June 2000.

19 Interview with Jerzy Milewski in *Polityk*, No. 25 (24 June 1995), cited by Agnieszka Gogolewska in *The Restructuring of Civil-Military Relations in Poland, Ukraine and Russia – A Comparative Study*, 20 June 1998, NATO Fellowship Report, pp. 64–65.

20 Koziej interview, Warsaw, 20 June 2000; Interview with COL Waldemar Czarnecki, Head, Force Policy Division, Strategic Planning Directorate, General Staff of the Polish Armed Forces, Warsaw, 19 June 2000; Interview with COL Stefan Czmur, Senior Expert, Force Policy Division, Strategic Planning Directorate, General Staff of the Polish Armed Forces, Warsaw, 19 June 2000.

21 *The Military Balance 1992–1993*, London: Brassey's for the International Institute of Strategic Studies, p. 80, and *The Military Balance 1995–1996*, p. 92.

22 Interview with LCOL Wladyslaw Staron, Main Military Expert, National Security Bureau, Office of the President, Department of the President's Supervisory of the Armed Forces, Warsaw, 12 June 2000.

23 From an address to the Sejm on security issues by Foreign Minister Krzysztof Skubiszewski, Warsaw Domestic Service, in Polish, 0833 GMT, FBIS-EEU-91-032, 14 February 1991.

24 *RFE/RL Research Report*, 15 February 1991, p. 49.

25 Interview with Krystian Piatkowski, Director for International Cooperation, Polish Chamber of National Defence Manufacturers, Warsaw, 14 June 2000.

26 Interview with COL Kysztof Osinski, Deputy Director, NATO Integration Department, Ministry of Defence, Warsaw, 13 June 2000.

27 Parliamentary Resolution 11/1993. 'Basic Principles of the Security Policy of the Republic of Hungary', *European Security*, Vol. 3, No. 2 (Summer 1994), pp. 352–358; 'The Basic Principles of National Defence of the Republic of Hungary', Budapest: Ministry of Foreign Affairs, Fact Sheets on Hungary No. 9, 1993.

28 Rudolf Joo discusses the goals of Hungarian defence reform in the changed geopolitical context of the early 1990s in *The Democratic Control of Armed Forces: The Experience of Hungary*, Paris: Institute for Security Studies, Western European Union, Chaillot Paper 23, February 1996, p. 37.

29 Zoltan Szenes, 'The Implications of NATO Expansion for Civil-military Relations in Hungary', Betz and Löwenhardt (eds), *Army and State* . . . , p. 83.
30 Interview with LTC Laszlo Szabo, (1) Head of Planning Section, Defence Policy Department, Ministry of Defence, Budapest, 2 December 1999.
31 Ibid.
32 This episode is covered by Zoltan Pecze in *Civil-Military Relations in Hungary 1989–1996*, Groningen, Netherlands: Centre for European Security Studies, Harmonie Paper 2, 1998, pp. 24–26.
33 Signing the *Partnership for Peace Framework Document* is the first step in joining the partnership. By signing the document countries reiterate their commitment to specific democratic norms of behaviour both in international relations and in respect to their system of defence management.
34 *The NATO Handbook*, 50th Anniversary Edition, Brussels, Belgium: NATO, Office of Information and Press, 1998–1999, p. 87.
35 Ujj interview, Budapest, 1 December 1999.
36 Staron interview, Warsaw, 12 June 2000; Interview with Slawomir Kaminski. Main Civilian Expert, National Security Bureau, Office of the President, Department of the President's Supervisory of the Armed Forces, Warsaw, 12 June 2000.
37 Ibid.
38 Interview with Professor Janos Matus. Head, Department of Security Studies, Miklos Zrinyi National Defence University, Budapest, 30 November 1999.
39 The 'right answer culture' will be familiar to any researcher who has spent a day being briefed at the ministry of defence or ministry of foreign affairs being told one thing only that evening to be told over a glass of vodka (more likely, several) something quite different by the same people.
40 Chris Donnelly, 'Civil-Military Relations in the New Democracies', in Betz and Löwenhardt (eds), *Army and State* . . . , p. 8.
41 Szabo (1) interview, Budapest, 2 December 1999.
42 Quoted in Dale Herspring, 'Civil-Military Relations in Post-Communist Poland: Problems in the Transition to a Democratic Polity', *Communist and Post-Communist Studies*, Vol. 33, No. 1 (March 2000), p. 71.
43 See the *Military Balance 1995–1996*, p. 73. The Stockholm Institute for Peace Research (SIPRI) gives a somewhat different budget estimate. They show 1993 as the first year in which defence spending rose to US$2.77 billion, followed by a decline in 1994 to US$2.67 billion. Sustained budgetary increases, however, began in 1995. Data is from the SIPRI military expenditure database: http://projects.sipri.org/milex/mex_database1.html (accessed 25 November 2003).
44 Henry Plater-Zyberk looks at Polish defence reform up to 1998, including a detailed consideration of *Armiia 2012*, in *Poland's Defence and Security: The Same Priorities, Different Approaches*, Sandhurst, UK: Conflict Studies Research Centre, Royal Military Academy, May 1998.
45 Breffni O'Rourke, 'NATO: New Members Had Military, Political Terms To Meet', *RFE/RL Research Report*, 12 March 1999.
46 This matter is discussed in some detail in *Report on Poland's Integration with NATO*, Warsaw, Ministry of Defence, 1998.
47 From an interview with Jerzy Szmajdzinski, Deputy Head of the Parliamentary Defence Affairs Committee and Romuald Szeremietiew, Secretary of State in the Defence Ministry, TV Polonia satellite service, Warsaw, in Polish, 0400 GMT, 17 August 1999, BBC Monitoring European – Political, London, 18 August 1999. See also, 'Army Fails to Provide Basic Needs for Servicemen – Audit Body', Polish Radio 1, Warsaw, BBC Monitoring International Reports, as provided by BBC Worldwide Monitoring, 15 March 1999.
48 Osinski interview, Warsaw, 13 June 2000.
49 SIPRI military expenditure database: http://projects.sipri.org/milex/mex_database1.html (accessed 25 November 2003).

50 This problem is widely misunderstood both in the West and the post-communist states. James Sherr wrote: 'The beginning of wisdom is to recognise that the principal problem is not resources – a constraint unlikely to change very soon – but the mismatch between resources and the force structure established.' See Sherr's chapter on Hungary in Harald von Riekhoff and Natalie Mychajlyszyn (eds), *Report on Specific Problems of Civil-Military Relations in the Czech Republic, Poland and Hungary*, Ottawa, Canada: Carleton University for the Department of National Defence, 1999, p. 84.
51 Figures are calculated on the basis of data from a table in *The Military Balance 1997–1998*, p. 37. Personnel costs were not broken down by categories: salaries, pensions and allowances. Polish figures for 1999–2000, however, show pensions and allowances accounting for 45 per cent of total personnel costs. See, *Basic Information on the MoND Budget for 2000*, Warsaw, Ministry of National Defence, Budget Department, 2000, pp. 13–14.
52 Bruce Jackson from the Lockheed-Martin aerospace company quoted in Jorgen Dragsdahl, 'NATO Resists Pressures to Militarise Central Europe', *BASIC Paper* 28 (July 1998).
53 Interview with an official of the Budget Department, Ministry of National Defence, Warsaw, 13 June 2000; Interview with a member of the Section for Cooperation with NATO, Ministry of National Defence, Warsaw, 13 June 2000.
54 Both an excerpt of the SACEUR report and a summary of the procurement plan are found in J. Dragsdahl, 'NATO Resists . . .'
55 Quoted in O'Rourke, 'NATO: New Members Had Military . . .'.
56 Ibid.
57 *The Military Balance 1995–1996* shows an increase in spending from 1994 to 1995 (p. 87). The SIPRI military expenditure database shows only a slowing of decline. Both agree that spending began to rise in 1998.
58 Figures are calculated on the basis of data from a table in *The Military Balance 1997–1998*, p. 37.
59 Interview with BGEN Zoltan Szenes, Deputy Chief (ACOS LOG), NATO HQ AFSOUTH, Glasgow, 20 March 2000.
60 'NATO Papers Belie Modest Expansion Cost', *Defense News* 8–14 (December 1997).
61 Institute for Strategic and Defence Studies, *The First Decade of the Independent Hungarian Security Policy 1989–1999*, Budapest: October 1999, p. 84.
62 Matus interview, Budapest, 30 November 1999.
63 Ujj interview, Budapest, 1 December 1999.
64 Parliamentary resolution 88/1995 (VII.6), cited in *The First Decade of the Independent Hungarian Security Policy*, p. 72.
65 Ibid., p. 74. Figures from the *Military Balance* for the same period are slightly different (presumably due to different ways of categorising personnel) but show roughly the same 45 per cent decline over four years.
66 Szabo 1 interview, Budapest, 2 December 1999.
67 *The Guardian*, 7 July 1997, gave an especially harsh assessment of the military fitness of the prospective members.
68 Ujj interview, Budapest, 1 December 1999.
69 Interview with Dr Kzysztof Jazwinski, Director, National Security Faculty, Institute of International Relations, Warsaw University, Warsaw, 12 June 2000.
70 Osinski interview, Warsaw, 13 June 2000.
71 *Security Strategy of the Republic of Poland*, 4 January 2000, can be found in English at http://www.polonya.org.tr/sec1-bezp-doc.html (accessed 25 November 2003).
72 An informal English translation of the *National Defence Strategy of the Republic of Poland*, 23 May 2000, was provided to me by the Ministry of National Defence.
73 Staron interview, Warsaw, 12 June 2000; Kaminski interview, Warsaw, 12 June 2000.
74 Introduction to the *Security Strategy of the Republic of Poland*.

75 Ibid.
76 *Security Strategy of the Republic of Poland*, 3.2.1 'Role of the Atlantic Alliance'.
77 Measured against analogous Western documents such as Canada's 1994 *Defence White Paper*, Britain's 1996 *Statement on Defence Estimates* or its 1998 *Strategic Defence Review*, Poland's efforts still seem rather general. However, compared with the 1992 documents they represent considerable progress.
78 Staron interview, Warsaw, 12 June 2000; Kaminski interview, Warsaw, 12 June 2000.
79 'NATO's 1999 Targets Not Achieved', *RFE/RL Poland, Belarus and Ukraine Report*, Vol. 2, No. 1 (4 January 2000).
80 *Basic Principles of Security and Defence Policy of the Hungarian Republic*, Parliamentary Act 94/1998, 29 December 1998.
81 I am indebted to MAJ GEN Wayne Knudsen for discussing the *Strategic Defence Review* and detailing to me his firm's recommendations to the Hungarian government: Interview with MGEN Wayne Knudsen (United States Army ret.), Team Leader-Hungary, Cubic Applications, Inc., Budapest, 1 January 2001.
82 Z. Szenes, in Betz and Löwenhardt, *Army and State . . .*, p. 92.
83 Ibid.
84 The text of the 7 May 1992 Presidential Decree creating the Russian armed forces was published in *Rossiyskaya Gazeta*, 9 May 1992.
85 For an overview of the security policy landscape in the Former Soviet Union (fSU) states in the early 1990s, see: Roy Allison, *Military Forces in the Soviet Successor States*, Oxford, UK: International Institute of Strategic Studies, Adelphi Paper No. 280, 1993.
86 The terms are a widely used convenience for categorising foreign policy views in Russia first coined in Neil Malcolm *et al.*, *Internal Factors in Russian Foreign Policy*, Oxford: Oxford University Press, 1996.
87 According to the *NATO Handbook*: 'The NATO-Russia Founding Act is the expression of an enduring commitment, undertaken at the highest political level, to work together to build a lasting and inclusive peace in the Euro-Atlantic area. It creates the framework for a new security partnership, as one step among others which are being taken to build a stable, peaceful and undivided Europe. It allows the Alliance and Russia to forge a closer relationship, not only in their own interests, but also in the wider interests of all other states in the Euro-Atlantic area.' *The NATO Handbook*, p. 87.
88 For example, Sergei Rogov, head of the USA/Canada Institute in *Izvestia*, 28 May 1997.
89 For a synopsis of the Russian debate see J.L. Black, *Russia Faces NATO Expansion: Bearing Gifts or Bearing Arms?* Lanham, MD: Rowman and Littlefield, 2000, section 1.
90 Margot Light and John Löwenhardt, 'Russian and Ukrainian Elite Attitudes to a Wider Europe', paper for the BASEES Conference, Fitzwilliam College, Cambridge, 1–3 April 2000, pp. 6–7.
91 Light and Löwenhardt, p. 6.
92 Ibid., p. 7.
93 E.g., 'Peace Shield' manoeuvres in 1995 and 1996, 'Sea Breeze' 1997 and 'Guards Partnership' 1998) – often despite Russian objections
94 Interview with COL George Bachman, Military Liaison Office, NATO Liaison Office to Ukraine, Kiev, 25 January 2001; Interview with LCDR James Greene, Russia/Ukraine Branch, Cooperation and Regional Security Division, NATO International Military Staff, Kiev, 25 January 2001; Interview with Natalie Melnyczuk, Head, NATO Information and Documentation Centre, Kiev, 24 January 2001.
95 Marybeth Peterson Ulrich looks at the impact of US-Russian military to military contacts in *Democratizing Communist Militaries: The Cases of the Czech and Russian Armed Forces*, Ann Arbor, MI: University of Michigan Press, 1999.
96 *The Military Balance*, 1993–1994.

97 Charles Dick described the Russian military as a 'hollow army'. See, C.J. Dick, 'A Bear Without Claws: The Russian Army in the 1990s,' *The Journal of Slavic Military Studies*, Vol. 10, No. 1 (March 1997), p. 2.

98 See, Roy Allison, 'The Russian Armed Forces: Structures, Roles and Policies', in V. Baranovsky (ed.), *Russia and Europe: The Emerging Security Agenda*, Oxford: Oxford University Press/SIPRI, 1997.

99 Quoted in Michael Orr, *Rodionov and Reform*, Sandhurst, UK: Conflict Studies Research Centre, Royal Military Academy, C92, January 1997, p. 3.

100 For a fuller discussion of Ukraine's strategic location see Sherman W. Garnett, *Keystone in the Arch: Ukraine in the Emerging Security Environment of Central and Eastern Europe*, Washington, DC: Carnegie Endowment, 1997.

101 Vitaliy Shlykov, 'The Budget and the Army', *Russian Politics and Law*, Vol. 35, No. 5 (September–October 1997), p. 72. Christopher Bluth cited general staff calculations that with realistic funding projections there were three alternatives for the Russian army: 1 a well-equipped army of at most 650,000–750,000 men; 2 a poorly-equipped army of 1.5 million men; or, 3 a substantial increase in the military share of national income. See, Christopher Bluth, 'Russian Military Forces: Ambitions, Capabilities and Constraints', in Roy Allison and Christopher Bluth (eds), *Security Dilemmas in Russia and Eurasia*, London, UK: Royal Institute of International Affairs, 1998, p. 81.

102 In Russia discharged officers with more than five years of service were legally entitled to a severance package which included a pension, an apartment, and payment of all wage arrears and allowances.

103 See, Michael Orr, *The Deepest Crisis: The Problems of the Russian Army Today*, Sandhurst, UK: Conflict Studies Research Centre, Royal Military Academy, Occasional Brief 48, 4 October 1996, p. 4. The situation was much the same in Ukraine. See, report in *Narodna Armiya*, 2 April 1999, cited in 'Military Reform in Ukraine: Start or Another False Start?' *National Security and Defence*, No 1 (2000), p. 22.

104 Prime Minister Viktor Chernomyrdin's description of the state's reform objectives included developing a core of well-trained, well-equipped, and well-funded troops with high strategic mobility and operational readiness. Reported by Interfax, 4 October 1996, FBIS-SOV-96-195.

105 The profound degradation of the Russian and Ukrainian armed forces has been covered widely and in minute detail. A few excellent studies include: C.J. Dick, 'A Bear Without Claws: The Russian Army in the 1990s,' *The Journal of Slavic Military Studies*, Vol. 10, No. 1 (March 1997), p. 2; Benjamin Lambeth, 'Russia's Wounded Military', *Foreign Affairs* (March/April 1995), pp. 86–98; and John Jaworsky, 'Ukraine's Armed Forces and Military Policy', in Lubomyr A. Hajda (ed.), *Ukraine in the World: Studies in the International Relations and Security Structure of a Newly Independent State*, Cambridge, MA: Ukrainian Research Institute of Harvard University, 1998, pp. 223–248.

106 For more detail on the plan for developing mobile forces, see Roy Allison, 'The Russian Armed Forces: Structures Roles and Politics', in Vladimir Baranovsky (ed.), *Russia and Europe: The Emerging Security Agenda*, Oxford: Oxford University Press, 1997, pp. 187–188.

107 Indeed, it was very much in line with the rhetoric about the 'revolution in military affairs' which was growing increasingly vogue in the West. Some of the better examples of the vast literature on the revolution in military affairs are Colin S. Gray, 'The Changing Nature of Warfare?', *Naval War College Review*, Vol. XLIX, No. 2 (Spring 1996), and Randall G. Bowdish, 'The Revolution in Military Affairs: The Sixth Generation', *Military Review*, (November–December 1995).

108 Interview with a Council Member, Council on Foreign and Defence Policy (Moscow), Geneva, Switzerland, November 2000.

109 Interview with Pavel Felgenhauer, Defence Correspondent, *Segodnya*, Moscow, December 1998.

110 Quoted in Vitaliy Shlykov, 'The War in Chechnya: Implications for Military Reform and Creation of Mobile Forces', in Mikhail Tsypkin (ed.), *War In Chechnya: Implications for Russian Security Policy*, Monterey, CA: Department of National Security Affairs, US Naval Postgraduate School, 1996, web version at: http://www.fas.org/man/dod-101/ops/war/docs/con-nps.htm (accessed 25 November 2003)

111 The military doctrine was passed by the Security Council and issued as a Decree of the President of the Russian Federation (No. 1833) on 2 November 1993. Initially the doctrine was not to be published but detailed summaries were published by *Izvestia*, 18 November 1993, and *Krasnaya Zvezda*, 19 November 1993. For a detailed summary and comment on the doctrine in English see Charles J. Dick, 'The Military Doctrine of the Russian Federation', *Journal of Slavic Military Studies*, Vol. 7, No. 3 (September 1994), pp. 481–506.

112 Quotes from the military doctrine are taken from Dick, 'Military Doctrine . . . ', pp. 485–486.

113 For a summary and analysis of the 1992 draft doctrine see: Charles J. Dick, 'Initial Thoughts on Russia's Draft Military Doctrine', *Journal of Slavic Military Studies*, Vol. 5, No. 4 (December 1992), pp. 552–566.

114 This was never published. Pavel Baev discusses it in *The Russian Army in a Time of Troubles*, London: Sage, 1996, p. 31.

115 'Expert Sees Hawks Win on Military Doctrine,' FBIS-SOV-EUR, 18 November 1993.

116 Pavel Baev, *Russian Military Development: 'Muddle Through' From 1992 to 1998 and Beyond*, Kjeller, Norway: Norwegian Defence Research Establishment, FFI/ Rapport-99/01229, 1999, p. 10.

117 Interview with Alexander Belkin, Deputy Executive Director, Council on Foreign and Defence Policy, Moscow, December 1998.

118 For a review of the early legislative acts concerning the establishment of the Ukrainian armed forces see: Stephen D. Olynyk, 'Ukraine as a Military Power', in Sharon L. Wolchik and Volodymyr Zviglyanich, *Ukraine: The Search for a National Identity*, Lanham, MD: Rowman and Littlefield Publishers, 2000, pp. 71–72; Bohdan Psykir, 'The Silent Coup: The Building of Ukraine's Military', *European Security*, Vol. 2, No. 2 (Spring 1993), pp. 149–155; and, John Jaworsky, *The Military-Strategic Significance of Recent Developments in Ukraine*, Ottawa, Canada: Directorate of Strategic Analysis, Department of National Defence, Report No. 645, pp, 79–80.

119 *Military Balance 1994–1995*, p. 103 and *Military Balance 1995–1996*, p. 100.

120 Interview with Anatoliy Grytsenko, President, Ukrainian Centre for Economic and Political Studies, Kiev, 1 February 2001; Interview with Leonid Polyakov, Director, Military Programmes, Ukrainian Centre for Economic and Political Studies, Kiev, 22 January 2001.

121 Polyakov interview, Kiev, 22 January 2001. The same may be said of Russia, though perhaps the even more extreme concentration of power in the presidency made cohabitation with parliament even less relevant there.

122 Article IX, 'On External and Internal Security' of the *Declaration of Sovereignty*, July 1990 stated: 'The Ukrainian SSR solemnly proclaims its intention to become in future a permanently neutral state, taking no part in military blocs and holding to three non-nuclear principles: not to accept, produce or acquire nuclear weapons.'

123 Quoted in Roman Wolczuk, 'The Evolution of Ukrainian Foreign and Security Policy, 1990–1994', *Journal of Slavic Military Studies*, Vol. 12, No. 3 (September 1999), p. 31.

124 Charles J. Dick, 'The Military Doctrine of Ukraine', *Journal of Slavic Military Studies*, Vol. 7, No. 3 (September 1994), p. 513.

125 *Economist*, 3 April 1993.

126 For more discussion of Ukraine's denuclearisation see: Roman Wolczuk, 'The Evolution of Ukrainian Foreign and Security Policy, 1990–1994', *Journal of Slavic*

Military Studies, Vol. 12, No. 3 (September 1999), pp. 18–37; and J.F. Dunn, *The Ukrainian Nuclear Weapon Debate*, Sandhurst, UK: Conflict Studies Research Centre, Royal Military Academy, March 1993.

127 Dick, 'Military Doctrine of Ukraine', p. 509.

128 Ibid., 510.

129 Polyakov interview (U27), Kiev, 22 January 2001.

130 Oleksiy Havrylenko, 'Does Ukraine Need a New Military Doctrine', *National Security and Defence*, No. 1 (2000), p. 45.

131 Quoted by Taras Kuzio in *Ukraine: The Unfinished Revolution*, Exeter: SR Press, Institute for European Defence and Strategic Studies, No. 16, 1992, p. 31.

132 For example, Andrea Chandler in 'Statebuilding and Political Priorities in Post-Soviet Ukraine: The Case of the Military', *Armed Forces and Society*, Vol. 22, No. 4 (Summer 1996), pp. 573–597.

133 As the Soviet joke went: 'Question: Why can't the son of a general become a marshal? Answer: Because the marshal has his own son.' Quoted in T.R.W Waters, *Crime in the Russian Military*, Sandhurst, UK: Conflict Studies Research Centre, Royal Military College, C90, November 1996.

134 Mark Galeotti, 'Russia's Rotten Army,' *Jane's Intelligence Review* (March 1996), p. 99.

135 *Kommersant Daily*, 21 May 1997.

136 Graham H. Turbiville, *Mafia in Uniform: The Criminalization of the Russian Armed Forces*, Fort Leavenworth, KS: US Army Foreign Military Studies Office, July 1995, p. 15.

137 According to a report of Taras Kuzio, 'The Ukrainian Armed Forces in Crisis', *Jane's Intelligence Review*, Vol. 7, No. 7 (July 1995), p. 305.

138 UNIAN, 22 June 1994.

139 Cited in Taras Kuzio, 'Ukrainian Civil-Military Relations and the Military Impact of the Ukrainian Economic Crisis', in Bruce Parrott (ed.), *Statebuilding and Military Power in Russia and the New States of Eurasia*, Armonk, NY: M.E. Sharpe, 1995, pp. 179–180.

140 Ibid., p. 180.

141 *Kievskie Vedomosti*, 26 January 1998.

142 M.J. Orr, *The Current State of the Russian Armed Forces*, Sandhurst, UK: Conflict Studies Research Centre, Royal Military College, D60, November 1996, p. 7.

143 Lambeth, 'Russia's Wounded Military', *Foreign Affairs* (March/April 1995), p. 91.

144 *Kommersant Daily*, 15 March 1997.

145 John Jaworsky, 'Ukraine's Armed Forces and Military Policy', in Lubomyr A. Hajda (ed.), *Ukraine in the World: Studies in the International Relations and Security Structure of a Newly Independent State*, Cambridge, MA: Ukrainian Research Institute, Harvard University, 1998, p. 231.

146 Kuzio, Ukrainian Civil-Military Relations . . .', p. 179.

147 'Military Reform in Ukraine: Start or Another False Start?', *National Security and Defence*, No. 1, 2000, p. 10.

148 Interview with COL Vladimir Konstantinov, Acting Chief, Main Organisational Department of the Russian General Staff, Moscow, December 1998.

149 *Kommersant Daily*, 15 February 1997.

150 Such reports are in no shortage in the Russian and Western press. These particular points were taken from the following: *Jamestown Monitor* Vol II, No 35 (19 February 1997); Waters, 'Crime in the Russian Military'; *Krasnaya Zvezda*, 11 April 1996; *Krasnaya Zvezda*, 24 July 1996; and 'Military Reform in Ukraine: Start or Another False Start?'

151 Quoted in Shlykov, 'The War in Chechnya'.

152 Ibid.

153 Orr, *Current State of the* . . . , p. 17.

154 *Krasnaya Zvezda*, 2 March 1996.
155 Pavel Felgengauer, 'Russian Military Reform: Ten Years of Failure', in Mikhail Tsypkin (ed.), *War In Chechnya: Implications for Russian Security Policy*, Monterey, CA: Department of National Security Affairs, US Naval Postgraduate School, 1996.
156 For a discussion of the size and character of the military electorate see Sven Gunnar Simonsen, 'Marching to a Different Drum? Political Orientations and Nationalism in Russia's Armed Forces', in Betz and Löwenhardt (eds), *Army and State . . .*, pp. 53–54.
157 Quoted in *New York Times*, 1 June 1996.
158 Quoted in Felgengauer, 'Russian Military Reform Ten Years of Failure . . .'.
159 Both are quoted in the *New York Times*, 1 June 1996. Trenin argued that a volunteer force was a goal worth striving for while conceding that the Yeltsin decree was wildly unrealistic. Gromov contended that the Russian army 'needs professionals rather than kids' adding that in this way there would be 'less mothers' tears'.
160 In the first round of balloting in the 1996 presidential elections Lebed garnered third place after Yeltsin and Communist Party leader Gennady Zyuganov. He withdrew from the race before the second ballot and endorsed Yeltsin.
161 Michael Orr suggested that Rodionov brought with him a 'radical and well-thought out programme of reform'. See Orr, *Rodionov and Reform*. To my mind, it is fair to say that Rodionov was a decidedly more capable military man than his predecessor with a superior intellectual approach. Nonetheless, though better argued the main points of his reform ideas seem not particularly different from those stated by Grachev.
162 Lebed's dismissal came amid allegations that he was preparing a coup made by the Interior Minister, General Anatoliy Kulikov – who was named by Lebed as the main guilty party for the poor performance of the security services in Chechnya. See interview with Lebed in *Nezavismaya Gazeta*, 18 October 1996.
163 *Sovremennaya Politicheskaya Istoria Rossii: Litsa Rossii*, (1985–1998), Vol. 2, Moscow: RAU – Korporatsiya, 1999, p. 676.
164 Ironically, given that it became such a thorn in his side, the creation of a Defence Council which could take on a unified decision-making and policy-making role in defence was one of Rodionov's main ideas for the basic direction of military reform. *Nezavisimaya Gazeta*, 22 April 1995.
165 *Rossiyskaya Gazeta*, 17 January 1997.
166 Quoted in Orr, *Rodionov and Reform*.
167 Quoted in *Nezavisimaya Gazeta*, 8 February 1997.
168 'Yeltsin Sacks Military Brass', Reuters, 22 May 1997.
169 Quoted in Anatoliy Grytsenko, *Civil-Military Relations in Ukraine: A System Emerging from Chaos*, Groningen, Netherlands: Centre for European Security Studies, Harmonie Paper 1, 1997, p. 15.
170 *Uryadovyy Kuryer*, 17 December 1996, cited in Grytsenko, *Civil-Military Relations in Ukraine . . .*, p. 3.
171 The 1996 reform programme was comprehensively critiqued by experts of the Ukrainian Centre for Economic and Political Studies in 'Military Reform in Ukraine . . .', passim.
172 'Military Reform in Ukraine . . .', p. 19.
173 Interview with a Senior Researcher at the Russian Institute of Strategic Studies, Moscow, January 1999.
174 Interview with a senior instructor of the Navy Training Centre (2), Ministry of Defence, Obninsk, January 1999.
175 This statement of the Council on Foreign and Defence Policy was published in *Nezavisimaya Gazeta*, 14 January 1997.
176 Interview with a Senior Researcher at the Russian Institute of Strategic Studies, Moscow, January 1999.
177 For a review of Rokhlin's agenda see Sven Gunnar Simonsen, 'Rokhlin Enters the Political Fray', *Jane's Intelligence Review*, January 1998, pp. 14–17.

178 Presidential Decree No. 725s, 16 July 1997. An excerpt of the decree was published in *Rossiiskaya Gazeta*, 19 July 1997. It was discussed in some detail by Pavel Anokhin in *Rossiiskiye Vesti*, 18 July 1997, in an article translated as 'Yeltsin Launches Controversial Military Reform', in *Current Digest of the Post-Soviet Press*, Vol. XLIX, No. 29 (20 August 1997), pp. 1–7.
179 Mark Galeotti, 'Russia's Military Under a New Master', *Jane's Intelligence Review* (September 1997), p. 387.
180 Igor Sergeyev, 'Reform the Armed Forces by the 21st Century', *Military News Bulletin*, Vol. VI, No. 12 (December 1997), pp. 1–3.
181 Polyakov interview, Kiev, 22 January 2001.
182 Sherr, 'Civil-Democratic Control of Ukraine's Armed Forces . . .', pp. 71–72.
183 Presidential Decree No. 1300, 17 December 1997. The text was published in *Rossiyskaya Gazeta*, 26 December 1997.
184 Mark Galeotti provided a scathing analysis in 'Russia's National Security Concept', *Jane's Intelligence Review*, (May 1998), pp. 3–4.
185 Sherr, 'Civil-Democratic Control of Ukraine's Armed Forces . . .', p. 71.
186 From an English translation of the concept found in Appendix B of Anatoliy Grytsenko's *Reforming the Military in States of Transformation: The Case of Ukraine*, Groningen, Netherlands: Centre for European Security Studies, EFP Working Paper No. 4, 2000, p. 119.
187 Ibid., Part III. 'Threats to the National Security of Ukraine', pp. 118–119.
188 Ibid., p. 120.
189 Published in *Nezavisimoye Voennoye Obozreniye*, 14 January 2000.
190 Published in *Nezavisimaya Gazeta*, 21 April 2000.
191 Pavel Baev, 'Putin's Military Reform: Two Trajectories for the First Presidency', Security Policy Library 6-2001, Oslo: Norwegian Atlantic Committee, 2001, p. 7.
192 *State Programme on Armed Forces Reform and Development Until 2005*, Kiev: Press of Ukraine, October 2000.
193 Sherr, 'Civil-Democratic Control of Ukraine's Armed Forces . . .', p. 75.
194 Interview with Alexander A. Parfionov, Executive Director, Ukrainian Centre for International Security Studies, Kiev, 24 January 2001.
195 Christopher Donnelly, 'Defence Transformation in the New Democracies: A Framework for Tackling the Problem' *NATO Review*, Vol. 45, No. 1 (January 1997), pp. 3–7.
196 I am aware of only a few serious commentators who voice a contrary opinion. Thomas M. Magstadt, 'Flawed Democracies: The Dubious Political Credentials of NATO's Proposed New Members' *Cato Policy Analysis*, No. 297, 6 March 1998, is one example.
197 Bachman interview, Kiev, 25 January 2001.
198 See Orr, *Rodionov and Reform*.
199 From an extract of the *Strategic Review Recommendations for the Government of Hungary*, 10 December 1999, provided to me by MAJ GEN Wayne Knudsen: Knudsen interview (H9), Budapest, 1 January 2000. (The capitalisation is as it appears in the report).
200 Interview with Leonid Belousov, President, Ukrainian Centre for International Security Studies, Kiev, 24 January 2001.

3 Civilian integration in the ministry of defence

1 For more on the problem of political control vs. administrative delegation, see: Peter Self, *Administrative Theories and Politics: An Enquiry into the Structure and Processes of Modern Government*, London: George Allen & Unwin Ltd., 1976, pp. 161–162.
2 This is not to suggest that management of the ministry of defence is completely the

same as, say, management of the ministry of health. The military profession is unique in that, in Richard Gabriel's words, 'only it has the awesome responsibility of legitimately spending the lives of others in order to render its service'. (See, Richard Gabriel, *To Serve with Honour: A Treatise on Military Ethics and the Way of the Soldier*, Westport, CT: Greenwood Press, 1982, p. 86.) That said, the distinction between civilian and military, particularly when looked at in terms of broad concepts of security where police and military functions are converging, is getting increasingly indistinct.

3 Douglas Bland, 'Managing the 'Expert Problem' in Civil-Military Relations', *European Security*, Vol. 8, No. 3 (Autumn 1999), pp. 38–39.

4 The most notable example of this view being William Odom. See, 'The Party–Military Connection: A Critique', in D. R. Herspring and I. Volgyes, *Civil-Military Relations in Communist Systems*, Boulder, CO: Westview Press, 1978, pp. 27–52.

5 On the structure of the Soviet ministry of defence and the general staff see: Ellen Jones, *Red Army and Society: A Sociology of the Soviet Military*, Boston, MA: Allen and Unwin, 1985, pp. 15–17; and, Harriet Fast Scott and William F. Scott, *Soviet Military Doctrine: Continuity, Formulation, and Dissemination*, Boulder, CO: Westview Press, 1988, pp. 216–217.

6 See Stephen M. Meyer, 'The Sources and Prospects of Gorbachev's New Political Thinking on Security', *International Security*, (Fall 1998), pp. 124–163.

7 *Literaturnaya Rossiya*, 6 May 1998. Quoted by Benjamin Lambeth, 'A Generation too Late: Civilian Analysis and Soviet Military Thinking', in Derek Leebaert and Timothy Dickinson, *Soviet Strategy and New Military Thinking*, Cambridge: Cambridge University Press, 1992, pp. 229–230.

8 Stephen Meyer, 'Soviet Perspectives on the Paths to Nuclear War', in Graham T. Allison, Albert Carnesale and Joseph S. Nye (eds), *Hawks, Doves and Owls: An Agenda for Avoiding Nuclear War*, New York, NY: Norton, 1985, p. 169.

9 Harry Gelman, *The Soviet Turn Toward Conventional Forces: The Internal Variables at Play*, Santa Monica, CA: RAND, R-3876-AF, 1989, p. 61.

10 Andrew Michta, *The Soldier-Citizen: The Politics of the Polish Army After Communism*, New York, NY: St. Martin's Press, 1997, p. 80. Michta said also that 'the issue of civilian control over the general staff was not in question under communism because the defence ministry was, by definition, a military organisation staffed by active-duty officers . . .', p. 85.

11 Zoltan Pecze, *Civil-Military Relations in Hungary*, Groningen, The Netherlands: Centre for European Security Studies, Harmonie Paper No. 2, February 1998, p. 7.

12 Zoltan Barany discusses this issue in some detail in *Soldiers and Politics in Eastern Europe, 1945–1990: The Case of Hungary*, New York, NY: St. Martin's Press, 1993, pp. 17–23.

13 Janos Szabo, 'Facts and Problems of the Civilian Control of Armed Forces in Hungary', in *Behind Declarations: Civil-Military Relations in Central Europe*, Budapest: Institute for Strategic and Defence Studies, 1996, p. 50.

14 Pecze, p. 7.

15 Michta, *The Soldier Citizen . . .* , p. 85.

16 Reka Szemerkenyi, *Central European Civil-Military Reforms at Risk: Progress in Establishing Democratic Controls Over the Military Has Not Been Sustained*, Oxford: Oxford University Press for the International Institute of Strategic Studies, Adelphi Paper No. 306, 1996, p. 11.

17 James Sherr, 'Hungary', in Harald von Riekhoff and Natalie Mychajlyszyn, (eds), *Report on Specific Problems of Civil-Military Relations in the Czech Republic, Poland and Hungary*, Ottawa, Canada: Department of National Defence, January 1999, p. 84.

18 Piotr Dutkiewicz, 'Poland', in von Riekhoff and Mychajlyszyn, *Report on Specific Problems . . .* , p. 44.

19 Szemerkenyi, *Central European . . .* , p. 42.

20 Szabo, 'Facts and Problems . . .', p. 52. Szemerkenyi referred to this phenomenon as 'Upton's disease: the expert military loses confidence in the factually incompetent civilians and wants to save itself from them. This disease has characterised Central Europe since the initial reforms in 1989–1990. See, Szemerkenyi, *Central European* . . . , p. 71.
21 *Wrpost*, 12 February 1995. Cited by Stefan Sarvas in 'Professional Soldiers and Politics: A Case of Central and Eastern Europe', *Armed Forces and Society*, Vol. 26, No. 1 (Fall 1999), p. 109.
22 Szemerkenyi, *Central European* . . . , p. 12.
23 Dutkiewicz, 'Poland'. p. 46.
24 From the 'Summarizing Conclusions' of the report reprinted as Appendix A in *The Hungarian Defence Force and Civil Control in the Reflection of British Trans-illumination*, Budapest: Ministry of Defence, Department for Education and Science, 1997, p. 101.
25 Ibid., pp. 101–102.
26 Zoltan Szenes, 'The Implications of NATO Expansion for Civil-Military Relations in Hungary', in David Betz and John Löwenhardt (eds), *Army and State in Post-Communist Europe*, London and Portland, OR: Frank Cass, 2001, p. 83.
27 *Law CX of 1993 on National Defence*, 7 December 1993, published in *Magyar Közlöny*, No. 186, 24 December 1993.
28 See, for example, Jeffrey Simon, Central European Civil-Military Relations and NATO Expansion, Washington, DC: Institute for National Strategic Studies, McNair Paper No. 39, 1995, p. 12.
29 Figures are from *Honvedelem '92*, Budapest: Ministry of Defence, 1992, cited by Alfred A. Reisch, 'Military Affairs: The Hungarian Army in Transition', *RFE/RL Research Report*, Vol. 2, No. 10 (5 March 1993), p. 50.
30 *Budapest Domestic Service*, 0700 GMT, 30 May 1991, FBIS-EEU, No. 91-064, 3 April 1991.
31 *Magyar Közlöny*, No. 103, 26 September 1991, pp. 2, 111–12,125, JPRS-EER, No. 91–168, 13 November 1991.
32 *Mala Konstytucya z komentarzem*, Warsaw: Wydawnictwo, 1993. The *Little Constitution* is analysed in Louisa Vinton, 'Poland's Little Constitution Clarifies Walesa's Powers', *RFE/RL Research Report*, Vol. 1, No. 35 (4 September 1992).
33 Michta, *The Soldier Citizen* . . . , pp. 79–80.
34 This law was actually passed by the Sejm in June 1995 only to be vetoed by Walesa. It was signed by his Kwasniewski in January 1996. See, 'Law Dated 14 December 1995 Detailing Duties of the Minister of National Defence', *Dziennik Ustaw*, No. 10, 30 January 1996, pp. 159–161, FBIS-EEU, No. 96–120, 30 January 1996.
35 Michta, *The Soldier Citizen* . . . , p. 91.
36 Eva Busza, 'Transition and Civil-Military Relations in Poland and Russia', *Communist and Post-Communist Studies*, Vol. 29, No. 2 (1996), p. 176.
37 Michta, *The Soldier Citizen* . . . , p. 82.
38 TVP, 1730 GMT, 6 April 1992, FBIS-EEU, No. 92–067, 7 April 1992.
39 PAP, 1056 GMT, 15 May 1992, FBIS-EEU, No. 92–097, 19 May 1992.
40 Michta, *The Soldier Citizen* . . . , p. 83.
41 Onyszkiewicz, a mathematician and Solidarity activist, was one of two civilian deputy ministers of defence appointed under the government of Prime Minister Tadeusz Mazowiecki in 1990. He resigned that post in 1992 when Jan Parys took over the ministry.
42 Interview with unnamed Polish defence official by Piotr Dutkiewicz, quoted in Dutkiewicz, 'Poland', p. 47.
43 Michta, *The Soldier Citizen* . . . , p. 87.
44 For an overview of Polish military educational reforms see, LCOL Piotr Sienkiewicz, COL Andzej Chijnacki and LCOL Slawomir Olezalek, 'Practical and Personnel

Conversion Aspects of Military Educational Reforms in Poland', in *Military Higher Education* (conference proceedings), Budapest: Ministry of Defence, Education and Sciences Department, 1999.

45 TV Polania Network, 1830 GMT, 11 October 1994, FBIS-EEU, No. 94–197, 12 October 1994; TV Polania Network, 1600 GMT, 14 October 1994, FBIS-EEU, No. 94–200, 17 October 1994; and article by Pawel Wronski in *Gazeta Wyborcza*, 11 October 194, FBIS-EEU, No. 94–197, 12 October 1994.

46 From comments of a member of the special committee interviewed in *Gazeta Poznanska*, 26 October 1994, FBIS-EEU, No. 92–214, 4 November 1994.

47 Szemerkenyi, *Central European . . .*, p. 13.

48 Directorate of Management Consultancy Services, *Review of Parliamentary Oversight of the Hungarian Ministry of Defence and Democratic Control of the Hungarian Armed Forces*, London: Ministry of Defence, 1996.

49 Paraphrased from Institute for Strategic and Defence Studies, *The First Decade of the Independent Hungarian Security Policy*, Budapest: October 1999, p. 49.

50 Interview with Professor Janos Matus. Head, Department of Security Studies, Miklos Zrinyi National Defence Uiversity, Budapest, 30 November 1999..

51 *At the Threshold of the New Millennium: Governmental Program for a Civilian Hungary*, Budapest: 1998; summarised and analysed in detail in *The First Decade of the Independent Hungarian Security . . .*, pp. 76–83.

52 Ibid., p. 82.

53 A record of the constitutional reforms in the defence sphere can be found in: MTI, 2107 GMT, 7 December 1993, FBIS-EEU, No. 93–236, 10 December 1993; the Constitution, especially Articles 19, Sections A, B and C, and Article 30, both dealing with presidential prerogatives in defence are found in English and Hungarian in *Constitutions of the Countries of the World*, Dobbs Ferry, NY: Oceana Publications, 1995.

54 Interview with Ilona Kiss, Program Manager, Constitutional and Legal Policy Institute, Open Society Institute, Budapest, 3 December 1999.

55 Interview with LTC Laszlo Kelemen, Professor, Legal Department, National Defence University, Budapest, 2 December 1999.

56 Intervew with LTC Andras Ujj, Deputy Director, Institute for Strategic and Defence Studies, National Defence University, Budapest, 1 December 1999.

57 Kelemen interview, Budapest, 2 December 1999 (emphasis added).

58 'Law Dated 14 December 1995 Detailing Duties of the Minister of National Defence', *Dziennik Ustaw*, No. 10, Warsaw, 30 January 1996, pp. 159–161, FBIS-EEU, 96–120, 30 January 1996. The law had been vetoed by Walesa in November 1995.

59 *Constitution of the Republic of Poland*, 2 April 1997, available on the Sejm website, http://www.sejm.gov.pl/english/konstytucja/ramka1.htm (accessed 25 November 2003).

60 *Constitution of the Republic of Poland*, Art. 26, Sec. 2.

61 Ibid., Art. 26, Sec. 1.

62 Ibid., Art 134, Sec. 2.

63 Numerous authors credit Onyszkiewicz with having earned the respect of the Polish military. Michta wrote that 'his tenure at defence won him uniform praise from both civilians and the military.' (Michta, *The Soldier Citizen . . .*, p. 97).

64 Szemerkenyi, *Central European . . .*, p. 11.

65 Hungarian figure is from Szemerkenyi, p. 12; Polish figure is from an interview in the personnel department of the ministry of defence: Jarmuszko interview(P13), Warsaw, 19 June 2000.

66 Ujj interview, Budapest, 1 December 1999.

67 Interview with Krystian Piatkowski. Director for International Cooperation, Polish Chamber of National Defence Manufacturers, Warsaw, 14 June 2000. This harsh estimate was only slightly at odds with the estimate of the personnel department of the

ministry of defence that of some 325 top management posts in the ministry, 45 were held by civilians: Interview with COL Stanislaw Jarmuszko, Personnel Department, Ministry of Defence, Warsaw, 19 June 2000.

68 Sarvas, 'Professional Soldiers . . .', p. 114.

69 Piatkowski interview, Warsaw, 14 June 2000.

70 Krysztof A. Zielke, 'NATO Expansion and Civil-Military Relations in Poland', in *Behind Declarations: Civil-Military Relations in Central Europe*, Budapest: Institute for Strategic and Defence Studies, 1996, pp. 73–76, p. 75. An interlocutor in Poland agreed that civilian defence officials had significantly less opportunity for training abroad under NATO or other bilateral programmes: Interview with a specialist in the Personnel Department, Ministry of Defence, Warsaw, 19 June 2000.

71 Szemerkenyi, *Central European . . .* , p. 67.

72 Interview with Professor Dr Janos Szabo (2), Deputy State Secretary for Human Resources, Ministry of Defence, 29 November 1999.

73 Interview with Dr Kzysztof Jazwinski, Director, National Security Faculty, Institute of International Relations, Warsaw University, Warsaw, 12 June 2000.

74 Dutkiewicz, 'Poland', p. 48.

75 Matus interview, Budapest, 30 November 1999.

76 Piatkowski interview, Warsaw, 14 June 2000.

77 Szabo (1) interview, Budapest, 2 December 1999.

78 Interview with COL Kysztof Osinski. Deputy Director, NATO Integration Department, Ministry of Defence, Warsaw, 13 June 2000. Moreover, within the ministry of defence military pay levels were 1.6–1.7 times higher than civilian pay levels: Jarmuszko interview, Warsaw, 19 June 2000.

79 Moreover, the defence economics department consisted of only one faculty member: Jazwinski interview, Warsaw 12 June 2000.

80 Matus interview, Budapest, 30 November 1999.

81 Matus interview, Budapest, 30 November 1999.

82 Ujj interview, Budapest, 1 December 1999.

83 Interview with Laszlo Nagy, Professor, Department of Security Studies, National Defence University, Budapest, 4 December 1999.

84 Nagy interview, Budapest, 4 December 1999.

85 Sarvas, 'Professional Soldiers . . .', p 114.

86 Ujj interview, Budapest, 1 December 1999.

87 Interview with MAJ Ferenc Molnar, Professor, Sociology Department, National Defence University, Budapest, 1–2 December 1999.

88 Szabo (1) interview, Budapest, 2 December 1999.

89 Michta, *The Soldier Citizen . . .* , p. 112.

90 In addition to the minister of defence and his office, the civilian side of the ministry of defence consists of 14 departments and two bureaus: the Administrative Coordination Department, the Department of International Security, the Budget Department, the Department of Ordinance and Military Equipment Supply, the Economics Department, the Department of Infrastructure, the Personnel and Military Educational Department, the Control Department, the Legal Department, the Department of Development and Implementation, the Social-Education Department, the Department of the Defence System, the Department of Foreign Military Affairs, and the Department of Cooperation with NATO, plus the Press and Information Bureau and the Complaints and Interventions Bureau.

The administrations which constitute the military side of the ministry of defence (i.e., those under the general staff) consist of 3 boards and 15 departments: the General Board, the Organisational Board, the Development Planning Board, the Strategic Planning Department, the Command and Training Systems Department, the Department of Logistics, the Mobilisation Department, the Command Department, the Material Department, the Territorial Defence Department, the Reconnaissance and

Electronic Warfare Department, the Logistic Support Planning Department, the Operational-Strategic Department, the Training Department, the Technical Department, the Topography Department, the Department of Signals and Informatics, and the Military Health service Department. See, *The Polish Defence Forces*, Warsaw: Press and Information Bureau, Ministry of Defence, 1998, pp. 10–11.

91 Ibid., p. 18.

92 Michta, *The Soldier Citizen . . .*, p. 113.

93 Rudolf Joo, *The Democratic Control of the Armed Forces: The Experience of Hungary*, Paris: Institute for Security Studies, Western European Union, Chaillot Paper No. 23, February 1996, p. 48. There is of course another interpretation of the reasons behind the separation of the general staff from the ministry of defence (i.e., it was in order to preserve some control of the armed forces by the reformed Communist Party which expected to win the 1990 presidential election). The two propositions are not mutually exclusive.

94 Pecze, *Civil-Military Relations . . .*, p. 39.

95 This quotation, and the longer one above are from the Kelemen interview, Budapest, 2 December 1999.

96 Matyas Szabo, ‘Hungarian Army Chief Resigns’, *RFE/RL Newsline Endnote*, 16 July 1999.

97 Ibid.

98 *Izvestia*, 30 June 1992. Earlier that year, in January 1992, First Deputy Minister of Finance Andrei Nechayev in an interview where cuts to the defence budget were being discussed pointed out, ‘we have to be clear-headed about this: we can’t demobilise a million soldiers a month. If the authorities cut back the army too hastily, the army will cut back the authorities.’ *Megalopolis-Express*, 1 January 1992.

99 David Mendeloff, ‘Explaining Russian Military Quiescence: The ‘Paradox of Disintegration’ and the Myth of a Military Coup’, *Communist and Post-Communist Studies*, Vol. 27, No. 3 (1994), pp. 225–246.

100 See, for example, David J. Betz, *If They Are Ordered ‘Die of Hunger!’ They Will Die*, Glasgow: Institute of Central and East European Studies, Glasgow Paper No. 2, 1999.

101 An interview with an Assistant First Deputy Prime Minister of the Russian Federation, Moscow, January 1999.

102 ‘One on One: Army Colonel General Oleksandr Kuzmuk, Ukraine’s Minister of Defence’, *Defence News* (26 May–1 June 1997), p. 30. In a *NATO Review* article in 1994, two analysts from the Ukrainian Centre for Independent Political Research quoted an unnamed senior defence official making a similar statement: ‘In early 1994 one senior Ukrainian officer described to the authors the principle of democratic accountability in Ukraine’s armed forces thus: ‘The president is commander-in-chief of our armed forces. The president is a democratically elected civilian. Therefore we have democratic, civil control of the armed forces.’ See, Vyacheslav Pikhovshek and Christopher Pett, ‘Transformation of the Ukrainian Armed Forces’, NATO Review, Vol. 42, No. 5 (October 1994), pp. 21–25.

103 James Sherr, ‘Civil-Democratic Control of Ukraine’s Armed Forces: To What Ends? By What Means?’, in Betz and Löwenhardt (eds), *Army and State . . .*, p. 67.

104 Presidential Directive 1068-PR, 30 July 1998. The reform plan was never published. However, a summary appeared in *Krasnaya Zvezda*, 5 August 1998, and *Kommersant-Daily*, 5 August 1998.

105 See ‘The Current State of the Armed Forces as an Impending Catastrophe’, a statement of the Council on Foreign and Defence Policy published in *Nezavisimaya Gazeta*, 14 February 1997.

106 ‘Ukraine Needs a New Type of Armed Forces’, English translation of a Ukrainian article by A. Pavlov, in (WPS) *Defence and Security*, 17 December 1997.

107 *Izvestia*, 1 June 1992.

108 Szemerkenyi, *Central European . . .*, p. 11.

109 It was only later that Grachev came to be loathed by many in the military as an over-promoted, easily corrupted, incompetent. In the beginning, he was quite well regarded. See, the chapter on Grachev in Viktor Baranets, *El'tsin i Ego Generaly*, Moscow: Sovershenno Sekretno, 1998, pp. 155–271.
110 Ibid., p. 197.
111 Interview with a Senior Researcher at the USA/Canada Institute interview, Moscow, January 1999.
112 Baranets, *El'tsin . . .*, p. 249.
113 Rokhlin is quoted in praise of Rodionov in *Sovremennaya Politicheskaya Istoriya Rossii: Litsa Rossii, 1985–1998*, Vol. 2, Moscow: RAU – Korporatsiya, 1999, p. 676.
114 Ibid., p. 676.
115 *Segodnya*, 10 January 1998.
116 See, for example, the article on his views about civilians in defence in *Nezavisimaya Gazeta*, 1 November 1994.
117 Interview with a Duma defence committee working group member, Moscow, December 1998.
118 Aleksandr Golts, 'Internal Strife in the Russian military: Plan Lands on Putin's Desk to Revamp the Armed Forces', *ITOGI/Newsweek*, (3 July 2000).
119 Olga Kuchkina, 'Ne khochu, chtoby v Rossii bylo ChP', *Mir za Nedeliu 15* (4–11 December 1999).
120 See Aleksandr Golts, 'Civilian Goes to the Top, But Same Old Approach', *Russia Journal* (31 March–6 April, 2001). Golts did not suggest that Ivanov was any more likely to succeed in his task of reforming the military than his predecessors.
121 *Zavtra*, 24 April 2001.
122 Some discussions of the pre-independence moves of the Ukrainian SSR towards creating an independent military include: Bohdan Pyskir, 'The Silent Coup: The Building of Ukraine's Military', *European Security*, Vol. 2, No. 1 (Spring 1993), p. 147; Taras Kuzio, 'Ukrainian Civil-Military Relations and the Military Impact of the Ukrainian Economic Crisis', in Bruce Parrott (ed.), *State-Building and Military Power in Russia and the New States of Eurasia*, Armonk, NY: M.E. Sharpe, 1995, pp. 159–162; and, Valeriy Izmalkov, 'Ukraine and her Armed Forces: The Conditions and Processes for their Creation, Character, Structure and Military Doctrine', *European Security*, Vol. 2, No. 2 (Summer 1993), pp. 282–283.
123 Interview with Alexander A. Parfionov, Executive Director, Ukrainian Centre for International Security Studies, Kiev, 24 January 2001.
124 *Constitution of Ukraine*, 28 June 1996, Chap. 5, Art. 106, Paras. 16–21.
125 Ibid., Chap. 5, Art. 107.
126 Pyskir, 'The Silent Coup . . .', pp. 140 and 147–149.
127 The opposition of senior military figures was reported by John Jaworsky, who cited an interview with Morozov as the source of this information in 'Ukraine's Armed Forces and Military Policy', in Lubomyr A. Hajda (ed.), *Ukraine in the World: Studies in the International Relations and Security Structure of a Newly Independent State*, Cambridge, MA: Ukrainian Research Institute of Harvard University, 1998, p. 226.
128 'Defence Minister Morozov Voices Opposition to Black Sea Fleet Accord', UNIAN, 9 October 1993.
129 Quoted by Anatoliy Grytsenko in *Civil-Military Relations in Ukraine: A System Emerging from Chaos*, Groningen, Netherlands: Centre for European Security Studies, Harmonie Paper 1, 1997, p. 28.
130 I am not aware of any opinion polls in the military on this question. However, most of the analysts cited here conclude the same, as have all the military officers whom I have interviewed.
131 Marta Kolomayets, 'Shmarov Defamation Case Halted as Language Becomes the Issue', *Ukrainian Weekly*, No. 20, Vol. LXIV (19 May 1996).
132 Grytsenko, *Civil-Military Relations . . .*, p. 31.

133 *RFE/RL Newsline*, 9 July 1996.
134 Interview with Leonid Polyakov, Director, Military Programmes, Ukrainian Centre for Economic and Political Studies, Kiev, 22 January 2001. Shmarov failed, according to another interviewee, because he 'was simply not competent enough in the military sphere when he was appointed'.: Interview with Leonid Belousov, President, Ukrainian Centre for International Security Studies, Kiev, 24 January 2001.
135 Pavel Baev and Tor Bukkvol, 'Ukraine's Army Under Civilian Rule', *Jane's Intelligence Review* Vol. 8, No. 1 (January 1996), p. 9.
136 Belousov interview, Kiev, 24 January 2001.
137 Interview with Hryhoriy Nemyria, Director, Institute of International Relations, Centre for European and International Studies, Taras Shevchenko University, Kiev, 31 January 2001.
138 Natalie Mychajlyszyn and Orest Subtelny, 'Ukraine' in Harold von Riekhoff and Natalie Mychajlyszyn (eds), *Report on Specific Problems . . .*, pp. 284–285.
139 Belousov interview, Kiev, 24 January 2001.
140 Interview with a Senior Researcher at the USA/Canada Institute (1), Moscow, January 1999.
141 Baranets, *El'tsin . . .*, p. 198.
142 Interview with Senior Researcher at the USA/Canada Institute (1), Moscow, January 1999.
143 Interview with a member of the Directorate of International Military Cooperation, Ottawa, March 1998 and Moscow, January 1999
144 Interview with an Assistant First Deputy Prime Minister of the Russian Federation, Moscow, January 1999.
145 Interview with a Senior Researcher of the USA/Canada Institute interview (2), Moscow, January 1999.
146 Interview with two instructors of the Navy Training Centre, Moscow, January 1999.
147 WPS Russian Military Analysis, No. 39 (6 April 2001).
148 According to Brian Taylor in 'The Duma and Military Reform,' PONARS Memo No. 154 (October 2000).
149 Polyakov interview, Kiev, 22 January 2001.
150 Baev and Bukkvol, 'Ukraine's Army . . .', p. 9.
151 Frank Cook and Yvan Zayets, 'Ukraine and its Armed Forces: A New Actor on the European Stage', *Report to the Defence and Security Committee of the NATO Parliamentary Assembly*, AS 253 DSC (99) 8, November 1999, p. 15.
152 The ministry of defence website (http:www.niss.dod.gov.ua) accessed in December 1999, listed only military officers at the deputy ministerial level.
153 Pavel Gazukin, *Vooruzhenye Sily Rossiiskoi Federatsi: Biograficheski Spravochnik*, Moscow: Panorama, 1996 and 1998 editions.
154 Interview a senior member of the Department of Contract Workers and Civilian Personnel, Ministry of Defence, Moscow, December 1998.
155 Interview with a member of the Law and Administration Program, The Open Society Institute, Soros Foundation, Moscow, January 1999.
156 Interview with a Chief Specialist in the Directorate of International Military Cooperation, Ministry of Defence, Ottawa, Canada, March 1998, and Moscow, January 1999.
157 *The State Programme of the Ukrainian Armed Forces Reform and Development until 2005*, Kiev: 'Press of Ukraine', 2000, p. 10.
158 Cook and Zayets, 'Ukraine and its Armed Forces . . .', p. 15.
159 Parfionov interview, Kiev, January 2001.
160 Interview with a member of the Law and Administration Program, The Open Society Institute, Soros Foundation, Moscow, January 1999.
161 Polyakov interview, Kiev, 22 January 2001.
162 Interview with a member of the Military Personnel Department of the Ministry of Foreign Affairs interview, Kiev, 23 January 2001.

163 Jaworsky, J. 'Ukraine's Armed Forces and Military Policy', in L. A. Hajda (ed.), *Ukraine in the World: Studies in the International Relations and Security Structure of a Newly Independent State*. Cambridge, MA: Harvard University Press, 1998, p. 234.
164 Interview with a member of the Department of Military-Political Studies, Institute of the USA and Canada, Moscow, January 1999.
165 Interview with a Senior Researcher at the Russian Institute of Strategic Studies, Moscow, January 1999.
166 Interview with MGEN (ret.) Vadim Grechaninov, President, Atlantic Council of Ukraine, Kiev, 24 January 2001.
167 Take, for example, the case of the Main Directorate for International Military Cooperation headed by General Ivashov in the Russian ministry of defence. Is it subordinate to the general staff or the minister of defence? In theory, to the minister. In practice, Ivashov reported to whoever was the stronger at any particular time: Interview with a Chief Specialist in the Directorate of International Military Cooperation, Ministry of Defence, Ottawa, Canada, March 1998, and Moscow, January 1999.
168 Felgenhauer interview, Moscow, December 1998.
169 See *Segodnya*, 13 January 1995; *Kommersant-Daily*, 17 January 1995; and, *Moskovskie Novosti*, 15–22 January 1995.
170 Interview with a Chief Specialist in the Directorate of International Military Cooperation, Ministry of Defence, Ottawa, Canada, March 1998, and Moscow, January 1999.
171 *RFE/RL Newsline*, 13 February 1996.
172 Baev and Bukkvol, 'Ukraine's Army . . .', p. 9.
173 Presidential Decree, *On the Division of Responsibilities of the Minister of Defence of Ukraine and the General Staff of the Armed Forces of Ukraine*, No. 888 97, 21 August 1997.
174 Taken from *The State Programme of the Ukrainian Armed Forces Reform and Development until 2005*, pp. 40–41.
175 Grytsenko, *Civil-Military Relations* . . . , p. 31.

4 Agencies of civilian oversight

1 Reka Szemerkenyi, *Central European Civil-Military Reforms at Risk: Progress in Establishing Democratic Controls Over the Military Has Not Been Sustained*, Oxford: Oxford University Press for the International Institute of Strategic Studies, Adelphi Paper No. 306, 1996, p. 72.
2 See, Julian Cooper, 'Management of the Defence Industry: The Soviet Union', in Carl G. Jacobsen (ed.), *Strategic Power USA/USSR*, London: Macmillan, 1990, pp. 325–326.
3 Quoted by Jeffrey Simon in 'Forging a Civilian Chain of Command for Poland's Military', *Transition*, 15 December 1995, p. 40.
4 Institute for Strategic and Defence Studies, *The First Decade of the Independent Hungarian Security Policy, 1989–1999*, Budapest: Institute for Strategic and Defence Studies, October 1999, pp. 21–23.
5 Leslie Holmes, *Post Communism: An Introduction*, Oxford: Blackwell Publishers, 1997, p. 174.
6 Article 32, paragraph 1 states 'The President shall exercise general supervision in the field of international relations'; similarly Article 34 states 'The President shall exercise general supervision with respect to the external and internal security of the State'. From the *Constitutional Act of 17th October 1992* (in English), Warsaw: Sejm Publishing Office, 1993.
7 Article 52, paragraph 8 of the *Constitutional Act of 17th October 1992* states 'The Council of Ministers, in particular, shall ensure the external and internal security of the state.'

8 Article 61of the *Constitutional Act of 17th October 1992* states 'The Prime Minister shall lay a motion to appoint the Minister of Foreign Affairs, of National Defence and of Internal Affairs after consultation of the President.' Previous prime ministers had not interpreted the words 'after consultation' to mean giving the president sole discretion over who was appointed. After Pawlak, however, constitutional lawyers could maintain that presidential authority over the security ministers was a matter of established constitutional practice.

9 Interview with a member of the International Affairs Group, Research Bureau, Chancellory of the Sejm, Warsaw, 14 June 2000.

10 Interview with two members of the Secretariat of the Defence Committee, Chancellory of the Sejm, Warsaw, 20 June 2000.

11 Interview with Dr Kzysztof Jazwinski, Director, National Security Faculty, Institute of International Relations, Warsaw University, Warsaw, 12 June 2000.

12 Interview with Krystian Piatkowski. Director for International Cooperation, Polish Chamber of National Defence Manufacturers, Warsaw, 14 June 2000.

13 Piatkowski interview, Warsaw, 14 June 2000.

14 Interviews with various staffers of the National Military Academy, Warsaw, 14 June 2000.

15 Piatkowski interview, Warsaw, 14 June 2000.

16 Andrew A. Michta, *The Soldier Citizen: The Politics of the Polish Army After Communism*, New York: St. Martin's Press, 1997, p. 113.

17 Zoltan Szenes, 'The Implications of NATO Expansion for Civil-Military Relations in Hungary', in David Betz and John Löwenhardt (eds), *Army and State in Postcommunist Europe*, London and Portland, OR: Frank Cass, 2001, p. 81.

18 Interview with Zoltan Martinusz, Institute for Central and East European Strategic Studies (former Head of the Department of Planning and Policy, Ministry of Defence of Hungary), The Hague, Netherlands, May 2001.

19 Interview with Professor Dr Janos Szabo (2), Deputy State Secretary for Human Resources, Ministry of Defence, 29 November 1999.

20 Interview with L.T.C. Laszlo Kelemen, Professor, Legal Department, National Defence University, Budapest, 2 December 1999.

21 At the time he wrote this Wachsler was a member of the defence committee, later he became the administrative state secretary of defence. See his contribution to *Behind Declarations: Civil-Military Relations in Central Europe*, Budapest: Institute for Strategic and Defence Studies, 1996, p. 17.

22 Szabo (2) interview, Budapest, 29 November 1999.

23 From Peter Deak in Zoltan Szenes (ed.), *The Hungarian Defence Force and Civil Control in the Reflection of British Transillumination*, Budapest: Ministry of Defence, Department for Education and Science, 1997, p. 45.

24 From Winfried Dunkel in Szenes (ed.), *The Hungarian Defence Force . . .*, p. 51.

25 Thomas Szayna and F. Stephen Larrabee, *East European Military Reform After the Cold War: Implications for the United States*, Santa Monica, CA: RAND, 1995, p. 26.

26 Interview with an official of the Budget Department, Ministry of National Defence, Warsaw, 13 June 2000.

27 Interview with LCOL Wladyslaw Staron. Main Military Expert, National Security Bureau, Office of the President, Department of the President's Supervisory of the Armed Forces, Warsaw, 12 June 2000.

28 Interview with Jakub Pinkowski, Director of Legal Department, Ministry of Defence, Warsaw, 12 June 2000.

29 Interview with Professor Janos Matus, Head, Department of Security Studies, Miklos Zrinyi National Defence University, Budapest, 30 November 1999.

30 Martinusz interview, The Hague, May 2001. Szemerkenyi claimed in 1996 that the budget submission was actually only one page long. See Szemerkenyi, p. 28.

31 Zoltan Pecze, *Civil-Military Relations in Hungary, 1989–1996*, Groningen, Netherlands: Centre for European Security Studies, Harmonie Paper 2, 1998, p. 58.
32 Piatkowski interview, Warsaw, 14 June 2000.
33 Eg., Ben Lombardi, 'An Overview of Civil-Military Relations in Central and Eastern Europe', *Journal of Slavic Military Studies*, Vol. 12, No. 1 (March 1999), p. 24.
34 From Sandor Kucson in Szenes (ed.), *The Hungarian Defence Force . . .* , p. 55.
35 Staron interview, Warsaw, 12 June 2000.
36 Pinkowski interview, Warsaw, 12 June 2000.
37 Ibid.
38 Ibid.
39 Staron interview, Warsaw, 12 June 2000.
40 Ibid.
41 *Nepszabadsag*, 26 May 1992, JPRS-EER, No. 92–088 (10 July 1992).
42 Kelemen interview, Budapest, 2 December 1999.
43 Interview with BGEN Zoltan Szenes, Deputy Chief (ACOS LOG), NATO HQ AFSOUTH, Glasgow, 20 March 2000.
44 See Jozsef Feher in Szenes (ed.), *The Hungarian Defence Force . . .* , p. 92.
45 Interview with Laszlo Nagy, Professor, Department of Security Studies, National Defence University, Budapest, 4 December 1999.
46 A subtle but important difference. See Marian Kowalewski, 'An Organisational Model of Civilian Control Over the Army in Polish Circumstances', Warsaw: NATO Research Fellowship Report 1995–1997, 10 June 1997, p. 20.
47 Staron interview (P28), Warsaw, 12 June 2000.
48 Ibid.
49 At the time interviews were conducted at the National Security Bureau in June 2000 there was only a single civilian staff member. Staron interview, Warsaw, 12 June 2000; Interview with Interview with Slawomir Kaminski, Main Civilian Expert, National Security Bureau, Office of the President, Department of the President's Supervisory of the Armed Forces, Warsaw, 12 June 2000.
50 Article 135 of the *Constitutional Act of 2 April 1997*.
51 Staron interview, Warsaw, 12 June 2000; Kaminski interview, Warsaw, 12 June 2000.
52 Interview with Andrzej Kierwinski, Director, Secretary of the Committee for Defence Affairs of the Council of Ministers, Chancellery of the Prime Minister, Department of Defence Affairs, 14 June 2001.
53 Z. Szenes, 'The Implications of NATO Expansion . . .', in Betz and Löwenhardt (eds), *Army and State . . .* , p. 80.
54 For example, the website of the OECD at http://www1.oecd.org/puma/sigmaweb/acts/cogprofiles/hun-cog.htm (accessed January 2001).
55 The other two directorates under Gyuricza were Defence Coordination (mainly for civil emergencies) and National Security Information Analysis (civil and military intelligence). After Gyuricza's death the secretariat has been headed by Reka Szemerkenyi.
56 *Law of the Russian Federation On Defence*, No. 3532-I, 24 September 1992, Chap. 2, Arts. 4 and 5.
57 *Constitution of the Russian Federation*, 12 December 1993, Chap. 4, Art. 83, Para. K.
58 Ibid., Chap. 4, Art. 87, Para. 2.
59 Ibid., Chap. 4, Art. 83, Para. G.
60 Ibid., Chap. 5, Art. 102, Paras A–C.
61 Ibid., Chap. 5, Art. 106. Paras A and F.
62 *Federal Law On Defence*, No. 61–F3, 31 May 1996, Chap. 2, Art. 4. Sec. 2, Paras 1–20.
63 Ibid., Chap. 2, Art. 5, Sec. 1, Paras 1–4.
64 Ibid., Chap. 2, Art. 5, Sec. 2, Paras 1 and 2.
65 The draft law is discussed in detail by one of its authors in Yuri Ivanov, 'Legal, Political

and Budgetary Aspects of Civilian Control of the Military in Russia', in Betz and Löwenhardt (eds), *Army and State* . . . , pp. 13–18. A copy of the draft was published in *Parlamentskii Kontrol' nad Voennoe Sferoi v Novykh Nezavisimykh Gosudarstvakh*, Moscow: Tsentr Politicheskikh i Mezhdunarodnykh Issledovanii, 1998, pp. 155–170.

66 The statute enacting the Security Council was published in *Rossiyskaya Gazeta*, 6 May 1992; the Defence Council statute can be found in *Rossiyskaya Gazeta*, 27 July 1996.

67 The enactment of the State Military Inspectorate was announced in *Krasnaya Zvezda*, 5 November 1996, but in actual fact it did not exist in law until the promulgation of the Presidential Decree *On Measures to Strengthen State Direction of Military Development in the Russian Federation*, No. 946, 28 August 1997.

68 *Constitution of Ukraine*, 28 June 1996, Art. 106, Para. 17.

69 Ibid., Art. 106, Para. 18.

70 Ibid., Art. 106, Para. 24.

71 Ibid., Art. 106, Paras 19 and 21.

72 Alexander Parfionov, *Rol' Struktur Ispolnitel'noi Vlasti v Sisteme Grazhdanskogo Kontrolya za Vooruzhennymi Silami v Ykraine*, Kiev: Ukrainian Centre for International Security Studies, 2000, p. 4.

73 *Constitution of Ukraine*, Art. 85, Para. 5.

74 Ibid., Art. 85, Para. 22.

75 Ibid., Art. 85, Para. 23.

76 Ibid., Art. 85, Para. 6.

77 Ibid., Art. 107.

78 Parfionov, *Rol' Struktur Ispolnitel'noi Vlasti*, p. 13.

79 The effectiveness of the committee is discussed in some detail in 'Democratic Civilian Control Over the Military in Ukraine: The Path from Form to Substance', *National Security and Defence*, No. 11 (2000), pp. 33–36. The 'unsatisfactory' quote is from Heorhiy Kriuchkov, a People's Deputy of Ukraine and former head of the defence committee, quoted in the journal on page 33.

80 Interview with Yuri B. Porkohnyavi, Deputy Head of the Secretariat of the Rada Committee on National Security and Defence, Kiev, Ukraine, 24 January 2001.

81 Interview with Duma defence committee working group member, Moscow, December 1998.

82 Quoted by O. A. Bel'kov, 'Rol' Parlamentskogo Kontrolya za Deyatel'nost'yu Cilovykh Struktur v Rossii', in *Parlamentskii Kontrol' nad Voennoe Sferoi* . . . , p. 217.

83 Interview with Duma defence committee working group member, Moscow, December 1998.

84 V.A. Grechaninov, 'Sostoyanie i Napravleniya Sovershenstvovaniya Demokraticheskogo Kontrolya nad Voennoi Sferoi v Ukraine', *Parlamentskii Kontrol' nad Voennoe Sferoi* . . . , p. 262.

85 Interview with MGEN (ret.) Vadim Grechaninov, President, Atlantic Council of Ukraine, Kiev, 24 January 2001.

86 Interview with a Senior Researcher at the Russian Institute of Strategic Studies, Moscow, January 1999.

87 Ibid. Another interviewee concluded that the defence committee which was 'ninety percent made up of generals' was 'in practice an effective military lobby in the Duma . . .': Interview with a Member of Duma International Affairs Committee, Moscow, January 1999. Indeed, the point that the defence committee acts as the lobby of the military was also made strongly in Yu. Fedorov, 'Grazhdanskii i Politicheskii Kontrol' Nad Vooryzhennymi Silami v Rossii: Osobennosti i Mekhanizmy', in *Parlamentskii Kontrol' nad Voennoe Sferoi* . . . , p. 190.

88 Interview with a ranking official of the Security Council of the Russian Federation, January 1999.

89 Interview with a senior researcher of the Institute of the USA and Canada (2), Moscow, January 1999.
90 Interview with Leonid Polyakov, Director, Military Programmes, Ukrainian Centre for Economic and Political Studies, Kiev, 22 January 2001.
91 Interview with Hryhoriy Nemyria, Director, Institute of International Relations, Centre for European and international Studies, Taras Shevchenko University, Kiev, 31 January 2001.
92 Interview with a member of staff of the Navy Training Centre (1), Ministry of Defence, Moscow, January 1999.
93 Interview with a member of the Partnership for Peace Directorate, Ministry of Defence, Kiev, 25 January 2001.
94 Ibid.
95 Interview with a senior researcher of the Institute of the USA and Canada (2), Moscow, January 1999.
96 Ukrainian Centre for Economic and Political Studies, 'Democratic Civilian Control Over the Military in Ukraine: The Path from Form to Substance', *National Security and Defence*, No. 11 (2000), p. 33.
97 Ibid., p. 33.
98 Porokhnyavi interview, Kiev, 24 January 2001.
99 Nemyria interview, Kiev, 31 January 2001.
100 Interview with Leonid Belousov, President, Ukrainian Centre for International Security Studies, Kiev, 24 January 2001.
101 Marco Carnovale, 'NATO Partners and Allies: Civil-Military Relations and Democratic Control of the Armed Forces', *NATO Review*, (March 1997), p. 33.
102 Interview with a Duma defence committee working group member interview, Moscow, December 1998.
103 Polyakov interview, Kiev, 22 January 2001.
104 Grechaninov, 'Sostoyanie i Napravleniya Sovershenstvovaniyav', p. 253.
105 Interview with Alexander A. Parfionov, Executive Director, Ukrainian Centre for International Security Studies, Kiev, 24 January 2001.
106 Interview with CDR Rick Williams, Defence Attache, Canadian Embassy, Kiev, 26 January 2001.
107 Jacob Kipp, *The Russian Military and the 1995 Parliamentary Elections: A Primer*, Fort Leavenworth, KS: US Army Foreign Military Studies Office, October 1995, p. 16.
108 Fedorov, pp. 189–190.
109 Interview with an Assistant First Deputy Prime Minister of the Russian Federation, Moscow, January 1999.
110 Interview with a member of the Law and Administration Program, The Open Society Institute, Soros Foundation, Moscow, January 1999.
111 Grechaninov interview, Kiev, 24 January 2001.
112 Interview with an Assistant First Deputy Prime Minister of the Russian Federation, Moscow, January 1999.
113 Belousov interview, Kiev, 24 January 2001. A NATO official resident in Kiev also pointed out that being replaced as secretary of the National Security and Defence Council was not necessarily a demotion for Gorbulin: Interview with Natalie Melnyczuk, Head, NATO Information and Documentation Centre, Kiev, 24 January 2001.
114 Parfionov, *Rol' Struktur Ispolnitel'noi . . .* , p. 4.
115 Interview with a member of the Military Personnel Department of the Ministry of Foreign Affairs interview, Kiev, 23 January 2001. This department manages the appointment of military attaches in Ukrainian embassies.
116 James Sherr, 'A Fresh Start for Ukrainian Military Reform', *Survival*, Vol. 43, No. 1 (Spring 2001), p. 118.

117 Nemyria interview, Kiev, 31 January 2001.
118 Interview with a defence attache of a NATO country, Kiev, 1 February 2001.
119 *Jamestown Monitor*, 29 October 1996.
120 Fedorov, p. 204.
121 Quoted by Steven Main in *The State Military Inspectorate*, Sandhurst, UK: Conflict Studies Research Centre, Royal Military Academy, C 93, December 1996.
122 Interview with a Senior Researcher at the Russian Institute of Strategic Studies, Moscow, January 1999.
123 Grytsenko, 'Democratic Civilian Control Over the Military in Ukraine: The Path from Form to Substance', p. 18.
124 Parfionov, *Rol' Struktur Ispolnitel'noi* . . . , p. 5.
125 Ibid., p. 5.
126 *Nezavisimaya Gazeta*, 12 August 1993.
127 The composition of the councils was exactly the same: president (chairman), secretary of the council, prime minister, head of FSB, minster of interior, minister of defence, security minister, minister of foreign affairs, head of border troops, and minister of finance.
128 Quoted in M. A. Smith, *The Defence Council of the Russian Federation*, Sandhurst, UK: Conflict Studies Research Centre, Royal Military Academy, C 95, March 1997.
129 *Nezavisimaya Gazeta*, 12 July 1996.
130 In October 1996 Lebed's most serious rival, Interior Minister Anatoli Kulikov, in tandem with the FSB and FAPSI, launched a mini coup against him. Accusing Lebed of planning a takeover, he severed inter-city communications on the night of 16–17 October and mobilised 100,000 interior troops to detain him. No charges were ever proven, but they provided sufficient pretext to oust him from his post as secretary of the Security Council. Far from being punished by Yeltsin for staging this coup, Kulikov was rewarded by being made the deputy prime minister for security affairs. See, Stephen Blank, *Towards the Failing State: The Structure of Russian Security Policy*, Sandhurst, UK: Conflict Studies Research Centre, Royal Military Academy, F56, November 1996, p. 2.
131 According to an article about Barsukov in *Kommersant-Daily*, 24 December 1998.
132 Interview with Alexander Belkin, Deputy Executive Director, Council on Foreign and Defence Policy, Moscow, December 1998.
133 Interview with a Duma defence committee working group member, Moscow, December 1998.
134 Parfionov, *Rol' Struktur Ispolnitel'noi* . . . , pp. 5–6.
135 Grytsenko, 'Democratic Civilian Control Over the Military in Ukraine: The Path from Form to Substance', p. 17.
136 Polyakov interview, Kiev, 22 January 2001.
137 Ibid.
138 'Military Reform in Ukraine: Start or Another False Start?' *National Security and Defence*, (Ukrainian Centre for Economic and Political Studies), No. 1 (2000).
139 According to a report in the newspaper *Holos Ukrayiny*, 9 February 2000, BBC Worldwide Monitoring, 9 February, 2000.
140 Belousov interview (U10), Kiev, 24 January 2001.
141 Matthew Shugart, 'Executive-Legislative Relations in Post-Communist Europe', *Transition* (13 December 1996), p. 6.
142 Yuri Popov, 'Grazhdanskii Kontrol' i Voennaya Reforma v Rossii', in *Grazhdanskii Kontrol' nad Vooruzhennymi Silami. Inostrannyi Opyt i Spetsifika Rossii, Materialy TACIS-proekta (1997–1998)*, Moskva: Russkii put', 1999, p. 149.
143 Peter Feaver, 'The Civil-Military Problematique: Huntington, Janowitz, and the Question of Civilian Control', *Armed Forces and Society*, Vol. 23, No. 2 (Winter 1996), p. 150.
144 Donnelly, 'Defence Transformation in the New Democracies: A Framework . . .'

145 Sherr, 'A Fresh Start . . .', p. 118.
146 Alfred Stepan, *Rethinking Military Politics: Brazil and the Southern Cone*, Princeton, NJ: Princeton University Publishers, 1988, p. 141.

Conclusion

1 Christopher Donnelly, 'Civil-Military Relations in the New Democracies', in David Betz and John Löwenhardt (eds), *Army and State in Postcommunist Europe*, London and Portland, OR: Frank Cass, 2001, p. 9.
2 I am aware of only a few serious commentators who voice a contrary opinion. Thomas M. Magstadt, 'Flawed Democracies: The Dubious Political Credentials of NATO's Proposed New Members' *Cato Policy Analysis*, No. 297, 6 March 1998, is one example.
3 These terms are taken from John Löwenhardt, Margot Light and Stephen White's research project entitled *The Outsiders: Russia, Ukraine, Belarus, Moldova and the New Europe* (project grant L213252007) which is part of the ESRC's 'One Europe or Several' Programme.
4 Sherr pointed to the significant impact of inertia on the attitudes of the Ukrainian military elite as well, noting the '. . . glaring discontinuity between the priorities put forward in the country's official national security concept and a situation where "sitting in classes, Ukrainian officers are rehearsing a situation in which a coalition of western and southern states comprising 50 divisions attacks Ukraine"'. James Sherr, 'Civil-democratic Control of Ukraine's Armed Forces: To What End? By What Means?', in Betz and Löwenhardt (eds), *Army and State . . .*, p. 74.
5 Many Western military officials, for example some officials at NATO, defence attaches, or advisers like those at the NATO Liaison Office in Kiev, have an excellent understanding of the issues from first-hand experience. On the other hand, they are rarely at liberty to use all this information for scholastic purposes. In other words, *participant observation* in the civil-military reform process might be the best way to get to the heart of the matter, but this option is not practically feasible for the academic researcher.
6 Douglas Bland, 'Protecting the Military From Civilian Control: A Neglected Dimension of Civil-Military Relations', in Ernest Gilman and Detlief Harold (eds), *Democratic and Civil Control Over Military Forces: Case Studies and Perspectives*, Rome: NATO Defence College Monograph Series, No. 3 (1995), p. 108.
7 E.N. Gladden, *The Essentials of Public Administration*, Third Edition, London: Staples Press Ltd., 1964, p. 69.
8 Carl von Clausewitz, *On War*, Middlesex: Penguin Books, 1968, p. 402.

Select bibliography

Reference annuals

The Military Balance. London: Brassey's for the International Institute of Strategic Studies. Various years.

Theoretical

Bacevich, A.J. 'Tradition Abandoned: America's Military in a New Era.' *National Interest*, 48 (Summer 1997), pp. 16–25.

Bland, Douglas. 'Discovering Westminster: The Transformation of Civil-Military Relations in Central Europe,' in D. Haglund, S. McFarland and J. Sokolski (eds). *NATO's Eastern Dilemmas*. Boulder, CO: Westview Press, 1994.

—— 'A Unified Theory of Civil-Military Relations.' *Armed Forces and Society*, Vol. 26, No. 1 (Fall 1999), pp. 7–26.

—— 'Managing the 'Expert Problem' in Civil-Military Relations.' *European Security*, Vol. 8, No. 3 (Autumn 1999), pp. 25–43.

—— 'A Unified Theory of Civil-Military Relations.' *Armed Forces and Society*, Vol. 26, No. 1 (Fall 1999), pp. 7–26.

Carnovale, Marco. 'NATO Partners and Allies: Civil-Military Relations and Democratic Control of the Armed Forces.' *NATO Review*, Vol. 45, No. 2 (March 1997), pp. 32–35.

Donnelly, Christopher. 'Defence Transformation in the New Democracies: A Framework for Tackling the Problem.' *NATO Review*, Vol. 45, No. 1 (January 1997), pp. 3–7.

Feaver, Peter D. 'The Civil-Military Problematique: Huntington, Janowitz and the Question of Civilian Control.' *Armed Forces and Society*, Vol. 23, No. 2 (Winter 1996), pp. 149–178.

Finer, Samuel. *The Man on Horseback: The Role of the Military in Politics*. 2nd edn. Boulder, CO: Westview Press, 1988.

Gabriel, Richard. *To Serve with Honour: A Treatise on Military Ethics and the Way of the Soldier*. Westport, CT: Greenwood Press, 1982.

Huntington, Samuel P. *The Soldier and the State: The Theory and Politics of Civil-Military Relations*. Cambridge, MA: Harvard University Press, 1957.

Janowitz, Morris. *The Professional Soldier*. Glencoe, IL: The Free Press, 1960.

Kemp, Kenneth and Charles Hudlin. 'Civil Supremacy Over the Military: Its Nature and Limits.' *Armed Forces and Society*, Vol. 19. No. 1 (Fall 1992), pp. 7–26.

Kohn, Richard H. 'How Democracies Control the Military.' *The Journal of Democracy*, Vol. 8, No. 4 (October 1997), pp. 140–153.

Machiavelli, Niccolo (W.K. Marriott trans.). *The Prince*. London: E.P. Dutton and Co., 1920.

Nelson, Daniel N. 'Civil Armies, Civil Societies and NATO's Enlargement.' *Armed Forces and Society*. Vol. 25, No. 1 (Fall 1998), pp. 137–160.

Nordlinger, Eric. *Soldiers and Politics: Military Coups and Governments*. Englwood Cliffs, NJ: Prentice-Hall, 1977.

Perlmutter, Amos. *The Military and Politics in Modern Times*. New Haven, CT: Yale University Press, 1977.

Schiff, Rebecca L. 'Civil-Military Relations Reconsidered: A Theory of Concordance.' *Armed Forces and Society*, Vol. 22, No. 1 (Fall 1995), pp. 7–24.

Stepan, Alfred. *Rethinking Military Politics: Brazil and the Southern Cone*. Princeton, NJ: Princeton University Press, 1988.

Sun Tzu (Thomas Cleary trans.). *The Art of War*. Boston, MA: Shambhala Publications, 1998.

von Clausewitz, Carl. *On War*. Middlesex: Penguin Books, 1968.

Welch, Claude (ed.). *Civilian Control of the Military*. Albany, NY: State University Press, 1976.

Communist era

Colton, Timothy. *Commissars, Commanders and Civilian Authority*. Cambridge, MA: Harvard University Press, 1979.

Cooper, Julian. 'Management of the Defence Industry: The Soviet Union,' in C.G. Jacobsen (ed.), *Strategic Power USA/USSR*. London: Macmillan, 1990.

Gelman, Harry. *The Soviet Turn Toward Conventional Forces: The Internal Variables at Play*. Santa Monica, CA: RAND, R-3876-AF, 1989.

Herspring, Dale R. and Ivan Volgyes (eds). 'The Military as Agent of Political Socialization in Eastern Europe: A Conceptual Framework'. *Armed Forces and Society*. Vol. 3, No. 4 (1977), pp. 249–270.

—— *Civil-Military Relations in Communist Systems*. Boulder, CO: Westview Press, 1978.

Jacobsen, Carl G. (ed.). *The Soviet Defence Enigma: Estimating Costs and Burden*. London: Oxford University Press, 1987.

—— *Strategic Power USA/USSR*. London: Macmillan Press, 1990.

Johnson, A. Ross, Robert W. Deen and Alexander Alexiev. *East European Military Establishments: The Warsaw Pact Northern Tier*. New York, NY: Crane Russak, 1980.

Jones, Ellen. *Red Army and Society: A Sociology of the Soviet Military*. Boston, MA: Allen and Unwin, 1985.

Karasek, Ted and William Green (eds). *Gorbachev and his Generals*. Boulder, CO: Westview Press, 1990.

Kolkowicz, Roman. *The Soviet Military and the Communist Party*. Princeton, NJ: Princeton University Press, 1967.

Kolkowicz, Roman and Andrzej Korbonski. *Soldiers, Peasants and Bureaucrats: Civil-Military Relations in Communist and Modernizing Societies*. London: Allen and Unwin, 1982.

Leebaert, Derek and Timothy Dickinson. *Soviet Strategy and the New Military Thinking*. New York, NY: Cambridge University Press, 1992.

Meyer, Steven. 'Soviet Perspectives on the Paths to Nuclear War,' in Graham T. Allison, Albert Carnesale and Joseph S. Nye (eds), *Hawks, Doves and Owls: An Agenda for Avoiding Nuclear War*. New York, NY: Norton, 1985.

—— 'The Sources and Prospects of Gorbachev's New Political Thinking on Security.' *International Security* (Fall 1998), 124–163.

—— 'Decision-making in Defence: The Soviet Case,' in G. Jacobsen (ed.), *Strategic Power USA/USSR*. London: Macmillan Press, 1990.

Nelson, Daniel N. (ed.). *Soviet Allies: The Warsaw Pact and the Issue of Reliability*. Boulder, CO: Westview Press, 1984.

Nicholls, Thomas. *The Sacred Cause: Civil-Military Conflict Over Soviet National Security*. Ithaca, NY: Cornell University Press, 1993.

Odom, William. 'The Militarization of the Soviet Society.' *Problems of Communism*, Vol. 25 (September–October 1976), pp. 34–51.

Sadkyewicz, Michael. *The Warsaw Pact Command Structure in Peace and War*. Santa Monica, CA: RAND, 1988a.

—— *Organizing for Coalition Warfare: The Role of the East European Warsaw Pact Forces in Soviet Military Planning*. Santa Monica, CA: RAND, 1988b.

Scott, Harriet Fast and William F. Scott. *Soviet Military Doctrine: Continuity, Formulation, and Dissemination*. Boulder, CO: Westview Press, 1988.

Snel, Gerald. *From the Atlantic to the Urals: The Reorientation of Soviet Military Strategy, 1981–1990*. Amsterdam, Netherlands: VU Press, 1996.

Volgyes, Ivan. *The Political Reliability of the Warsaw Pact Armies: The Southern Tier*. Durham, NC: Duke University Press, 1982.

Transition states

Barany, Zoltan. 'East European Armies in the Transition and Beyond.' *East European Quarterly*, Vol. 26, No. 1 (Spring 1992), pp. 1–30.

Bebler, Anton (ed.). *Behind Declarations: Civil-Military Relations in Central Europe*. Budapest: Institute for Strategic and Defence Studies, 1996.

—— *Civil-military Relations in Post-communist States: Central and Eastern Europe in Transition*. Westport, CT: Praeger, 1997.

Betz, David and John Löwenhardt (eds). *Army and State in Post-Communist Europe*. London and Portland, OR: Frank Cass, 2001.

Cottey, Andrew. *East-Central Europe After the Cold War: Poland, the Czech Republic, Slovakia and Hungary in Search of Security*. London: Macmillan Press, 1995.

Crane, Keith, Steven Popper and Barbara Kliszewski. *Civil-Military Relations in a Multiparty Democracy*. Santa Monica, CA: RAND Corporation, R-3941-RC, 1990.

Danopoulos, Constantine P. and Daniel Zirker (eds). *Civil-Military Relations in the Soviet and Yugoslav Successor States*. Boulder, CO: Westview Press, 1996.

—— *The Military and Society in the Former Eastern Bloc*. Boulder, CO : Westview Press,1998.

Donnelly, Chris. 'Civil-Military Relations in the New Democracies,' in D. Betz and J. Löwenhardt (eds), *Army and State in Post-Communist Europe*. London and Portland, OR: Frank Cass, 2001.

Dragsdahl, Jorgen. 'NATO Resists Pressures to Militarise Central Europe.' *BASIC Paper* 28 (July 1998).

Elster, Jon, Claus Offe and Ulrich K. Preuss. *Institutional Design in Post-Communist Societies: Building the Ship at Sea*. Cambridge, UK: Cambridge University Press, 1998.

Garton Ash, Timothy. 'Refolution: The Springtime of Two Nations.' *New York Review of Books*, Vol. 36, No. 10 (15 June 1989), pp. 3–4, 6, 8, 10.

Gogolewska, Agnieszka. *The Restructuring of Civil-Military Relations in Poland, Ukraine and Russia – A Comparative Study*. 20 June 1998, NATO Fellowship Report.

Gow, James and Carole Birch. *Security and Democracy: Civil Military Relations in Central and Eastern Europe*. London: Brassey's for the Centre for Defence Studies/University of London Press, London Defence Studies No. 40, 1997.

Herspring, Dale. ''Refolution' in Eastern Europe: The Polish, Czech, Slovak and Hungarian Militaries.' *European Security*, Vol. 3, No. 4 (Winter 1994), pp. 664–690.

Hockaday, Sir Arthur. 'Parliamentary Control of Defence: The Role of Select Committees.' *RUSI Journal*, Vol. 135, No. 1 (Spring 1990), pp. 7–10.

Holmes, Leslie. *Post Communism: An Introduction*. Oxford: Blackwell Publishers, 1997.

Lombardi, Ben. 'An Overview of Civil-Military Relations in Central and Eastern Europe.' *Journal of Slavic Military Studies*, Vol. 12, No. 1 (March 1999), pp. 13–33.

Military Higher Education. (Conference proceedings) Budapest: Ministry of Defence, Education and Sciences Department, 1999.

Parlamentskii Kontrol' nad Voennoe Sferoi v Novykh Nezavisimykh Gosudarstvakh. Moscow: Tsentr Politicheskikh i Mezhdunarodnykh Issledovanii, 1998.

Parrott, Bruce (ed.). *State Building and Military Power in Russia and the New States of Eurasia*. Armonk, NY: M.E. Sharpe, 1995.

Peterson Ulrich, Marybeth. *Democratizing Communist Militaries: The Cases of the Czech and Russian Armed Forces*. Ann Arbor, MI: University of Michigan Press, 1999.

Šarvas, Stefan. 'Professional Soldiers and Politics: A Case of Central and Eastern Europe.' *Armed Forces and Society*, Vol. 26, No. 1 (Fall 1999), pp. 99–118.

Simon, Jeffrey. 'Central European Civil-Military Relations and NATO Expansion.' Washington, DC: Institute for National Strategic Studies, National Defence University, McNair Paper No. 39, 1995.

Study on NATO Enlargement. Brussels: NATO, 1995.

Szayna, Thomas and F. Stephen Larrabee. *East European Military Reform After the Cold War: Implications for the United States*. Santa Monica, CA: RAND, 1995.

Szemerkenyi, Reka. *Central European Civil-Military Reforms at Risk: Progress in Establishing Democratic Controls Over the Military Has Not Been Sustained*. Oxford: Oxford University Press for the International Institute for Strategic Studies, Adelphi Paper No. 306, 1996.

von Riekhoff, Harald and Natalie Mychajlyszyn (eds). *Report on Specific Problems of Civil-Military Relations in the Czech Republic, Poland and Hungary*. Ottawa, Canada: Carleton University for the Department of National Defence, 1999a.

—— *Report on Specific Problems and Developments in Civil-Military Relations in the Baltic Republics, Bulgaria, Romania, Russia, Slovakia, Slovenia and Ukraine*. Ottawa, Canada: Carleton University for the Department of National Defence, 1999b.

Hungary

Barany, Zoltan. *Soldiers and Politics in Eastern Europe, 1945–1990 : The Case of Hungary*. New York, NY: St. Martin's Press, 1993.

Directorate of Management Consultancy Services. *Review of Parliamentary Oversight of the Hungarian Ministry of Defence and Democratic Control of the Hungarian Armed Forces*. London: Ministry of Defence, 1996.

Gorka, Sebestyen. 'Hungarian Military Reform And Peacekeeping Efforts.' *NATO Review*, Vol. 43, No. 6 (November 1995), pp. 26–29.

Institute for Strategic and Defence Studies. *The First Decade of the Independent Hungarian Security Policy 1989–1999*. Budapest: October 1999.

Joo, Rudolf. *The Democratic Control of Armed Forces: The Experience of Hungary*. Paris: Institute for Security Studies, Western European Union, Chaillot Paper 23, February 1996.

Pecze, Zoltan. *Civil-Military Relations in Hungary 1989–1996*. Groningen, Netherlands: Centre for European Security Studies, Harmonie Paper 2, 1998.

Sherr, James. 'Hungary,' in H. von Riekhoff and N. Mychajlyszyn (eds), *Report on Specific Problems of Civil-Military Relations in the Czech Republic, Poland and Hungary*. Ottawa, Canada: Carleton University for the Department of National Defence, 1999a.

Szabo, Janos. 'Facts and Problems of the Civilian Control of Armed Forces in Hungary,' in *Behind Declarations: Civil-Military Relations in Central Europe*. Budapest: Institute for Strategic and Defence Studies, 1996.

Szenes, Zoltan (ed.). *The Hungarian Defense Force and Civil Control in the Reflection of British Transillumination*. Budapest: Ministry of Defence, Department for Education and Science Management,1997.

Szenes, Zoltan. 'The Implications of NATO Expansion for Civil-military Relations in Hungary,' in D. Betz and J. Löwenhardt (eds), *Army and State in Post-Communist Europe*, London and Portland, OR: Frank Cass, 2001.

Poland

Busza, E. 'Transition and Civil-military Relations in Poland and Russia.' *Communist and Post-communist Studies*. Vol. 29, No. 2 (June 1996), pp. 167–184.

Coughlan, Elizabeth. 'Democratizing Civilian Control: the Polish Case.' *Armed Forces and Society*. Vol. 24, No. 4 (Summer 1998), pp. 519–533.

Davies, Norman. *God's Playground: A History of Poland*. Oxford: Oxford University Press, 1981.

Dutkiewicz, Piotr. 'Poland,' in H. von Riekhoff and N. Mychajlyszyn (eds), *Report on Specific Problems of Civil-Military Relations in the Czech Republic, Poland and Hungary*. Ottawa, Canada: Carleton University for the Department of National Defence, 1999a.

Herspring, Dale. 'The Polish Military and the Policy Process,' in Maurice Simon and Roger E. Kanet (eds), *Background to Crisis: Policy and Politics in Gierek's Poland*. Boulder, CO: Westview Press, 1981.

—— 'Civil-Military Relations in Post-Communist Poland: Problems in the Transition to a Democratic Polity.' *Communist and Post-Communist Studies*, Vol. 33, No. 1 (March 2000), pp. 71–100.

Korbonski, Andrzej. 'The Dilemmas of Civil-Military Relations in Contemporary Poland: 1945–1981.' *Armed Forces and Society*, Vol. 8, No. 4 (1981), pp. 3–20.

Kowalewski, Marian. 'An Organisational Model of Civilian Control Over the Army in Polish Circumstances.' Warsaw: Nato Research Fellowship Report 1995–1997, 10 June 1997.

Malcher, George C. *Poland's Politicized Army: Communists in Uniform*. New York, NY: Praeger, 1984.

Michta, Andrew. *Red Eagle: The Army in Polish Politics, 1944–1988*. Stanford, CA: Hoover Institution Press, 1990.

—— 'Civil-Military Relations in Poland After 1989: The Outer Limits of Change.' *Problems of Post-Communism*, Vol. 25 (September–October 1996), pp. 34–51.

—— *The Soldier-Citizen: The Politics of the Polish Army After Communism*. New York, NY: St. Martin's Press, 1997.

Piatkowski, Krystian. 'Outline and Timetable for the Integration of Poland into NATO (January 1994).' *European Security*, Vol. 3, No. 3 (Autumn 1994), pp. 501–528.

Plater-Zyberk, Henry. *Poland's Defence and Security: The Same Priorities, Different Approaches*. Sandhurst, UK: Conflict Studies Research Centre, Royal Military Academy, May 1998.

The Polish Defence Forces. Warsaw: Press and Information Bureau, Ministry of Defence, 1998.

Wiatr, Jerzy. *The Soldier and the Nation: The Role of the Military in Polish Politics, 1918–1985*. Boulder, CO: Westview Press, 1998.

Russia

Allison, Roy. 'The Russian Armed Forces: Structures, Roles and Policies,' in V. Baranovsky (ed.), *Russia and Europe: The Emerging Security Agenda*. Oxford: Oxford University Press/SIPRI, 1997.

Allison, Roy and Christopher Bluth (eds). *Security Dilemmas in Russia and Eurasia*. London: Royal Institute of International Affairs, 1998.

Arbatov, Alexei. *The Russian Military in the 21st Century*. Carlisle Barracks, PA: US Army War College, Conference paper, June 1997.

Arnett, Robert. 'Can Civilians Control the Military?' *Orbis*, Vol. 38, No. 1 (Winter 1994), pp. 41–57.

Azrael, Jeremy. 'The Soviet Civilian Leadership and the Military High Command, 1976–1986.' RAND R-3251-AF, June 1987.

Baev, Pavel. *The Russian Army in a Time of Troubles*. London: Sage, 1996.

—— *Russian Military Development: 'Muddle Through' From 1992 to 1998 and Beyond*. Kjeller, Norway: Norwegian Defence Research Establishment, FFI/Rapport-99/01229, 1999.

Ball, Deborah Yarsike. 'How Reliable are Russia's Officers?' *Jane's Intelligence Review*, (May 1996), pp. 205–207.

—— 'The Political Attitudes of Russian Field Grade Officers.' *Post-Soviet Affairs*, Vol. 12, No. 2 (1996), pp. 161–183.

Baranets, Viktor. *El'tsin i Ego Generaly*. Moscow: Sovershenno Sekretno, 1998.

Baranovsky, V. (ed.). *Russia and Europe: The Emerging Security Agenda*. Oxford: Oxford University Press/SIPRI, 1997.

Barylski, Robert. 'The Soviet Military Before and After the August Coup.' *Armed Forces and Society*, Vol. 19, No. 1 (Fall 1992), pp. 27–45.

—— *The Soldier in Russian Politics: Duty, Dictatorship and Democracy Under Gorbachev and Yeltsin*. New Brunswick, NJ: Transaction Publishers, 1998.

Belkin, Alexander. *The War in Chechnya: The Impact on Civil-Military Relations*. Monterey, CA: US Naval Postgraduate School, Conference on Russian Defence Policy Toward the Year 2000, March 1997.

Bel'kov, O. A. 'Rol' Parlamentskogo Kontrolya za Deyatel'nost'yu Cilovykh Struktur v Rossii,' in *Parlamentskii Kontrol' nad Voennoe Sferoi* Moscow: Tsentr Politicheskikh i Mezhdunarodnykh Issledovanii, 1998.

Betz, David J. *If They Are Ordered 'Die of Hunger!' They Will Die*. Glasgow: Institute of Central and East European Studies, Glasgow Paper No. 2, 1999.

—— 'Russia,' in H. von Riekhoff and N. Mychajlyszyn (eds), *Report on Specific Problems and Developments in Civil-Military Relations in the Baltic Republics, Bulgaria, Romania, Russia, Slovakia, Slovenia and Ukraine*. Ottawa, Canada: Carleton University for the Department of National Defence, 1999b.

Black, J.L. *Russia Faces NATO Expansion: Bearing Gifts or Bearing Arms?* Lanham, MD: Rowman and Littlefield, 2000.

Blank, Stephen. *Russian Defense Legislation and Russian Democracy*. Fort Leavenworth, KS: US Army Foreign Military Studies Office, August 1995.

—— *Towards the Failing State: The Structure of Russian Security Policy*. Sandhurst, UK: Conflict Studies Research Centre, Royal Military Academy, F56, November 1996.

Bluth, Christopher. 'Russian Military Forces: Ambitions, Capabilities and Constraints,' in R. Allison and C. Bluth (eds), *Security Dilemmas in Russia and Eurasia*. London: Royal Institute of International Affairs, 1998.

Brusstar, James and Ellen Jones. *The Russian Military's Role in Politics*. Washington, DC: Institute for National Strategic Studies, National Defence University, McNair Paper No. 34, January 1995.

Dallin, Alexander. *Russian and Soviet History 1500–1991: Civil-Military Relations in the Soviet Union*. New York, NY: Garland Publishing, 1992.

Davenport, Brian. 'Civil-Military Relations in the Post-Soviet State: 'Loose Coupling' Uncoupled?' *Armed Forces and Society*, Vol. 21, No. 2 (Winter 1995): 175–194.

Derleth, William J. 'The Evolution of the Russian Polity: The Case of the Security Council.' *Communist and Post-Communist Studies*, Vol. 29, No. 1 (1996), pp. 43–58.

Dick, Charles J. 'Initial Thoughts on Russia's Draft Military Doctrine.' *Journal of Slavic Military Studies*, Vol. 5, No. 4 (December 1992), pp. 552–566.

—— 'The Military Doctrine of the Russian Federation.' *Journal of Slavic Military Studies*, Vol. 7, No. 3 (September 1994), pp. 481–506.

—— 'A Bear Without Claws: The Russian Army in the Nineties.' *Journal of Slavic Military Studies*, Vol. 10, No. 1 (March 1997), pp. 1–10.

Efimov, Nikolai. 'The Army, Society and Reforms.' *Russian Politics and Law*, Vol. 34, No. 4 (July/August 1996), pp. 7–21.

Epperson, Robert. 'Civil-Military Relations: Russian Military Intervention in Politics, 1991–96.' *Journal of Slavic Military Studies*, Vol. 10, No. 3 (September 1997), pp. 90–108.

Erickson, John. *The Soviet High Command: A Military-Political History 1918–1941*. New York, NY: St. Martin's Press, 1962.

Fedorov, Yu. 'Grazhdanskii i Politicheskii Kontrol' Nad Vooryzhennymi Silami b Rossii: Osobennosti i Mekhanizmy.' in *Parlamentskii Kontrol' nad Voennoe Sferoi* Moscow: Tsentr Politicheskikh i Mezhdunarodnykh Issledovanii, 1998.

Felgengauer, Pavel. 'Russian Military Reform Ten Years of Failure,' in M. Tsypkin (ed.), *War In Chechnya: Implications for Russian Security Policy*. Monterey, CA: Department of National Security Affairs, US Naval Postgraduate School, 1996.

Fitch, Raymond. *The Strange Case of Russian Peacekeeping Operations in the Near Abroad*. Fort Leavenworth, KS: US Army Foreign Military Studies Office, July 1996.

—— *Why the Russian Army Failed in Chechnya*. Fort Leavenworth, KS: US Army Foreign Military Studies Office, May 1997.

Garnett, Sherman. 'A Wedged Bear in Great Tightness: Understanding the Constraints on Russian Power.' *Pro et Contra*, Vol. 2, No. 1 (Winter 1997), pp. 5–20.

Gatty, Clifford. *The Price of the Past: Russia's Struggle with the Legacy of a Militarized Economy*. Washington, DC: Brookings Institution, 1996.

Gazukin, Pavel. *Vooruzhenye Sily Rossiiskoi Federatsi: Biograficheski Spravochnik*, Moscow: Panorama, 1996 and 1998 editions.

Goldman, Stuart D. *Russian Conventional Armed Forces: On the Verge of Collapse?* Washington, DC: Congressional Research Service Report, 97–820F, September 1997.

Goldstein, Lyle. 'Russian Civil-Military Relations in the Chechen War, December 1994–February 1995.' *Journal of Slavic Military Studies*, Vol. 10, No. 1 (March 1997), pp. 109–127.

Golovkov, Alexander and Sergei Leskov. 'Top Guns: Who's Who in the Russian Military.' *Bulletin of the Atomic Scientist* (May/June 1995), pp. 51–54.

Hamburg, Roger. 'After the Abortive Coup and What is to be Done?: The Post-Soviet Military.' *Journal of Political and Military Sociology* (Winter 1992), pp. 305–322.

Herspring, Dale. 'The Russian Military: Three Years On.' *Communist and Post-Communist Studies*, Vol. 28, No. 2 (1995), pp. 163–182.

—— *Russian Civil-military Relations*. Bloomington IN: Indiana University Press, 1996.

—— 'The Future of the Russian Military.' *Problems of Post Communism*, Vol. 44 (March/April 1997), pp. 47–56.

Jacobsen, Carl G. 'Russia's Revolutionary Arbiter? Arms and Society, 1988–1994.' *Arms and Society*, Vol. 1 (May 1995), pp. 101–146.

Kaminski A. and A. Gogolewska. 'Civilian Control of the Russian Military Since 1991.' *European Security*, Vol. 5, No. 4 (Winter 1996), pp. 588–603.

Kennaway, A. *The Russian Black Hole* Sandhurst, UK: Conflict Studies Research Centre, Royal Military Academy, E90, November 1996.

Kipp, Jacob. *The Russian Military and the 1995 Parliamentary Elections: A Primer*. Fort Leavenworth, KS: US Army Foreign Military Studies Office, October 1995.

—— *Military Pluralism and the Crisis of Russian Military Professionalism*. Washington, DC: Heritage Foundation, Conference on The Future of the Russian Military: Managing Geo-Political Change and Institutional Decline, December 1996.

Lambeth, Benjamin. 'Russia's Wounded Military.' *Foreign Affairs*, Vol. 74, No. 2 (March/April 1995), pp. 86–98.

Leppingwell, John W. 'Soviet Civil-Military Relations and the August Coup.' *World Politics*, Vol. 44, No. 4 (July 1992), pp. 539–572.

Lunev, Stanislav. 'Is the Russian Army Starving?' *Prism*, Vol. 1, No. 24 (17 November 1995).

Main, S.J. *The State Military Inspectorate*. Sandhurst, UK: Royal Military Academy, Conflict Studies Research Centre, C93, December 1996.

Mendeloff, David. 'Explaining Russian Military Quiescence: The 'Paradox of Disintegration' and the Myth of a Military Coup.' *Communist and Post-Communist Studies*, Vol. 27, No. 3 (1994), pp. 225–246.

Meyer, Stephen. 'How the Threat (and the Coup) Collapsed: The Politicization of the Soviet Military.' *International Security*, Vol. 16, No. 3 (Winter 1991/1992), pp. 5–37.

—— 'The Devolution of Russian Military Power.' *Current History*, Vol. 94 (October 1995), pp. 322–328.

Nichols, Thomas M. 'An Electoral Mutiny? Zhirinovsky and the Russian Armed Forces.' *Armed Forces and Society*, Vol. 21, No. 3 (Spring 1995), pp. 327–347.

Odom, William. 'The Party–Military Connection: A Critique,' in D.R. Herspring and I. Volgyes (eds), *Civil-Military Relations in Communist Systems*. Boulder, CO: Westview Press, 1978.

Orr, Michael. *The Deepest Crisis: The Problems of the Russian Army Today*. Sandhurst, UK: Conflict Studies Research Centre, Royal Military Academy, Occasional Brief 48, October 1996.

—— *The Current State of the Russian Armed Forces*. Sandhurst, UK: Conflict Studies Research Centre, Royal Military Academy, November 1996.

—— *Rodionov and Reform*. Sandhurst, UK: Conflict Studies Research Centre, Royal Military Academy, C92, January 1997.

Shakirov, M. 'Mercenaries: Conversations with Military Personnel on the Road from Dushanbe to the Forgotten Russians at Sary-Pulak.' *Russian Politics and Law*, Vol. 34, No. 4 (July–Auust 1995), pp. 23–32.

Shlykov, Vitaliy. 'The War in Chechnya: Implications for Military Reform and Creation of Mobile Forces,' in M. Tsypkin (ed.), *War In Chechnya*. Monterey, CA: Department of National Security Affairs, US Naval Postgraduate School, 1996.

—— 'The Budget and the Army.' *Russian Politics and Law*, Vol. 35, No. 5 (September–October 1997).

Simonsen, Sven Gunnar. 'Marching to a Different Drum? Political Orientations and Nationalism in Russia's Armed Forces,' in D. Betz and J. Löwenhardt (eds), *Army and State in Post-Communist Europe*. London and Portland, OR: Frank Cass, 2001.

Smith, M.A. *The Security Council*. Sandhurst, UK: Conflict Studies Research Centre, Royal Military Academy, C94, January 1994.

—— *The Defence Council of the Russian Federation*, Sandhurst, UK: Conflict Studies Research Centre, Royal Military Academy, C95, March 1997.

Sovremennaya Politicheskaya Istoria Rossii: Litsa Rossii, (1985–1998). Vol. 2, Moscow: RAU – Korporatsiya, 1999.

Taylor, Brian D. 'Russian Civil-Military Relations After the October Uprising.' *Survival*, Vol. 36, No. 1 (Spring 1994), pp. 3–29.

Thomas, Timothy. 'Fault Lines and Factions in the Russian Army.' *Orbis*, Vol. 39, No. 4 (Fall 1995), pp. 531–548.

—— 'The Russian Military and the December 1995 Duma Elections: Dissatisfaction Continues to Grow in the Armed Forces.' *Journal of Slavic Military Studies*, Vol. 9, No. 3 (September 1996), pp. 519–547.

Thomas, Timothy and Lester Grau. 'A Military Biography: Russian Minster of Defence General Igor Rodionov: In With the Old, In With the New.' *Journal of Slavic Military Studies*, Vol. 9, No. 2 (June 1996), pp. 443–452.

Tishin, I. 'National Interests and Geopolitics: A Primer on "The Basic Provision of the Military Doctrine of the Russian Federation".' *European Security*, Vol. 4, No. 1 (Spring 1995), pp. 107–131.

Tsypkin, Mikhail (ed.). *War In Chechnya: Implications for Russian Security Policy*. Monterey, CA: Department of National Security Affairs, US Naval Postgraduate School, 1996.

—— 'Will the Military Rule Russia?' *Security Studies*, Vol. 2, No. 1 (Autumn 1997), pp. 51–55.

Turbiville, Graham H. *Mafia in Uniform: The Criminalization of the Russian Armed Forces*. Fort Leavenworth, KS: US Army Foreign Military Studies Office, July 1995.

Vallance, Brenda. 'Corruption and Reform in the Soviet Military.' *Journal of Slavic Military Studies*, Vol. 7, No. 4 (December 1994), pp. 703–724.

Volkogonov, Dmitri. 'The Army in the Political System.' *Russian Politics and Law* (Summer 1992), pp. 49–55.

Waters, T.R.W. *Crime in the Russian Military*. Sandhurst, UK: Conflict Studies Research Centre, Royal Military Academy, C90, November 1996.

Wilson, Andrew. 'Russian Military Haunted by Past Glories.' *Jane's International Defence Review* (May 1996), pp. 25–28.

Ukraine

Allison, Roy. *Military Forces in the Soviet Successor States*. Oxford: Oxford University Press for the International Institute for Strategic Studies, Adelphi Paper No. 280, 1993.

Arel, Dominique. 'Ukraine: The Muddle Way.' *Current History*, Vol. 97, No. 620 (October 1998), pp. 342–346.

Baev, Pavel and Tor Bukkvol. 'Ukraine's Army under Civilian Rule.' *Jane's Intelligence Review*, Vol. 8, No. 1 (January 1996).

Chandler, Andrea. 'Statebuilding and Political Priorities in post-Soviet Ukraine: The Case of the Military.' *Armed Forces and Society*, Vol. 22, No. 4 (Summer 1996), pp. 573–597.

Cook, Frank and Yvan Zayets. 'Ukraine and its Armed Forces: A New Actor on the European Stage.' *Report to the Defence and Security Committee of the NATO Parliamentary Assembly*, AS 253 DSC (99) 8, November 1999.

Dick, Charles J. 'The Military Doctrine of Ukraine.' *Journal of Slavic Military Studies*, Vol. 7, No. 3 (September 1994).

Dunn, J.F. *The Ukrainian Nuclear Weapon Debate*. Sandhurst, UK: Conflict Studies Research Centre, Royal Military Academy, March 1993.

Foye, Stephen. 'The Ukrainian Armed Forces: Prospects and Problems.' *RFE/RL Research Report*, Vol. 1, No. 26 (26 June 1992).

—— 'Civil-Military Tension in Ukraine.' *RFE/RL Research Report*, Vol. 3, No. 25 (18 June 1993).

Garnett, Sherman W. *Keystone in the Arch: Ukraine in the Emerging Security Environment of Central and Eastern Europe*. Washington, DC: Carnegie Endowment, 1997.

Grechaninov, V.A. 'Sostoyanie i Napravlleniya Sovershenstvovaniya Demokraticheskogo Kontrolya nad Voennoi Sferoi v Ykraine,' in *Parlamentskii Kontrol' nad Voennoe* Moscow: Tsentr Politicheskikh i Mezhdunarodnykh Issledovanii, 1998.

Grytsenko, Anatoliy S. *Civil-Military Relations in Ukraine: A System Emerging From Chaos*. Groningen, Netherlands: Centre for European Security Studies, Harmonie Paper 1, 1997.

—— *Reforming the Military in States of Transformation: The Case of Ukraine*. Groningen, Netherlands: Centre for European Security Studies, EFP Working Paper No. 4, 2000.

Hajda, Lubomyr A. (ed.). *Ukraine in the World: Studies in the International Relations and Security Structure of a Newly Independent State*. Cambridge, MA: Harvard University Press, 1998.

Havrylenko, Oleksiy. 'Does Ukraine Need a New Military Doctrine.' *National Security and Defence*, No. 1 (2000), p. 45.

Izmalkov, Valeriy. 'Ukraine and Her Armed Forces: The Conditions and Process for their Creation, Character, Structure and Military Doctrine.' *European Security*, Vol. 2, No. 2 (Summer 1993), pp. 279–319.

Jaworsky, John. 'Ukraine's Armed Forces and Military Policy,' in L.A. Hajda (ed.), *Ukraine in the World*. Cambridge, MA: Harvard University Press, 1998.

Krawciw, Nicholas. 'Ukrainian Perspectives on National Security and Ukrainian Military Doctrine,' in B. Parrott (ed.), *State Building and Military Power in Russia and the New States of Eurasia*. Armonk, NY: M.E. Sharpe, 1995.

Kuzio, Taras. 'Ukraine – A New Military Power?' *Jane's Intelligence Review*, Vol. 4, No. 2 (February 1992).

—— *Ukraine: The Unfinished Revolution*. Exeter: SR Press, Institute for European Defence and Strategic Studies, No. 16, 1992.

—— 'Ukraine Approves New Military Doctrine.' *Jane's Intelligence Review Pointer*, No. 2 (December 1993).

—— 'New Ukrainian Military Legislation.' *Jane's Intelligence Review Pointer*, No. 10 (August 1994).

—— 'Ukrainian Civil-Military Relations and the Military Impact of the Ukrainian Economic Crisis,' in B. Parrott (ed.), *State Building and Military Power in Russia and the New States of Eurasia*. Armonk, NY: M.E. Sharpe, 1995.

—— 'Civil-Military Relations in Ukraine, 1989–1991.' *Armed Forces and Society*, Vol. 22, No. 1 (Fall 1995), pp. 25–48.

—— 'The Organization of Ukraine's forces.' *Jane's Intelligence Review*, Vol. 8, No. 6 (June 1996).

Mychajlyszyn, Natalie and Orest Subtelny. 'Ukraine,' in H. von Riekhoff and N. Mychajlyszyn (eds), *Report on Specific Problems and Developments in Civil-Military Relations in the Baltic Republics, Bulgaria, Romania, Russia, Slovakia, Slovenia and Ukraine*. Ottowa, Canada: Carleton University for the Department of National Defence, 1999.

Olynyk, Stephen D.'Emerging Post-Soviet Armies: The Case of the Ukraine.' *Military Review*, Vol. 34, No. 3 (March 1994), pp. 5–18.

—— 'Ukraine as a Military Power,' in S.L. Wolchik and V. Zviglyanich (eds), *Ukraine: The Search for a National Identity*. Lanham, MD: Rowman and Littlefield Publishers, 2000.

Parfionov, Alexander. *Rol' Struktur Ispolnitel'noi Vlasti v Sisteme Grazhdanskogo Kontrolya za Vooruzhennymi Silami v Ykraine*. Kiev: Ukrainian Centre for International Security Studies, 2000.

Pikhovshek, Vyacheslav and Christopher Pett, 'Transformation of the Ukrainian Armed Forces.' *NATO Review*, Vol. 42, No. 5 (October 1994), pp. 21–25.

Pyskir, Bohdan. 'The Silent Coup: The Building of Ukraine's Military.' *European Security*, Vol. 2, No. 1 (Spring 1993), pp. 140–160.

Sauerwein, Brigitte. 'Rich in Arms, Poor in Tradition: The Ukrainian Armed Forces.' *International Defense Review*, Vol. 24, No. 4 (1993), pp. 317–318.

Sherr, James. *Management And Supervision of Defence in A Society in Transition*. Sandhurst, UK: Conflict Studies Research Centre, Royal Military Academy, 1997.

—— 'Russia-Ukraine Rapprochement?: The Black Sea Fleet Accords.' *Survival*, Vol. 39, No. 3 (Autumn 1997), pp. 33–50.

—— 'Civil-democratic Control of Ukraine's Armed Forces: To What End? By What Means?,' in D. Betz and J. Löwenhardt (eds), *Army and State in Post-Communist Europe*. London and Portland, OR: Frank Cass, 2001.

—— 'A Fresh Start for Ukrainian Military Reform.' *Survival*, Vol. 34, No. 1 (Spring 2001), pp. 107–126.

The State Programme of the Ukrainian Armed Forces Reform and Development until 2005. Kiev: 'Press of Ukraine', 2000.

Ukrainian Centre for Economic and Political Studies 'Military Reform in Ukraine: Start or Another False Start?' *National Security and Defence*, No. 1 (2000).

Ukrainian Centre for Economic and Political Studies, 'Democratic Civilian Control Over the Military in Ukraine: The Path from Form to Substance.' *National Security and Defence*, No. 11 (2000).

Wolchik, Sharon L. and Volodymyr Zviglyanich. (eds). *Ukraine: The Search for a National Identity*. Lanham, MD: Rowman and Littlefield Publishers, 2000.

Wolczuk, Roman. 'The Evolution of Ukrainian Foreign and Security Policy, 1990–1994.' *Journal of Slavic Military Studies*, Vol. 12, No. 3 (September 1999), pp. 18–37.

Index